New Jersey

New Jersey School Laws

New Jersey

New Jersey School Laws

ISBN/EAN: 9783744666916

Printed in Europe, USA, Canada, Australia, Japan

Cover: Foto ©Suzi / pixelio.de

More available books at **www.hansebooks.com**

New Jersey

SCHOOL LAWS

With

Notes, Blanks and Forms

For the

Use and Government of School Officers

Prepared by the

State Superintendent of Public Instruction.

∽∽∽∽

To be Preserved and Delivered by Each Officer to His Successor.

TRENTON, N. J.
MacCrellish & Quigley, Book and Job Printers
1894

Extracts

From the State Constitution Respecting the Public Schools.

Section VII.

6. The fund for the support of free schools, and all money, stock and other property which may hereafter be appropriated for that purpose, or received into the treasury under the provision of any law heretofore passed to augment the said fund, shall be securely invested and remain a perpetual fund; and the income thereof, except so much as it may be judged expedient to apply to an increase of the capital, shall be annually appropriated to the support of public free schools, for the equal benefit of all the people of the State; and it shall not be competent for the Legislature to borrow, appropriate or use the said fund, or any part thereof, for any other purpose, under any pretence whatever. The Legislature shall provide for the maintenance and support of a thorough and efficient system of free public schools for the instruction of all the children in this State between the ages of five and eighteen years.

11. The Legislature shall not pass private, local or special laws providing for the management and support of free public schools.

The School Law.

An Act to establish a System of Public Instruction.

STATE BOARD OF EDUCATION.

1. BE IT ENACTED *by the Senate and General Assembly of the State of New Jersey,* That the general supervision and control of public instruction in the State of New Jersey shall be vested in a state board of education, which board shall consist of two members from each congressional district, only one of whom shall be a member of the same political party, and no two of whom shall reside in the same county, except where a congressional district lies entirely within one county; said members shall be appointed by the governor, by and with the consent of the senate, and shall hold office severally for the term of five years, and until their successors shall be appointed as aforesaid, and hereafter, in the place of those whose terms expire, successors in like manner and for a like term shall be appointed, so that there shall always be two members from each congressional district; and in case of any vacancy by death, resignation or otherwise, a successor for the unexpired term shall in like manner be appointed.

State board, how composed. P. L. 1894. Chap. CCCIX, § 1.

2. The members of the state board of education already appointed shall continue in office, severally for the terms for which they have been appointed; provided, however, that this section shall not apply to any congressional district which now has two members of said state board of education who are both members of the same political party, but the terms of office of each of said members shall terminate upon the passage of this act, and two members shall be appointed from said district in the manner provided in the first section of this act, one of whom shall be appointed for the full term of five years and one for the term for which the members from said district would have served as mem-

bers of said board had their terms of office not been terminated by this act.

<small>Trustees of state normal school.
P. L. 1892.
Chap. CI, § 2.
[See sec. 79 to 87.]</small>

3. The board of trustees of the state normal school is hereby abolished; all the duties and offices of such board shall hereafter be exercised and performed by the state board of education, provided for in the first section of this act.

<small>Trustees of deaf-mute school.
P. L. 1891.
Chap. XCVII, § 2.
[See sec. 88 to 95.]</small>

4. Said institution (New Jersey school for deaf-mutes) shall be under the control and management of the state board of education; such board shall have all the powers and perform all the duties of the board of trustees created by the act to which this is a supplement, which board of trustees is hereby abolished.

(For the powers and duties of the state board of education as trustees of the state normal school and trustees of the New Jersey school for deaf-mutes, see "Normal School" and "Deaf-Mute School.")

<small>Quorum.
P. L. 1875.
Chap. LXIX, § 1.
[See sec. 40.]</small>

5. A quorum of the state board of education shall consist of eight members.

<small>Powers and duties.
P. L. 1867.
Chap. CLXXIX, § 2.
Make rules
[See sec. 76, 77, 152, 235, 240 and 248.</small>

6. The state board of education shall have power, and it shall be their duty:

I. To frame and modify at pleasure such by-laws as may be deemed expedient for their own government, not inconsistent with the provisions of this act, and to prescribe and cause to be enforced all rules and regulations necessary for carrying into effect the school laws of this state;

<small>Recommend laws.
[See sec. 21.]</small>

II. To consider the necessities of the public schools, and recommend to the legislature, from time to time, such additions and amendments to the laws as are deemed necessary for perfecting the school system of the state;

<small>Appoint county superintendents.
P. L. 1889.
Chap CLXV, § 1.
[See sec 25.]
Make rules for institutes.
P. L. 1867.
Chap. CLXXIX, § 2.
Authorize payment of expenses of state superintendent.
Ibid. § 2.</small>

III. To appoint the county superintendents of the several counties of the state;

IV. To prescribe all rules and regulations for holding teachers' institutes;

V. To authorize the payment by the treasurer of the school fund, upon the warrant of the state comptroller, of all the necessary incidental expenses incurred by the state superintendent in the performance of his official duties;

VI. To decide all appeals from the decision of the state superintendent of public instruction. <small>Decide appeals. [See sec. 17.]</small>

7. The members of the board shall receive no compensation for their services, but the treasurer of the school fund shall pay the necessary expenses of the said members, upon the warrant of the state comptroller. <small>Compensation. Ibid. ¿ 3. P. L. 1885, Chap. CLXIV, § 1, div 4. [See sec. 136, div. 3.]</small>

8. The board shall report annually to the legislature in regard to all matters committed to their care. <small>Annual report. P. L. 1867. Chap. CLXXIX, ¿ 4</small>

STATE SUPERINTENDENT OF PUBLIC INSTCUCTION.

9. The state superindendent of public instruction shall be appointed by the governor, by and with the advice and consent of the senate, for the term of three years, and until his successor is appointed, and shall receive annually a salary of three thousand dollars, to be paid out of the income of the school fund; *provided*, that nothing herein contained shall prevent his re-appointment. <small>State superintendent, how appointed, term of office, salary. P. L. 1889 Chap. V, ¿ 1.</small>

<small>Proviso.</small>

10. He shall be required to have his office in the state house, at Trenton. <small>Location of office. P. L. 1867, Chap. CLXXIX, ¿ 6.</small>

11. It shall be his duty to carry out the instructions of the board, and to enforce all rules and regulations prescribed by them. <small>To carry out instructions of state board. Ibid. 7.</small>

12. He shall be, *ex officio*, secretary of the board of education, president of the state association of school superintendents, and a member of the state board of examiners, and of all county and city boards of examiners. <small>Officer ex-officio. Ibid. ¿ 8. [See sec. 35.]</small>

13. He shall have the supervision of all the schools of the state receiving any part of the state appropriation, and shall be the general adviser and assistant of the county superintendents; he shall, from time to time, as he shall deem for the interests of the schools, address circular letters to said superintendents, giving advice as to the best manner of conducting schools, constructing school houses, furnishing the same, and procuring competent teachers. <small>Supervision of schools. Ibid. ¿ 9.</small>

14. The state superintendent, under the direction of the trustees of the school fund, shall apportion to the several counties the state school moneys to which each may be entitled, which apportionment shall be made in the ratio of the <small>Apportionment of school moneys Ibid. ¿ 10 [See sec. 152.]</small>

number of children between the ages of five and eighteen in the said counties, as ascertained by the last annual report of the state superintendent; he shall furnish to the state comptroller, and to the county superintendent and the county collector of each county, an abstract of such apportionment, and shall draw his order on the state comptroller for the amount to which each county is entitled, in favor of the county collector of said county.

<small>Power of withholding school moneys.
Ibid. § 11
[See secs. 23, 33, 110 and 344.]</small>

15. He shall have power, and it shall be his duty to direct and cause the county superintendent of any county, or any board of trustees or other school officers, to withhold from any officer, or district, or teacher, that part of the state appropriation derived from the revenue of the state, until such officer, district or teacher shall have complied with the provisions of this act and its supplements, relating to his, its or their duties, and with all the rules and regulations made in pursuance thereof by the state board of education; he shall forbid the payment of said part of the state appropriation to any district in which the school or schools have not been kept according to law, or in which a public school <small>[See sec. 141.]</small> has not been kept for at least [nine] months during the year next preceding the demand for payment.

<small>Blanks and forms, how furnished
Ibid. § 12.
[See sec. 180.]</small>

16. He shall prepare, and cause to be printed, suitable forms for making all reports and conducting all necessary proceedings under the school laws of this state, and shall transmit them to the local school officers and teachers; he shall cause all school laws to be printed in pamphlet form, and shall annex thereto forms for making reports and conducting school business.

<small>To decide disputes.
Ibid. § 13.
[See secs. 6, div. vi. and 34.]</small>

17. He shall decide, subject to appeal to the state board of education, and without cost to the parties, all controversies or disputes that may arise under the school laws of the state or under the rules and regulations prescribed by the state board of education, the facts of which controversies or disputes shall be made known to him by written statements by the parties thereto, verified by oath or affirmation, if required, and accompanied by certified copies of all documents necessary to a full understanding of the question in

dispute; and his decision shall be binding until a different decision shall be given by the state board of education.

18. He shall preserve in his office such school books, apparatus, maps, charts, works on education, plans for school buildings, and other articles of interest to school officers or teachers, as may be secured without expense to the state. Preserve books and apparatus Ibid. § 14

19. He shall file all school reports of this state and of other states which may be sent to his office, and shall keep a record of all the acts connected with his official duties, and preserve copies of all the decisions given by him. File reports, &c. Ibid. § 15.

20. He shall provide a seal, with suitable device, for use in his office, by which all his official acts and decisions may be authenticated. Official seal. Ibid. § 16.

21. He shall report to the state board of education, at its annual meeting in December of each year, a statement of the condition of the public schools and of all the educational institutions receiving support from the state, which report shall contain full statistical tables of all items connected with the cause of education that may be of interest to the school officers or people of the state, together with such plans and suggestions for the improvement of the schools and the advancement of the public instruction in the state as he shall deem expedient. Annual report. Ibid. § 17. [See sec. 6, div. II.]

22. He shall, at the expiration of his term of office, deliver to his successor his official seal, together with all property, books, documents, maps, records, reports and other papers belonging to his office, or which may have been received by him for the use of his office. Deliver property to successor. Ibid. § 18.

23. He shall (unless the state board of education shall, for good cause shown, otherwise direct) have power, and it shall be his duty, to direct and cause the county collector of any county to withhold from any county superintendent any portion of his salary until he has fully complied with the provisions of the act to which this is a supplement, or any of its supplements, relating to his duties; and (unless the state board of education shall, for good cause shown, otherwise direct) it shall be his duty to direct and cause the county superintendent of any county, or any board of trus- Power of withholding school moneys. P. L. 1872. Chap. DXXVIII, § 1. [See secs. 15, 33, 110 and 344.]

tees or school officers, to withhold from any officer, or district, or teacher, that part of the state appropriation derived from the revenue of the state until such officer, district or teacher shall have complied with the provisions of the act to which this is a supplement, or any of its supplements, relating to his, its or their duties, and with all the rules and regulations made in pursuance of any of these acts by the state board of education; and by and with the advice and consent of the state board of education, he shall have power, and it shall be his duty, to suspend or revoke the license of any teacher, when the county superintendent shall make formal report that such teacher does not possess the attainments or qualifications which are essential to his office, or that the school or department of a school under the charge of such teacher is suffering from his or her incompetency, or from his or her failure or inability to govern or instruct the children who are under his or her care.

Suspend or revoke teacher's certificate.

24. The state superintendent of public instruction shall cause to be prepared and printed in convenient form plans and general specifications for the construction of schoolhouses of the various sizes and styles adapted to the needs of this state, with such general directions as to heating, lighting, ventilation and other sanitary conditions and details as may be desirable, and shall furnish such plans and directions, upon application, to school trustees and other school officers of this state; *provided*, that not more than five hundred dollars shall be expended for this purpose in any one year, and that the same shall be paid on the warrant of the comptroller out of the income of the school fund.

Prepare plans for school houses. P. L. 1889. Chap. LXXVII, § 1.

Proviso.

COUNTY SUPERINTENDENTS.

25. The state board of education shall appoint for each county a person of suitable attainments to be the county superintendent of the public schools of that county, who shall hold office for the term of three years and until his successor shall have been appointed as aforesaid, unless sooner removed for cause by the state board of education.

County superintendent, how appointed. P. L. 1889. Chap. CLXV, § 2. [See sec. 6, div. 3.] Term.

SCHOOL LAW.

26. In order to enable county superintendents of schools to devote more time to the discharge of the duties of their office, and to properly examine and direct the schools under their charge, by frequent visits to said schools and counsel and direction to teachers in the proper method of instruction, their yearly salary shall be at the rate of twelve and a half cents for each child in the county between the ages of five and eighteen, as ascertained from the last annual report of the state superintendent; *provided*, that the salary shall in no case be less than eight hundred dollars, nor more than thirteen hundred dollars; *and provided*, that the salary of a superintendent having fifty or more district schools to visit shall not be less than one thousand dollars; *and provided*, that in case any city or town shall have a city or town superintendent of schools, the children belonging to such city or town shall not be counted in determining the salary of the county superintendent, and the supervision of the schools of said city or town, which would otherwise belong to the county superintendent, shall devolve upon the city or town superintendent. Salary of county superintendents. P. L. 1892. Chap. CCXXVIII, § 1. Proviso. Proviso. Proviso.

27. In order to enable county superintendents of schools to discharge their duties with greater efficiency, they shall receive annually, in addition to the salary now allowed them, such sums as they may need to pay the actual expenses incurred by them in the performance of their official duties, which sums shall be paid by the collector of the county on the order of the state superintendent of public instruction; *provided*, that no such order shall be given in favor of any county superintendent until such county superintendent shall have furnished the state board of education a certified statement, under oath, by items, of the expenses he has incurred, and that, during the year for which such order is drawn, he has performed faithfully all the duties imposed by the school law and by the regulations of the state board of education; *and provided further*, that in no case shall the expenses aforesaid exceed three hundred dollars annually. Expenses of county superintendents. P. L. 1871. Chap. DCX, § 1. Proviso. Proviso.

28. The county superintendent shall have power to administer all necessary oaths or affirmations to district clerks and County superintendent authorized to administer oath.

P. L. 1871.
Chap. DXXVII
§ 13.
other school officers, for which he shall receive no compensation.

County superintendent to issue orders.
P L. 1894.
Chap. CCCXXXV, § 1.
[See sec. 153.
29. He shall issue orders on the county collector in favor of each township collector or receiver of taxes, and of each city treasurer for that portion of the state appropriation to which said township, city, town or borough is entitled.

License teachers, fix boundaries of districts, &c.
Ibid. § 2.
[See sec. 6.]
30. He shall **examine and license teachers** and discharge other duties of general supervision and superintendence over the public schools of the county in accordance with the regulations prescribed from time to time by the state board of education.

Appointment of trustees.
Ibid. § 3]
[See sec. 32.]
31. He shall have power, and it shall be his duty, to appoint trustees for any district which, for any cause, fails to elect at the regular time and to appoint trustees to fill vacancies: provided, the terms of office of trustees so appointed shall expire at the next regular election for school trustees, and that the trustees elected to fill vacancies shall be elected for the unexpired term.*

Removal of district clerk.
P. L. 1888
Chap. LVIII,
§ 1.
32. Whenever any county superintendent of schools shall receive satisfactory evidence that any district clerk in his county has neglected or refused to perform any official duty assigned to him by law, he may declare the office of said district clerk vacant, and proceed to fill, by appointment,

Proviso.
such office for the unexpired term; *provided*, that due notice of his proposed action shall be sent by the county superintendent to such district clerk, who shall have opportunity to present satisfactory reasons for such neglect or refusal, and that the office of such district clerk shall not be declared vacant until the expiration of three weeks from the date of

Proviso.
said notice; *and provided further*, that the action of the county superintendent shall be approved by the state superintendent of public instruction.

Power of withholding school moneys.
P. L. 1883.
Chap. CXXXVIII § 1.
[See secs. 15, 23, 110, 121 and 344.]
33. He shall have power to withhold that part of the state appropriation derived from the revenue of the state from any district in which the inhabitants fail to provide a suitable school building and outhouses; *provided*, that no building of two or more stories, used for the purpose of

---

*The office of trustee is not vacated by an unaccepted resignation. *Townsend* v. *Trustees, &c.*, 12 Vr. 312.

public instruction, in which any of the doors at places of exit are so constructed as to open inwardly, shall be considered a suitable school building within the meaning of this section. *Doors to open outwardly.*

34. In all controversies arising under the school law, the opinion and advice of the county superintendent shall first be sought, and from him appeal may be made, if necessary, to the state superintendent of public instruction.* *To give advice. P. L. 1867 Chap. CLXXIX, § 28. Appeal to state superintendent*

35. The county and city superintendents shall together constitute an association, to be called "The State Association of School Superintendents," which association shall meet annually, at such times and places as the state board of education may appoint, and at such other times as they may agree upon. *State association of school superintendents. Ibid. § 29. P. L. 1872. Chap. DXXVIII, § 3.*

36. Each county superintendent and each city superintendent, in his annual report to the state superintendent, in the manner and form prescribed by him, shall specifically set forth any and all such facts within his purview as touch and describe the location and capacity of each school healthfully to accommodate the pupils in attendance, to the end that a full observation may be deduced, favorable or otherwise, as to an ample supply of sittings, suitability of conveniences, eligibility of position, attention to ventilation, and as to all such other pertinent subjects as may clearly and fully exhibit the sanitary condition of the public schools under his official inspection. *Annual report by county and city superintendents. P. L. 1873, Chap. DXCIX, § 1. [See sec. 37.]*

37. The annual reports required of city superintendents, district clerks and township collectors shall be made on or before the first day of August, and that the reports of the county superintendents shall be made on or before the first day of September of each and every year. *When reports shall be made. P. L. 1874, Chap. CCCLV, § 4.*

---

*1. In controversies arising under the school law, the appeal is to be made to the county superintendent, and not to the city superintendent. *Macfarland* v. *Gloucester City*, 16 Vr. 100.

2. A county superintendent has no authority, under the public school act, to decide controversies, so as to bind the parties. He can merely express an opinion and give advice after such investigation as seems to him reasonable. *Buren* v. *Albertson*, 25 Vr. 72.

SCHOOL CENSUS.

<small>Census takers, appointment of. P. L. 1894, Chap. CCCXXXIV, § 1.</small>

38. The board of school trustees, or other body having control of the schools in the respective school districts in the State, shall annually designate the district clerk, or some other suitable person or persons, to act as school census enumerators, who shall personally canvass the school, the school district or portion thereof for which they have been appointed, and take, in each year, during the month of <small>Time of taking census.</small> May, an exact census of all children residing in the district between the ages of five and eighteen, not including the children who may be inmates of poorhouses, asylums or almshouses, and shall specify the names and ages of such children and the names of their parents or guardians (all children who may be absent from home attending colleges, boarding schools and private seminaries of learning shall be included in the census list of the city, town or district in which their parents or guardians reside, and not be taken by the district clerk or other person or persons appointed to take the census in the city, town or district where they may be attending such institutions of learning); and the person or persons authorized to take the same shall make a full re- <small>Report to state superintendent.</small> port thereof, verified by him or them under oath or affirmation that the same is correct and true to the best of his knowledge and belief, on the blanks furnished for that purpose, to the State superintendent of public instruction, on or before the fifteenth day of June next, after the taking of such census, and shall file a copy of the same with the board of school trustees, board of education, board of school commissioners or other body having charge and control of the schools, for the use of the district, and said district clerk or other person or persons appointed as aforesaid, making and <small>Compensation.</small> reporting said census, shall be entitled to such compensation, not exceeding five cents for the name of each child on said census list, as the board of school trustees, board of education, board of school commissioners, or other body having charge of the schools may allow, which compensation shall be paid by the district on the certificate of the state superintendent of public instruction.

39. When satisfactory evidence is presented to the state superintendent of public instruction that the census of any district or any portion thereof has been incorrectly taken or reported, as provided in this act, or when he has reason to believe that the same is incorrect, he shall return the report to the enumerator for correction; provided, that in case any enumerator shall neglect or refuse to make such correction as is necessary to secure an accurate census, it shall be the duty of the state superintendent of public instruction to designate a suitable person, who shall be a resident of the district for which he is appointed, to act as enumerator in the place of the enumerator whose report was found to be inaccurate, and the person so appointed shall take the said census, and the said census so taken shall be deemed the census of such district and shall be used in place and stead of the census taken under the provisions of the first section of this act, and the person or persons appointed by him shall receive such compensation as he may deem proper, not exceeding five cents a name, which compensation shall be paid by the district, if it appears that the census taken under the provisions of the first section of this act was incorrect, but if the census so taken is found to be correct, then and in that case the compensation for retaking the census shall be paid from the income of the school fund, on warrant of the state comptroller, on bills duly certified to him by the state superintendent of public instruction. *Census retaken in certain cases. Ibid. § 2.*

40. The state board of education, on the first Tuesday in December next and every two years thereafter, shall appoint a suitable person who shall have charge, under the direction of the state superintendent of public instruction, of all the details connected with the taking of the annual school census; and the person so appointed shall hold his office for the term of two years, unless sooner removed for inefficiency by the state board of education, and shall be paid an annual compensation of fifteen hundred dollars, which compensation shall be paid out of the income of the school fund. *Supervisor of census, how appointed. Ibid. § 3.* *Compensation.*

41. The provisions of this act shall apply to all districts in this state whether acting under the provisions of the act to which this is a supplement, or under any special charter,

or the charter of any city, town, borough or other municipality.

<small>Unvaccinated children to be designated on census roll
P. L. 1887.
Chap. LXVIII, § 23.</small>

42. At the enrollment of the children by the clerk of the school districts in the townships of this state, or by other proper officers in the cities or municipalities, inquiry shall be made as to how many of the children within the school age are unvaccinated, and the same shall be designated by a mark on the said roll, and in case any are found to be unvaccinated whose parents desire them to be protected from small-pox, and who, in the judgment of the board of education or the trustees of the school districts, are unable to pay therefor, the clerk of said district, or other authorized

<small>Children may be vaccinated at expense of township.</small>

person, may give to the said child or children a permit to appear at the office of any regularly licensed physician in said district or municipality to be vaccinated, and such physician, on presentation of said permit, with his certificate appended thereto that the said vaccination has been by him successfully performed, shall be entitled to receive from the said township or local municipal authority the sum of fifty cents for each case so certified, and the same shall be paid in the same manner that other bills for current expenses are paid therein.

SCHOOL TRUSTEES.

<small>Trustees when elected.
P. L. 1894.
Chap. CCCXXXV, § 4.</small>

43. An annual meeting for the election of school trustees shall be held in each district, on the third Tuesday in March, at the school-house or in such other convenient public place within the district as may be selected by the board of education, and notices thereof, specifying the day,

<small>Notices posted.</small>

time, object and place of such meeting, shall be posted on each school-house within the district, and at such other public places as shall be deemed necessary, at least ten days

<small>Proviso.</small>

before the date of such meeting; *provided*, that not less than seven notices shall be posted in each district, and that a copy

<small>Elections advertised in papers.
[See sec. 44.]</small>

of such notice shall be printed in such papers published in the county as are designated, for the time being, to print the pamphlet laws, in the last issue of such papers printed prior to the third Tuesday in March; the voters shall be the

SCHOOL LAW.

legal voters of the district, and a plurality of votes shall elect; and no person shall be eligible to the office of trustee unless he or she is above twenty-one years of age, is a resident of the district and can read and write; any district clerk who shall fail to post and cause to be printed notices of the election of trustees, as required by this section, shall pay a fine of twenty dollars, to be recovered in an action of debt in the court for the trial of small causes, by any person resident of said school district.

<small>Penalty for failure of district clerk to post notices.</small>

44. Every citizen of the United States, of the age of twenty-one, who shall have been a resident of this state for one year, and of the county in which he or she claims a vote for five months next before said meeting, shall have the right to vote at any school meeting in any school district of the state wherein they may reside; *provided*, that no person in the military, naval or marine service of the United States, by being stationed in any garrison, barrack or military or naval force or station within the state, and no pauper, idiot, insane person, or person convicted of a crime, which now excludes him or her from being a witness, unless pardoned or restored by law to the right of suffrage, shall enjoy the right to vote in any school meeting.

<small>Legal voters at school meetings. P. L. 1887, Chap. CXVI, § 1.</small>

<small>Proviso.</small>

45. All elections for school trustees shall be by ballot, that the legal voters shall appoint two tellers who shall receive the votes, and with the chairman of the meeting shall count the ballots, and it shall be the duty of the secretary of the meeting to record the name of each person voting at such meeting; the polls for such election shall remain open at least one hour, and as much longer as may be necessary to enable all the legal voters present to cast their ballots; the ballots may be either printed or written, and in case a trustee is to be elected to fill an unexpired term, the ballots shall designate which of the persons voted for is for the full term and which for the unexpired term.

<small>Elections to be by ballot. P. L. 1894, Chap. CCCXXXV, § 18.</small>

46. In any school district in this state where the school trustees, commissioners, board of education or other body having charge of the public schools of such district are elected by ballot at a special election held for school purposes only, by virtue of any general or special law or charter for

<small>Notices to designate time for opening and closing polls. P. L. 1894, Chap. LXXIII, § 1.</small>

such district, the trustees, commissioners, board of education or other body having charge or control of the public schools of such district, shall have the power and it shall be their duty to designate, in the notice calling such meeting for the election of such officers, the time for opening and closing the polls for such election.

<small>Number of trustees in districts not divided into wards.
P. L. 1894, Chap. CCCXXXV, § 14.</small>

47. In any township, city, town, borough or other municipality acting under the provisions of this act, which is not divided into wards, there shall be a school board consisting of nine trustees, all of whom shall be elected at the annual school meeting next after the passage of this act; at the first meeting of said trustees they shall proceed by lot to divide

<small>Members to divide into classes.</small>

themselves into three classes of three members each, who shall hold office for one, two and three years respectively; and annually thereafter three trustees shall be chosen at each annual school meeting, who shall hold office for the term of three years.

<small>Number of trustees in districts divided into wards.
Ibid § 15.</small>

48. In any township, city, town, borough or other municipality which is divided into wards there shall be a school board consisting of two trustees from each ward, all of whom shall be chosen at the annual school meeting next after the passage of this act, and at such election one person shall be chosen from each ward to serve for a term of one year, and one person to serve for a term of two years, and annually thereafter one person shall be chosen from each ward to serve for the term of two years.

<small>Time for election for 1894.
Ibid. § 16.</small>

49. The terms of office of the school trustees now in office shall expire on the first day of July next, and that it shall be the duty of the county superintendents of the several counties in this state to designate the time and place in each district for holding a special election for the selection of trustees, in accordance with the provisions of sections fourteen and fifteen of this amendatory act, and that it shall be the duty

<small>[See secs. 47 and 48.]</small>

of the several district clerks now in office to post three notices in public places within their respective districts (one of which shall be the school house, if there be one), stating the time, place and object of said meeting; and it shall be the duty of the state superintendent of public instruction to cause to be printed in each paper designated to print the session laws a notice of said meeting; and such election shall be taken to be the annual election for the year one thousand eight hundred and ninety-four; *provided*, that in any town- _{Proviso.} ship, city, town, borough or other municipality now having a board of school trustees organized as provided in sections fourteen and fifteen of this amendatory act, the terms of _{See secs. 47 and 48.]} office of such trustees shall not terminate, but such trustees shall continue in office for the terms for which they were severally elected; *and provided furth.r*, that the election pro- _{Proviso.} vided for in this section shall be held within thirty days after this act takes effect.

50. The trustees elected as provided for in sections four- _{Trustees a corporate body.} teen and fifteen of this act, shall be a body corporate, and _{Ibid. § 17.} shall be called and known as "the board of education of the _[See secs. 47 and 48.] township (city, town, or borough, as the case may be) of ———, in the county of ———."*

51. Each board of education created under the provisions _{Organization of board.} of this act shall organize within ten days after the annual _{Ibid § 34.} election, by the election of one of its members as president and one of its members as district clerk, and shall have the power to fix the compensation of said clerk, and on its _{Compensation of district clerk.} failure to organize the county superintendent shall appoint such president and district clerk.

52. He shall record, in a suitable book, all proceedings _{Duties of district clerk.} of the board, and of the annual school meetings, and of _{P. L. 1867, Chap CLXXIX, § 35.} special school meetings, and pay out, by orders on the township collectors, in the manner prescribed by law, all school moneys of the district, received from the state, township or district; he shall keep a correct and detailed account of all expenditures of school moneys in his district, and report the same to the county superintendent and also to the township committee; at each annual school meeting he shall present his record books and his accounts for public inspection, and shall make a statement of the financial condition of the district and of the action of the trustees.

---

*1. The action must be brought against the district by its corporate name, and not against the trustees in their individual names, with description appended of "Trustees, &c." *Sprout* v. *Smith*, 11 Vr. 314. The trustees of a school district, in their corporate capacity, are not liable to be sued in a justice's or district court. *Townsend* v. *Trustees, &c.*, 12 Vr. 312; *Trustee, &c*, v. *Stocker*, 13 Vr. 115.

SCHOOL LAW.

Powers of boards of education. P. L., 1894, Chap. CCCXXXV, §6.
Employ teachers, &c.

53. The board of education shall have power, and it shall be its duty:

I. To employ and dismiss teachers, janitors, mechanics and laborers, and to fix, alter and order paid their salaries and compensations; *

Make rules.

II. To make and enforce rules and regulations, not in conflict with the general regulations of the state board of education, for the government of schools, pupils and teachers;

Erect buildings, buy land and borrow money.

III. To erect, enlarge or improve school buildings and grounds, and purchase, lease, mortgage or sell school lots or school buildings; to borrow, with or without mortgage, and to raise money by taxation for any such purpose, or to pay debts incurred therefor or for the current expenses of the schools; *provided*, that for any such acts they shall have the previous authority of a vote of the district;

Proviso.

Rent buildings,

IV. To rent, furnish and repair school buildings and keep the same insured;

Purchase property.

V. To purchase personal property, and to receive, lease and hold in fee, in trust for the district, any and all real or personal property for the benefit of the schools thereof;

Enforce rules of state board. Prescribe course of study and series of text books.

VI. To enforce the regulations prescribed by the state board of education, and, in connection with the county superintendent, to prescribe the course of study to be pursued and a uniform series of text books to be used in the school or schools under their charge;

Suspend and expel pupils.

VII. To suspend or expel pupils from school;

Provide text books and supplies.

VIII. To provide text books and other necessary school supplies and loan the same free to all the pupils in the schools under their control;

Call special meetings of voters

IX. To call a special meeting of the legal voters of the district at any time when, in the judgment of the trustees, the interests of the school may require it, which meeting shall be called in the manner provided in section eighty-six of this act, and no business shall be transacted at such

---

* The employment of teachers by school corporations is an act judicial in its character, and should be done at a meeting of the trustees, of which all should have notice and in which all have an opportunity to participate. *Townsend* v. *Trustees, &c.*, 12 Vr. 312. An appointment, by a body authorized by statute to appoint, of one of their own number, is a mere nullity. 33 Barber 287.

special meetings except such as has been set forth in the notices by which said meeting was called ; *

X. To call a special meeting of the legal voters of such district whenever one-fourth of such legal voters shall request them by petition so to do; and in the notices calling such special meeting shall be inserted the purpose or purposes named in said petition, so far as the same are in conflict with the school laws of this state ; Call special meetings of voters upon petition.

XI. To permit a school-house to be used for other than school purposes when a majority of the trustees shall consent thereto at a regularly called meeting of the board of education ; Permit school house to be used for other purposes.

XII. To make an annual report, on or before the first day of August, to the county superintendent, in the manner and form prescribed by the state superintendent of public instruction. Make reports.

54. In case of the failure of any district clerk or city superintendent to send his annual report to the county superintendent of his county in the form prescribed, on or before the first of August, such county superintendent shall make up his report for such district or city from the last published report of the state superintendent; in making up such report, however, he shall deduct one-fifth from the school census; *provided, however*, that all such cases of delay or negligence shall be reported to the state superintendent of public instruction, whose duty it shall be to investigate the Penalty for failure of district clerk to report. P. L. 1871, Chap. DXXVII, § 12.

Proviso.

---

*1. A special meeting of the legal voters of a school district, duly called, may vote to raise money for school purposes, although such appropriation has been refused at the annual meeting. *State, Trustees, &c., v. Lewis*, 6 Vr. 377. Special meetings of the voters of a school district cannot be called unless ordered by the board of trustees regularly convened. *Bogert v. Trustees, &c.*, 14 Vr. 358. Where money is ordered to be raised by taxation at a special meeting the previous action of the trustees in calling such meeting in pursuance of authority here given, must appear in the certificate of the clerk to the assessor. *Lamb v. Hurff*, 9 Vr. 310; *Slack v. Palmer*, 10 Vr. 250.

2. Notices for special school meetings to raise special school taxes should be put up at least ten days before the time of meeting. *Davis v. Rapp*, 14 Vr 594.

3. At a special district meeting called by the board of trustees of a school district to build an addition to a school house, a majority of the votes of the taxable residents present at a meeting is sufficient authority to act. *Crandall v. Trustees, &c.*, 22 Vr. 138.

4. A special school tax, ordered by a special meeting of the voters, which was not called by the board of trustees and of which the district clerk did not give notice, will be set aside. *Apgar v. Van Syckle*, 17 Vr. 492.

5. A special meeting can vote to raise money to build a school house, although a similar proposition has been rejected at a previous special meeting held in the same year. *Stackhouse v. School Dist. 43, Sussex Co*, 23 Vr. 29:.

same, and to restore the number deducted from the school census in all cases when he receives satisfactory reasons for such delay or negligence.

<small>Trustees of public schools, when to meet P. L. 1880. Chap. CXVIII. § 1.</small>

55. The trustees of the public schools, elected in each school district in this state, shall meet for the transaction of business connected with the public schools in their respective districts, on the first Tuesday after the first Monday in March, June, September and December, or oftener if the business of the board require it.

<small>Bills and demands to be passed on in open session. Ibid. § 2.</small>

56. All bills and demands for money expended for school purposes, and contracts entered into, shall be presented and passed on in open session of the board of school trustees, and no bills or demands for money on that account shall be paid which have not been thus passed on and approved.

<small>Unlawful for trustees to pay any bills or demands unless the same are itemized. Ibid. § 3.</small>

57. It shall be unlawful for any board of school trustees or board of education of this state, to pay or disburse, out of the school moneys under their control, any sum for school supplies, books, maps, charts, globes, fuel, erecting, enlarging, repairing or improving school buildings and grounds, and janitors' salaries, unless the person claiming or receiving the said moneys shall first present to the board of trustees or board of education a detailed bill of items or demand, specifying particularly how such bill or demand is made up, and the dates thereof, and the names of the persons to whom

<small>Proviso.</small>

the amount composing such bill or demand is due; *provided*, that the district clerk, as he may be authorized by the board of trustees, is empowered to purchase for the school or schools under their control, such supplies as may be necessary, and shall present an itemized bill of the same, with affidavit attached, which shall be acted on and paid as other bills; and said itemized bill shall be considered as satisfying all the provisions of this act.

<small>Affidavit to be made to all bills. Ibid. § 4.</small>

58. Any person or persons presenting any such bill or demand, shall make an affidavit that the goods or services, itemized in said bill or demand, have been delivered or rendered, that no bonus has been given or received by any person or persons with the knowledge of the deponent in connection with the claim, and that the same is correct and

<small>Proviso.</small>

true; *provided*, that the clerk of any board of trustees or board of education is hereby authorized to take said affidavit without cost.

59. Any board of school trustees or board of education who shall willfully violate the provisions of this act, shall be deemed guilty of a misdemeanor, and on conviction thereof shall be punished by a fine not to exceed one hundred dollars, or as the court may direct. Penalty for violation of sections 55, 56, 57 and 58. Ibid. § 5.

60. The board of health of any township, or any city, borough, town or other local municipal government in this state, shall have the right to declare any epidemic or cause of ill health to be so injurious or hazardous as to make it necessary to close any or all of the public or private schools in the limits of such township, or of such city, borough, town or other local municipal government; but in case of public schools, the same shall not be closed except by the direction of the board of education, school trustees or other body having the control or direction thereof; any such board of education, school trustees or other body having control of public schools may, in such case, cause any or all of the schools under their control to be closed, if, in their judgment, such closing be necessary for sanitary purposes. Local boards authorized to declare epidemics, &c. P. L. 1887, Chap. LXVIII, § 21. Public schools may be closed.

61. Any board of education, school trustees or other body having control of the public schools, may, on account of the prevalence of any contagious disease, or to prevent the spread of such contagious disease, prohibit the attendance of any teacher or scholar upon any school under their control, and may specify the time during which such teacher or scholar shall remain away from such school, and may prohibit the attendance of any unvaccinated child who has not had the small-pox, and shall also have power to decide how far re-vaccination shall be required if a case or cases of small-pox have occurred in the city or district. Trustees may prohibit attendance of unvaccinated children. P. L. 1887, Chap. LXVIII, § 22.

62. When any execution shall be issued against any school district of this state, or against the trustees of any such school district as a body corporate representing such school district, by any court authorized to issue the same, whether upon a judgment recovered before or subsequent to Executions against school districts. P. L. 1881, Chap. LXXVII, § 1

SCHOOL LAW.

the passing of this act, and there shall be no property belonging to said school district or body corporate sufficient to satisfy the same liable to be levied on, then the officer authorized to execute such process shall serve a copy of the same upon the assessor or assessors of the township or townships in which said school district is situate, and also upon the collector or collectors of such township or townships; and upon receipt of such copy or copies, it shall be the duty of such assessor or assessors, at the time of the next regular assessment of school taxes in such school district, to assess and levy, in addition to said regular school taxes, the amount due upon said execution with interest to the time when the same shall be paid to the officer serving such process, upon the inhabitants of said school district and their estates, and upon the taxable property therein; and this tax shall be assessed and collected at the same time and in the same manner and under the same conditions, restrictions and regulations upon the assessor or assessors, collector or collectors, as other taxes for school purposes are required to be assessed and collected in such school district; and the amount of this tax, when collected, shall be a separate fund, and shall be paid over by the collector of the township in which such school district shall be situate, and if such school district be situate in two or more townships, then by the collector of that township in which the fraction of the school district containing the school house is situate, to the officer serving the process.

Assessors to assess amount of executions.

Tax, how assessed and collected and to whom paid.

TEACHERS.

School register, how kept. Ibid. § 41.

63. Every teacher of a public school shall keep a school register in the manner provided therefor, and no salary shall be paid to such teacher until said register is exhibited to the district clerk or other officer authorized to make payment, and until said officer finds, by examination, that the register has been properly kept for the time for which salary

is demanded, and enters upon the register a certificate to that effect.*

64. Every teacher who shall leave a school before the close of the school year shall, at the time of leaving, make to the county superintendent a report of the school for all that portion of the current school year that the school has been in his or her charge, and shall, at the same time, give a duplicate of said report, and surrender the school register to the district clerk, and any teacher who may be teaching any school at the close of the school year shall, in his or her annual report, include all the statistics from the school register for the entire school year, notwithstanding any previous report for a part of the year; no school money shall be paid to any teacher for the last month of his or her services, until the report herein required shall have been made and received, and the register exhibited; *provided,* that in graded schools, in which there are more teachers than one, the principal teacher alone shall be responsible for the school report and register. Report of county superintendent. Ibid. § 42.
School register left with district clerk.
Proviso.

65. No teacher shall be entitled to any salary unless such teacher shall be the holder of a proper teacher's certificate in full force and effect. When not entitled to salary. Ibid. § 43.

66. In every contract, whether written or verbal, between any teacher and board of trustees, a school month shall be construed and taken to be twenty school days, or four weeks of five school days each; and no teacher shall be required to teach school on the first day of January, the twenty-second day of February, thirtieth day of May, fourth day of July, first Monday in September (to be known as Labor Day), Thanksgiving Day, twenty-fifth day of December and any day upon which a general election shall be held for members of assembly in each year, and also any day set apart by proclamation of the governor of this state or by the president School month and holidays. Ibid. § 44.
P. L. 1887, Chap. CXIV, § 1.

---

* 1. A school teacher who has rendered services according to the requirements of the school law, and is refused compensation out of the fund specially provided for that purpose, is entitled to a mandamus to compel the proper officers to perform their duty, and to make payment of what is justly due. *Apgar* v. *School Trustees, &c.,* 5 Vr 308.

2. In an action brought by a teacher to recover of the trustees of a school district for services as a teacher an objection that the plaintiff was not the holder of a proper teacher's certificate in full force and effect cannot be made after the evidence is closed and the cause being summed up. *Sproul* v. *Smith,* 11 Vr. 314.

of the United States for the purpose of public observance; and no deduction from the teacher's time or wages shall be made by reason of the fact that a school day happens to be one of the days referred to in this section; any contract made in violation of this section shall have no force or effect as against the teacher.

Teacher's authority over pupils.
P. L. 1867, Chap. CLXXIX, § 45.

Proviso.

[See sec. 71.]

67. Every teacher shall have power to hold every pupil accountable in school for any disorderly conduct on the way to or from school, or on the play grounds of the school, or during recess, and to suspend from school any pupil for good cause; *provided*, that such suspension shall be reported by the teacher to the trustees as soon as practicable; and if such action is not sustained by them, the teacher may appeal to the county superintendent, whose decision shall be final.

Corporal punishment forbidden.
P. L. 1893, Chap. CIX, § 1.

68. No principal, teacher or other person employed or engaged in any capacity in any school or educational institution within this state, whether public or private, shall be permitted to inflict, or direct, or cause to be inflicted, corporal punishment upon any child or pupil attending or that they may attend the same.

Resolutions authorizing corporal punishment void.
Ibid. § 2.

69. Any and every resolution, by-law, rule, ordinance or other act or authority heretofore or hereafter passed, adopted, approved, made or given, by any person or persons whomsoever, natural or artificial, permitting or authorizing corporal punishment to be inflicted upon any child or pupil attending or that may attend any school or educational institution in this state, is hereby made and shall be henceforth absolutely void and of no force or effect.

Dismissal of teacher.
P. L. 1867, Chap. CLXXIX, § 46.

70. In case of the dismissal of any teacher before the expiration of any contract entered into between such teacher and trustees, the teacher shall have the right of appeal to the county superintendent, and if the county superintendent shall decide that the removal was made without good cause, said teacher shall be entitled to compensation for the full time for which the contract was made; but it shall be optional with the trustees whether he or she shall or shall not teach for the unexpired term.

PUPILS.

71. The pupils of the public schools shall comply with the regulations established in pursuance of law for the government of such schools; shall pursue the course of study, and use the series of text-books prescribed by the trustees and county superintendent, and shall submit to the authority of the teachers; continued and willful disobedience, or open defiance of the authority of the teacher, the use of habitual profanity or obscene language, shall constitute good cause for suspension or expulsion from school; any pupil who shall in any way cut, deface or otherwise injure any school house, fences or outbuildings thereof, shall be liable to suspension and punishment, and the parents of such pupil shall be liable for damages to the amount of injury, on complaint of the teacher, the amount to be determined by the trustees, and collected by the district clerk, by an action in debt therefor, in any court having jurisdiction, in his name as district clerk, together with the costs of said action.   *Pupils to submit to authority of teacher. Ibid. § 47. [See sec 67]*   *Parents liable for damages.*

72. No child between the age of five and eighteen years of age shall be excluded from any public school in this state on account of his or her religion, nationality or color. *   *No child to be excluded from any public school. P. L. 1881, Chap. CXLIX, § 1.*

73. Any member of any board of trustees of any school district, or any member of any board of education in this state, who shall vote to exclude from any public school in this state, any child between the age of five and eighteen years of age, on account of his or her religion, nationality or color, shall be deemed guilty of a misdemeanor, and on conviction thereof shall be punished by a fine of not less than fifty dollars, nor more than two hundred and fifty dollars, or by imprisonment in the county jail, workhouse or penitentiary of the county in which the offense is committed, not less than thirty days, nor more than six months, or both fine and imprisonment may be imposed in the discretion of the court.   *Penalty for voting to exclude any child from any public school. Ibid. § 2.*

74. It shall not be lawful to charge tuition fees for the support of public schools in this state, but that all such   *Tuition fees not allowed P. L. 1871, Chap. DXXVII, § 9.*

---

* School trustees cannot exclude children from any public school on the ground that they are of the negro race. *Pierce v. Union District Trustees*, 17 Vr. 76; 18 Vr. 348.

schools shall be free to all persons over five and under eighteen years of age residing within the district, so long as such schools can be thus maintained with the public school funds.

Ages of pupils.
P. L. 1889,
Chap LI, § 1.

75. The trustees of all public school districts within this state be and they are hereby authorized and required to admit to such public schools, all pupils between the ages of five and twenty years, residing in their respective districts;

Proviso.

provided, always, that attendance shall not be compulsory in the case of any pupil under the age of six or over the

Proviso.

age of eighteen years; *and provided further,* that in taking the school census only pupils between the ages of five and eighteen years shall be enrolled, as heretofore.

BOARDS OF EXAMINERS.

State board of examiners.
P. L. 1867,
Chap.
CLXXIX, § 48.

76. There shall be a state board of examiners, consisting of the state superintendent of public instruction and the principal of the state normal school; they shall have power, and it shall be their duty, to hold examinations of teachers, and to grant state certificates, or revoke the same, under such rules and regulations as the state board of education may

Certificates of state board.

prescribe; and a certificate thus granted shall entitle the holder, without further examination, to teach in any part of the state, so long as the certificate remains valid by the terms thereof, and in any school not of a higher grade than that for which the certificate represents him as qualified.

County boards of examiners.
P. L. 1893,
Chap.
CLXXVI, § 1.

77. There shall be in each county a county board of examiners, which shall be composed of the county superintendent, who shall, *ex-officio,* be chairman, and of a number of teachers, not to exceed three, to be appointed by him, who shall hold for one year from the time of their respective appointments; but no person shall be appointed as county examiner unless he holds either a state or a first grade county certificate; the county superintendent shall fill vacancies that occur from absence or other cause, but if he cannot find any teacher in his county qualified under the provisions of this section willing to serve, he shall conduct the examination

SCHOOL LAW.

himself; the board shall meet at such places as may be designated by the chairman, and shall hold at least three regular sessions each year; each member of the county board of examiners, except the county superintendent, shall receive for his services, in addition to traveling expenses, such compensation as may be fixed by the state board of education, not exceeding ten dollars for each regular examination, to be paid by the county collector on the order of the county superintendent; *provided*, that whenever said board shall hold sessions at any other time than as appointed by the state board of education, no compensation shall be allowed from the county; but in case of special examinations said board may charge each applicant an examination fee not exceeding two dollars; the county board of examiners shall have power to conduct examinations and to grant certificates of different grades, in accordance with the general regulations on the subject prescribed by the state board of education. Compensasion. Proviso.

78. In every city having a board of education governed by special laws there may be a city board of examiners, to consist of such members as said board of education of that city may appoint; said examiners shall have power, subject to such rules and regulations as may be prescribed by the city board of education, to grant certificates of qualification, which shall be valid for all schools of that city, and no teacher shall be employed in any of the schools of that city unless possessing such certificate, or a state certificate, nor in any school of a higher grade than that for which such certificate represents the holder to be qualified; any city board of examiners may recognize the certificates of any other city, and, without examination, issue to the holders certificates of a corresponding grade. City boards of examiners.
P. L. 1885,
Chap. LXXIV, § 1.

SCHOOLS.

State Normal School.

79. There shall be a normal school, or seminary, for the training and education of teachers in the art of instructing and governing the common schools of this state, the object Normal school.
P. L. 1867,
Chap. CLXXIX, § 51.
[See sec. 3.]

of which normal school or seminary shall be the training and education of its pupils in such branches of knowledge, and such methods of teaching and governing, as will qualify them for teachers of our common schools.

<small>Supervision of normal school.
Ibid. § 54.
[See sec. 3.]</small>

80. To the said board of trustees shall be committed the control and use of the buildings and grounds owned and used by the state for the use of the normal school, the application of the funds for the support thereof, the appointment of teachers and the power of removing the same, the power to prescribe the studies and exercises of the school, and rules for its management, to grant diplomas, to appoint some suit-

<small>Treasurer.</small>

able person treasurer of the board, and to frame and modify at pleasure such by-laws as they may deem necessary for

<small>Annual report.</small>

their own government; and they shall report annually to the legislature their own doings and the progress and condition of the school.

<small>Repairs, &c., to normal school.
P. L. 1867,
Chap. CLXXIX, § 2, div. 6.
P. L. 1885, Chap CLXIV, § 1, div. 3.</small>

81. To order all necessary repairs to the grounds, buildings and furniture of the state normal school, and to keep said buildings and furniture insured, and the comptroller shall draw warrants on the treasurer of the school fund for the payment of the same, upon the certificate of the president of said board.

<small>Pupils, how admitted.
P. L. 1867,
Chap. CLXXIX, § 56.</small>

82. At the opening of each term of the normal school the principal, with his assistants, shall proceed to examine applicants, and to admit to the school such as appear to be possessed of the proper qualification to the number to which each county may be entitled.

<small>Number of pupils.
P. L 1893,
Chap XLIX,
§ 3.</small>

83. Each county shall be entitled to at least six times as many pupils in the school as it has representatives in the legislature; and in case any county is not fully represented additional candidates may be admitted from other localities on sustaining the requisite examination; the applicants shall give on admission a written declaration signed with their own hands, that their object in seeking admission to the school is to qualify themselves for the employment of public school teachers, and that it is their intention to engage in that employment in this state for at least two years or refund to the state the cost of their tuition.

84. The board of trustees shall appoint and procure the number of teachers which may be necessary to carry out, in the best and highest sense, the purposes and designs of this act, and shall furnish for the use of the pupils the necessary apparatus and text-books, so far as the funds hereafter to be named and appropriated for the support of the school will allow; and the tuition in the normal school shall be gratuitous. Teachers, how appointed. P. L. 1867, Chap. CLXXIX, § 58. [See sec. 3.]

85. The board of trustees are authorized to maintain a model school, under permanent teachers, in which the pupils of the normal school shall have opportunity to observe and practice the modes of instruction and discipline inculcated in the normal school, and in which pupils may be prepared for the normal school. Model school Ibid. § 59. [See sec. 3.]

86. For the support of the normal school and to carry out the purpose and designs of this act, there is appropriated hereby the annual sum of twenty-eight thousand dollars, to be paid out of the income of the school fund upon the warrant of the comptroller. Appropriation. P. L. 1893, Chap. XLIX, § 4.

87. The school year, so far as regards the state normal school, shall hereafter terminate on the last day of June. School year for normal school. P. L. 1872, Chap. CCCCXCI, § 1.

Deaf-Mute School.

88. The property lately used as a home for soldiers' children shall be taken and set apart to be used as an institution for the maintenance and instruction by the state of its indigent deaf and dumb. Property designated and uses prescribed. P. L. 1882, Chap. CLXXXVII, § 1.

89. The name and title of the institution shall hereafter be "the New Jersey school for deaf-mutes." Name of institution. P. L. 1884, Chap. CIII, § 2.

90. Indigent deaf and dumb persons of suitable age and capacity for instruction, who are legal residents of this state, shall be entitled to the privilege of the school without charge, and for such a period of time in each individual case as may be deemed expedient by the board of trustees; *provided,* that whenever more persons apply for admission at one time than can be properly accommodated in the said school, the trustees shall so apportion the number received that each county may be represented in the ratio of its deaf and dumb population Qualifications of pupils. P. L. 1882, Chap. CLXXXVII, § 6. Term of instruction. [See sec 92.] Proviso. Apportionment to counties.

to the total population of such persons in the state; application for admission into the said school shall be made to the board of trustees in such manner as they may direct, but the board shall require each application to be accompanied by a certificate from a county judge or county clerk of the county, or the chosen freeholder, or clerk of the township, or the mayor of the city where the applicant resides, setting forth the applicant is a legal resident of the town, township or city, county and state, claimed as his or her residence, and the age, circumstances and capacity of such pupil, and the ability or inability of the parent or guardian of such pupil to pay any part of the expense of tuition, care and maintenance of the person in whose behalf such application may be made; the primary object of the school shall be to furnish to the indigent deaf and dumb children of this state the best known facilities for the enjoyment of such a share of the benefits of the system of free public education established in this state as their afflicted condition will admit of; the board of trustees shall have charge of all the affairs of the school, with power to make such by-laws and regulations for the government and the proper management thereof, as well as for the admission of pupils, as shall be approved by the state board of education; they shall elect from their own number a president, treasurer and secretary, together with such standing committees as they may deem necessary; the treasurer shall have the custody of all the funds of the said school, and pay out the same only on proper authenticated orders of the board, or its executive committee; before entering upon the duties of his office he shall give bond, with at least two sureties, to be approved as hereinafter stated, to the people of the state of New Jersey, in the penal sum of ten thousand dollars conditioned for the faithful discharge of his trust, which bond shall be approved by the board of trustees of this state [institution], and deposited in the office of the secretary of state; the board of trustees shall have power to appoint a competent and experienced superintendent, who shall be the chief executive officer of the school, together with an efficient corps of teachers and subordinate officers, prescribe the duties and terms of service of the same, fix and pay their salaries, and for just cause remove any or all of them; they shall likewise employ the requisite number of servants and other assistants in the various departments of the school, and pay the wages of the same; and they shall purchase all furniture, school books, school apparatus; and other supplies necessary to the equipment and carrying on of the same, and in the manner hereinafter described. *Terms of service and salaries. May be removed by trustees. Employment of assistants and servants. Payment of their wages. Purchase of furniture, books and supplies. [See sec. 94.]*

91. The trustees of said institution shall receive no compensation for their services except in the case of the treasurer, who may be fairly compensated at the discretion of the board, but they shall be paid all necessary expenses incurred by them in the discharge of their duties, to be paid by the treasurer of said board of trustees on the order of the governor. *Trustees to receive no compensation. Ibid. § 7. Payment of their expenses. Treasurer may be paid.*

92. That any indigent deaf-mute of suitable capacity, who shall be a legal resident of this state, and who shall be not less than eight years nor more than twenty-one years of age, may be admitted to and be entitled to the benefits of the institution, subject to such rules and regulations as have been or may be established by the state board of education; the term of instruction shall be three years, but in any case in which it may be proper, in the judgment of the said board, the term may be thereupon extended by said board for a period not exceeding eight years, which said term may be further extended by said board in meritorious cases for a period not exceeding three additional years; *and provided, further,* that when it shall be found, in the judgment of said board, that any pupil now in the institution, or hereafter admitted, shall be, from want of capacity or other cause, not capable of receiving the benefits designed to be conferred, or that the retention of any pupil is or may be detrimental to the interests of the school, the said board shall have power to shorten the term of, or to dismiss from the school such pupil upon reasonable notice given to his or her parents or guardians. *Who may be admitted. P. L. 1892, Chap. CCIII, § 1. Term of instruction. Proviso.*

93. Whenever the board of trustees shall be satisfied that the resources of any person applying for the benefits of this act, or those of his or their parents or guardians, are *Tuition and maintenance of pupils not indigent.*

sufficient to defray a part of the expense of instructing and maintaining such person, but not sufficient to defray the whole expense, then the board of trustees may cause to be paid such proportion as to them may seem just and equitable of the annual expense of educating such person.

P. L. 1882, Chap CLXXXVII, § 9.

94. All improvements, additions and repairs to the buildings to be used for the purposes of this act, together with the furnishing of the same, shall be by contract, after due notice is given and specifications furnished; and that it shall be the duty of the superintendent, under the direction of the board of trustees, to invite proposals twice in each year, at intervals of six months, for supplying the institution with dry goods, wearing apparel, groceries, provisions, vegetables, fuel, illuminating material, and all other articles the necessity of which it is practicable to determine as being needed for the ensuing six months, the standard quality of which shall be determined by the board, and standard sample grades of non-perishable articles shall be kept in the office of the superintendent, for the inspection of bidders; the inviting of proposals shall be advertised ten consecutive days in two daily newspapers published in the city of Trenton, and which advertisement shall classify the articles which shall be grouped in each bid, and also state, as near as practicable, the amount and quantity needed and that said goods are to be delivered during the ensuing six months, as wanted, on the order of the superintendent; and it shall be the duty of the board to award the contract to the lowest average bidder on each class or group of articles advertised for, and to require the contractors to enter into suitable bonds for the faithful performance of the same; *it is further provided*, that the board of trustees reserve the right to reject any or all bids not considered to be in the interest of the state.

Additions and repairs to buildings to be made by contract. Ibid. § 10.

Supplies to be contracted for.

Proposals to be invited by advertisement.

Bonds to be given by contractors.

Trustees may reject all bids.

95. It shall be the duty of the trustees of the New Jersey school for deaf-mutes to submit a quarterly report to the governor of the state showing the number of pupils taught and maintained in the school in each quarter, and upon the approval of the said report by the governor, there shall be paid to the said trustees, for such expenses, the sum

Trustees to make quarterly report to governor. P. L. 1888, Chap CCXXXVII, § 1.

or sums required to defray the expenses of teaching, maintaining and clothing the said pupils for the said quarter; *provided*, the said sum shall not exceed for any three months the sum of seventy-six dollars for each pupil taught, maintained and clothed within the said period, the same to be paid by the state treasurer, out of the income of the school fund, upon the warrant of the comptroller.

Appropriation.

Proviso

DISTRICT SCHOOLS.

96. The several school districts in each township shall be consolidated into one school district, and that all property, real and personal, of said several school districts shall become and be the property of the consolidated district, in its corporate capacity, and shall be held in its corporate name, and the several obligations and debts of said districts, whether secured by bonds or otherwise, shall be assumed by and shall become the obligations and debts of said consolidated district.*

Consolidation of school districts. P. L. 1894, Chap. CCCXXXV. § 13.

97. Each city, borough and incorporated town shall be a school district, separate and distinct from the township school district; *provided*, that whenever any borough or any district acting under a special charter, or under the provisions contained in the charter of any city, town, borough or other municipality, desires to consolidate with the township and form but a single school district, such consolidation shall take effect when the board of education of such borough or district shall file with the county superintendent a certificate that at a meeting of the legal voters of such borough or district a majority of the legal voters present voted in favor of such consolidation, which meeting shall be specially called for that purpose by the board of education in the manner provided for calling other special meetings of the legal voters of the district.

Districts, how constituted. Ibid. § 24.

Boroughs and districts with special charters may unite with township.

98. Wherever the word "district" is used in this act, or in the act to which this is an amendment, it shall be taken

Word "district," how construed. Ibid. § 25. [See secs. 97 and 98.]

---

*The fact that a debt was contracted by the trustees of a district, which was subsequently consolidated with another district, will not bar the right to recover; the new district having become entitled to all the property, rights and assets of and liab'e to all just claims against the several districts. *Sproul* v. *Smith*, 11 Vr. 314.

as applying only to districts constituted as provided in sections thirteen and twenty-four of this act.

Children to attend school in district where they reside. Ibid. ₴ 21.

99. All children shall be required to attend the schools in the district in which they reside; *provided*, that any child living remote from any public school in the district in which he resides may be allowed to attend the public schools in an adjoining district, but only with the consent of the county superintendent, which consent must be in writing, and one copy thereof filed with the district clerk of the district in which such child resides, and one copy filed with the district clerk of the district in which such child attends school; and in case the districts are not in the same county, the consent of the superintendent of each county must be obtained; and *provided further*, that the money apportioned to the district for such child on the basis of the school census shall be paid over by the township collector of the township in which such child resides to the township collector of the township in which such child attends school on the order of the county superintendent.

May be transferred to other districts in certain cases.

Proviso.

District may provide transportation for children in certain cases. Ibid. ₴ 22.

100. When in any district there are children living remote from the school house, and who are unable on that account to attend such school, such district may order raised by special district tax an amount of money sufficient to enable the board of education to transport such children to and from the school, under such rules and regulations as may be deemed necessary by the board of education of such district; that the moneys expended in accordance with the provisions of this section shall be entered as a separate item in the accounts kept by the district clerk, and that the total sum expended for the purpose of transporting such children shall not exceed the amount ordered to be raised for said purpose.

District Schools.

Suitable school buildings repaired. P. L. 1867, Chap. CLXXIX, ₴ 62. [See sec. 33.]

101. The inhabitants of every school district shall be required to provide a suitable school building and outhouses for the accommodation of their children; and in case such buildings are not provided, or those already in use shall be pronounced by the county superintendent unfit

for the purposes for which they are applied, such district shall be deprived of the benefit of that part of the state appropriation derived from the revenues of the state until suitable buildings shall be erected. Penalty.

102. Every building now or hereafter used in whole or in part as a school house shall be provided with proper ways of egress or other means of escape from fire sufficient for the use of all persons assembling in such building, and such ways of egress and means of escape shall be kept free from obstruction, in good repair and ready for use; all doors in any building subject to the provisions of this section shall open outwardly, if the inspector or one of his deputies shall so direct in writing; no portable seats shall be allowed in the aisles or passageways of such building during any service or entertainment held therein. School houses to be provided with fire escapes. P. L. 1889, Chap. CCLXXXVII, § 1. [See sec. 33]

103. A copy of this act shall be kept posted in a conspicuous place in every such building by the person occupying the premises. Copy of law to be posted. Ibid. § 2.

104. Every story above the second story of a building subject to the provisions of section one of this act shall be supplied with means of extinguishing fire, consisting either of pails of water or other portable apparatus, or of a hose attached to a suitable water supply, and capable of reaching any part of such story; and such means of extinguishing fire shall be kept at all times ready for use and in good condition. Fire extinguishers. Ibid. § 7. [See sec 102.]

105. All buildings now or hereafter erected in which twenty or more persons live or congregate or are employed, temporarily or otherwise, above the first or ground floor thereof, shall have one or more, as the proper authority shall direct, external wrought-iron fire escapes, of such dimensions and character and subject to such regulation and construction as the said proper authority shall designate. Fire escapes on buildings P. L. 1890, Chap. LXIII, § 1.

106. In all incorporated municipalities the board of aldermen, city council or borough commissioners shall provide for the enforcement of the provisions of this act by ordinance. Who to enforce in municipalities. Ibid. § 2.

107. In all sections outside of incorporated municipalities, township committees shall have power to enforce the provisions of this act. Who to enforce in townships. Ibid § 3.

Time schools must be maintained.
P. L. 1867, Chap. CLXXIX, § 63.
[See sec. 141.]
Proviso.

108. No school district shall be entitled to receive any part of the school appropriation which shall not have maintained a public school for at least nine months during the then next preceding school year; *provided,* that any new district, or a district in which the school is discontinued on account of the repairing of an old or the erection of a new school building, shall not be deprived of its full share of the public school funds on account of the restrictions of this section.

Power of school district to borrow money to pay teachers' salaries.
P. L. 1886, Chap. LXXII, § 1.

109. Any school district may, after the first day of September and before the thirty-first day of December, in any year, borrow a sum not exceeding four-tenths of the amount apportioned to such district from the state school moneys for such year, for the purpose of paying teachers' salaries falling due within said year; and that the said district may pay the amount so borrowed, together with interest thereon at a rate not exceeding six per centum per annum, out of the state school moneys apportioned to said district for the then current school year, as soon as the same shall have been received by the township collector of the township in which said district is situated.

Power of withholding school money.
P. L. 1881, Chap. CLXXX, § 1.
[See secs. 15, 23, 110 and 344.]

110. In case any school district or city shall use any of the school money apportioned to it for any other than public school purposes, as these purposes are defined and limited in the ninety-first section of this act, such district or city shall forfeit out of the next annual apportionment a sum equal to twice the amount thus used; and it shall be the duty of the county superintendent to re-apportion the money thus forfeited among the other districts and cities of his county;

Proviso.

provided, the state superintendent may remit such penalty for cause.

Preamble.

WHEREAS, Certain school districts in this state are subject to the provisions of special or local laws applicable to such

P. L. 1886, Chap. CCXXX.

districts, and it is deemed desirable that such districts should be governed solely by the provisions of the general school law of this state; therefore,

Districts having local laws may adopt the general law.
Ibid. § 1.

111. Any such district may be relieved from the provisions and limitations of such special or local laws upon the adoption of the provisions of this act by the legal voters of said

district at any meeting of such voters called for the purpose, as hereinafter provided.

112. Whenever the trustees of any such district shall by resolution decide to submit the question of the adoption of this act to the voters of the district, they shall call a meeting for that purpose, giving notice of the time, place and object of said meeting, in the manner provided for the calling of school meetings by the eighty-sixth section of the "Act to establish a system of public instruction" [Revision], approved March twenty-seventh, one thousand eight hundred and seventy-four, and if at any such meeting a majority of the legal voters present shall vote to adopt the provisions of this act, thereafter said district shall be governed solely by the general school laws of this state applicable thereto, instead of the special act, and the said trustees shall forthwith file a certificate with the county school superintendent setting forth the determination of such meeting.

Special meetings to vote on questions of abandoning special school laws. Ibid. § 2.

[See sec. 164.]

113. In case of the adoption of this act by any district, the said district shall retain all its property, real and personal, and be subject to any lawful obligations it may have incurred, in the same manner and to the same extent as if the provisions of this act had not been adopted.

Obligations of districts not changed. Ibid § 3.

114. The school year shall begin on the first day of July and end on the last day of June.

School year. P. L. 1893. Chap. CLXXVI, § 2

TEXT BOOKS AND SUPPLIES.

115. School trustees and boards of education shall purchase text books and other necessary school supplies for use in the public schools of their respective school districts, as such new text books and supplies are required in addition to those at present in use in the hands of pupils or owned by the school districts, out of a free text book fund of the district, to be raised by special school tax, which shall be assessed and collected in the same manner as moneys for public school purposes are now raised by law, and when so procured the necessary books and school supplies shall be furnished free of cost for use in the public schools of said districts, subject to the orders of the school

School boards to supply books and supplies to pupils. P. L. 1894, Chap. CLXXXVII, § 1.

trustees and boards of education thereof, whose duty it shall be to provide for the return of and for the safe keeping and care of the books, which shall be returned at the close of the annual school term in each year, or as the board may direct.

Separate account of expenses incurred for books, &c.
Ibid. § 2.

116. The board shall keep an account of all moneys expended under the above section, and report it under separate items in the annual financial accounts as authorized by law.

School officers not to act as agents.
Ibid. § 3.

117. It shall not be lawful for the county superintendents, school trustees or boards of education, or any other person officially connected with the common school system, to become agents for the sale, or in any way unlawfully promote the sale, of any school books, maps, charts, school apparatus or stationery, or to receive unlawful compensation for such sale, or promotion of sale, in any manner whatsoever, and any violation of the provisions of this section shall be deemed a misdemeanor, and punishable with removal from office.

Officers not to be interested in furnishing books, &c.
Ibid. § 4.

118. It shall not be lawful for any director or president of any school board in this state to be interested in the furnishing of books or any other supplies for said schools.

SCHOOL FUND.

Trustees of school fund.
P. L. 1894.
Chap. CII, § 1.

119. The governor of this state, the president of the senate, the speaker of the house of assembly, the attorney general, the secretary of state, the comptroller and the treasurer and their successors in office, be and they are hereby constituted and appointed trustees of the fund for the support of public schools in this state arising either from appropriation heretofore made or which may hereafter be made by law, or which may arise from the gift, grant, bequest or devise of any person or persons whatsoever, which trustees shall be known by the name, style and title of "the trustees for the support of public schools;" *provided*, that it shall not be lawful for any teacher, trustee or trustees to introduce into or have performed in any school receiving its proportion of the public money, any religious service, ceremony or forms whatsoever, except reading the Bible and repeating the Lord's prayer.

120. The public stocks and moneys heretofore appropriated by law shall constitute the funds in the hands of the trustees appointed by the foregoing section of this act, and shall be held by the said trustees in trust, the interest and dividends arising therefrom to be applied by the said trustees, or a majority of them, for the support of public schools in this state, in the mode now prescribed or hereafter to be prescribed by any act or acts of the legislature, and for no other use or purpose whatsoever.

<small>School fund, how constituted. P. L. 1867, Chap. CLXXIX, § 66.</small>

121. All moneys hereafter received from the sales and rentals of land under water, belonging to the state, shall be paid over to the trustees of the school fund, and appropriated for the support of free public schools, and shall be held by them in trust for that purpose, and shall be invested by the treasurer of the state, under their direction, in the same manner as the funds now held by them are invested; the same to constitute a part of the permanent school fund of the state, and the interest thereof to be applied to the support of public schools, in the mode which now is, or hereafter may be, directed by law, and to no other use or purpose whatever.

<small>Riparian funds appropriated to schools. P. L. 1871, Chap. DXXX, § 1.</small>

122. All leases which have been made by this state, or any board or officer of this state, in pursuance of the provisions of an act entitled "An act to provide for the use of the proceeds of riparian sales, grants and leases," approved March nineteenth, one thousand eight hundred and ninety, of lands belonging to the state now or formerly lying under water, be and the same are hereby transferred to the trustees of the school fund of this state, to become a portion of the free school fund, and that the annual income arising from such leases shall be distributed by the said trustees for the support of free public schools in the same manner that other moneys are now distributed for that purpose.

<small>Riparian leases transferred to school fund. P. L. 1894, Chap. LXXI, § 2.</small>

123. All leases which shall hereafter be made of lands belonging to the state, now or formerly lying under water, or which have been made since the sixth day of April, eighteen hundred and seventy-one, shall be transferred to the trustees of the school fund of this state, and become a portion of the free school fund; and the annual income

<small>Money derived from leases added to school fund. P. L. 1872, Chap. CCCCXXXIV, § 1.</small>

arising from said leases shall be distributed by the said trustees for the support of free public schools, in the same manner that other moneys are now distributed for that purpose.

Investment of school fund. P. L. 1886, Chap CXIX, § 1.

124. The fund above mentioned, together with all the moneys which shall be received by the treasurer in payment of the principal or interest of the bank or turnpike stock belonging to the fund for the support of free schools, all the taxes which may hereafter be received into the treasury from any of the banking and insurance companies in this state, the capital stock of which now is, or may hereafter be liable by law to be taxed, all appropriations to said fund made or to be made by any law of this state, and the amount of all gifts, grants, bequests or devises hereafter made by any person or persons to the said trustees, for the purpose contemplated by this act, shall be invested by the treasurer of this state, under the direction of said trustees, or a majority of them, in the bonds of the United States, or of New Jersey, or in the bonds of any county, city, town or township of this state, in any case where the total indebtedness of such county, city, town or township does not exceed in the aggregate fifteen per centum of the total assessable valuation of all taxable property within such county, city, town or township, the interest thereof to be applied to the support of the public schools in the mode which now is, or may hereafter be, directed by law, and to no other use or purpose whatsoever; *Report to Legislature.* an account of the management of the said fund shall be laid before the legislature with the annual statement of the treasurer's account; *Compensation* and no compensation shall be made to said trustees or treasurer for any service performed in pursuance of the direction of this act; and all investments of money and property belonging to said fund now held or existing in the name of "The Trustees for the Support of Free Schools," are hereby and shall hereafter be vested in and held, and any proceeding or action whatever relative thereto may be taken, had, made and maintained by said trustees, in the name of the trustees for the support of public schools.

125. Whenever, in the judgment of the trustees for the support of free schools of this state, or a majority of them, it shall not be deemed advisable or for the best interests of the school fund to invest the income of the said fund in bonds secured by mortgage on land, they shall have the power to invest the said income, or any portion thereof, in the bonds of the United States and of this state, and of the several counties, townships, boroughs and cities of the same.

<small>School fund may be invested in U. S. and municipal bonds. P. L. 1878, Chap. CIII, ¶ 69.</small>

<small>[See sec. 126]</small>

126. From and after the passage of this act, it shall not be lawful for the trustees of the school fund to invest any part of the principal or interest of said fund in bonds secured by mortgage on lands in this state, except in such cases as hereinafter provided.

<small>State school fund not to be loaned on mortgage. P. L. 1883, Chap. XCIV, ¶ 1.</small>

127. The "trustees for the support of public schools" be and they are hereby authorized and empowered to bid for and purchase any lands and premises exposed to sale under the order and decree of any court, for the payment and satisfaction of any mortgage encumbrance thereon held by the said trustees, and to take and hold the title to the lands and premises so purchased in and by their official name, style and title, and as part of the assets of the school fund of New Jersey; *provided*, that said trustees shall not bid a higher price for such lands and premises than shall be sufficient to save the amount due upon their said mortgage encumbrance and costs, the taxed costs attending such proceedings and sale, if any, to be paid by the treasurer of this state, on warrant of the comptroller, out of the income of the school fund.

<small>Trustees of school fund may purchase land at foreclosure sale. P. L. 1875, Chap. CCCLXXXIII, ¶ 1</small>

<small>Proviso.</small>

<small>P. L. 1885, Chap. CLXIV, ¶ 1, div. xi.</small>

128. All real estate now held by the trustees of the school fund shall be sold, either at private or public sale, at such times and at such prices as will, in their judgment, be for the best interests of the state; and the said trustees are hereby authorized to loan to the purchaser of said property, or other properties which may come into their possession by foreclosure, one-half the amount of the purchase money, the same to be secured by bond and mortgage on the premises so purchased, and that they shall be empowered to advertise such properties, either at private or public sale in such manner as to them seems judicious; and the proceeds arising

<small>Real estate belonging to the fund to be sold. P. L. 1883, Chap. XCIV, ¶ 2.</small>

from such sales shall be paid into the fund and be invested by the trustees as provided for by existing laws.

<small>Real estate acquired under foreclosure to be sold.
Ibid § 3.
[See sec. 128]</small>

129. In case the trustees of the school fund shall further acquire real estate under foreclosure proceedings, that the same shall be disposed of at public or private sale, in the manner provided by section two of this act, and the proceeds arising from such sales shall be invested as hereinbefore directed.

<small>Foreclosure proceedings to be begun when interest is in arrears six months.
Ibid. § 4.</small>

<small>Proviso.</small>

130. The trustees are hereby directed and required to cause foreclosure proceedings to be commenced without delay, in all cases where the interest on bonds, secured by mortgage, is or may become due and remain unpaid for the space of six months; *provided*, that in case foreclosure proceedings shall have been commenced, the said trustees may, in their discretion, discontinue the same upon the payment of accrued interest and the cost of such proceedings.*

<small>Loans for building schoolhouses
P. L. 1872, Chap. DXLI, § 1.</small>

<small>[See sec. 124]</small>

131. The treasurer of this state, under the direction of "The Trustees for the Support of Public Schools," is authorized to invest the fund for the support of public schools in this state, in addition to the securites mentioned in section sixty-nine of this act, in the bonds of the several school districts of this state, and in the bonds of any city or municipality of this state, legally issued, for the purpose of building school houses, either by authority of special acts of the legislature, or by the consent of the inhabitants of the district, as hereafter herein provided for.

<small>Rate of interest on loans to school district.
P. L. 1886, Chap. XLV, § 1.</small>

132. The treasurer of this state, under the direction of the "trustees for the support of public schools," is authorized to invest the fund for the support of the public schools of this state in the bonds of the several school districts legally issued for the purpose of building school houses, at a rate of interest not less than five per centum per annum, payable half yearly.

<small>Report concerning school fund.
P. L. 1867, Chap. CLXXIX, § 63.</small>

133. The treasurer of this state shall annually make and furnish to the board of trustees for the support of public schools, on the first day of the stated annual meeting of the legislature, and at such other times as the majority of the

---

* Money belonging to the state is not liable to taxation. *Trustees of the School Fund v. Trenton*, 3 Stewart, 618-667.

said trustees shall require the same, a particular statement of the school fund, containing an account of the securities belonging to said fund, with the dates of investment, their value, and the interest arising from each denomination of securities, together with an account of the moneys in the treasury belonging to said fund.

134. The secretary of state is hereby constituted and appointed secretary of the said board of trustees, whose duty it shall be to record, in a book to be kept for that purpose, the proceedings of the said board, and the accounts to be furnished by the treasurer as hereinbefore directed. Secretary
Ibid. ¿ 69.

135. It shall be the duty of the trustees of the school fund of this state, on or before the first Monday of April of every year, to appropriate out of the annual income of the fund for the support of public schools the sum of one hundred thousand dollars; and if the annual income of said fund shall not have been received in full, or shall be insufficient for that purpose, then the said trustees are hereby authorized and empowered to draw for any sum necessary to make up the deficiency, by warrant, signed by the comptroller, upon the treasurer of the state, who is directed to pay the same; which sum, so drawn from the treasury aforesaid, shall be replaced from the annual income of said school fund so soon as the same shall be received. Appropriation of school fund to schools.
P. L. 1878.
Chap. XXXV, § 1.

Deficiency, how provided for.

136. The trustees of the school fund of this state shall have authority to divide the aforesaid sum of one hundred thousand dollars into two or more annual installments, which shall be paid by the state treasurer to the several county collectors on the warrants of the state comptroller. Payment of appropriation to schools.
P. L. 1867, Chap CLXXIX, § 75.

137. For the purpose of defraying the expenses of teachers' institutes and procuring teachers and lecturers for said institutes and other necessary expenses of the same, there may be paid annually to the state superintendent of public instruction, out of the income of the school fund, upon the warrant of the comptroller upon itemized accounts rendered to him by the state superintendent of public instruction of the expenses incurred, a sum not exceeding one hundred dollars to one teachers' institute in any county; and where two or more counties join in holding a union institute there Teachers' Institutes.
P. L. 1886,
Chap. LXXIII, § 1.

Union institute.

may be paid a sum not exceeding one hundred dollars for each county joining in such union institute.

<small>Appropriations from income of school fund.
P. L. 1885 Chap. CLXIV, § 1.</small>

188. There shall be annually appropriated from the income or revenue of the fund for the support of public free schools of this state, so much of the said income or revenue as shall be required to meet the following named disbursements, to wit:

<small>State normal school.
P. L. 1893, Chap. XLIX, § 4.</small>

I. The sum of twenty-eight thousand dollars for the support of the state normal school.

<small>Repairs to normal school.</small>

II. The sum required to be paid for the necessary repairs to the grounds, buildings and furniture of the state normal school, and for keeping the said buildings and furniture insured, and for the payment of the necessary incidental expenses of the state superintendent of public instruction.

<small>Expenses of state superintendent.</small>

<small>Expenses of state board of education. [See sec. 7.]</small>

III. The sum required to pay the expenses of the members of the state board of education.

<small>Salary of state superintendent.</small>

IV. The sum required to pay the salary of the state superintendent of public instruction.

<small>Teachers' institutes.</small>

V. The sum required to defray the expenses of teachers' institutes.

<small>School libraries.</small>

VI. The sum required to pay the appropriations for free public school libraries.

<small>Assistants in state superintendent's office.
P. L. 1889, Chap CXCIII.</small>

VII. The sum required to pay the salary of the assistants in the office of the state superintendent of public instruction.

<small>Farnum school.</small>

VIII. The sum required to pay the appropriation for the support of the Farnum Preparatory School at Beverly.

<small>Technical schools.</small>

IX. The sum required to pay the amount to be contributed by the state to any technical schools now established or hereafter to be established in this state.

<small>Costs of foreclosure.</small>

X. The sum required to pay the taxed costs attending foreclosure proceedings in the case of lands or premises bought by the trustees for the support of public schools.

<small>School fund expenses.</small>

XI. The sum required to defray such legal and other expenses as may be incurred by or under the direction of the trustees for the support of public schools in the investment and protection of the school fund, and in the collection of the income thereof.

139. The comptroller is hereby directed to draw his warrants upon the treasurer of the school fund for the above-mentioned appropriations and expenditures when they shall severally become due and payable, and the said treasurer is directed to pay the same out of any moneys now in his hands or which may come to his hands as income or revenue from the investments of the school fund, from rentals or leases of lands under water, or from grants of lands under water; *provided*, that nothing in this act shall be construed to authorize the expenditure of any portion of the principal of the said school fund; *and provided further*, that nothing in this act shall be so construed as to prevent, hinder or in any way interfere with the payment of the annual appropriation of one hundred thousand dollars toward the support of public schools out of the income of the said fund as now provided by law. Payment by comptroller. Ibid. § 2.

Principal of fund not to be expended.
Annual appropriations to schools.

140. If at any time the payments hereby authorized to be made from the income of the school fund shall become due and payable, the said income shall not have been collected to a sufficient amount to meet the required payments, the necessary sum shall be drawn from the state treasury upon the warrant of the comptroller. Payments to be paid by state in certain cases. Ibid. § 3.

TAXATION.

State School Tax.

141. For the purpose of maintaining free public schools there shall be assessed, levied and collected annually, upon the taxable real and personal property in this state, as exhibited by the latest abstract of ratables from the several counties, made out by the several boards of assessors and filed in the office of the comptroller of the treasury, a state school tax equal to five dollars for each child in this state between the ages of five and eighteen years, as exhibited by the next preceding school census, which tax shall be assessed, State tax imposed. P. L. 1894, Chap. CCCXXXV, §7.

levied and collected at the same time and in the same manner in which other taxes are assessed, levied and collected.*

<small>Comptroller shall apportion tax among counties.
P. L. 1881, Chap. CVI, § 2</small>

142. It shall be the duty of the comptroller aforesaid to apportion the said tax among the several counties, in proportion to the amount of taxable real and personal estate of said counties respectively, as shown by the ratables respectively as aforesaid, and it shall be his further duty to transmit, on

<small>Transmit statement.</small>

or before the first day of April of each year, to the county collector of each county, a statement of the amount of said

<small>[See P. L. 1866, Chap CCCCLXXXVII.]</small>

tax apportioned to and payable by said county, and said county collector shall lay said statement before the board of assessors of the townships and wards within his county at their next annual meeting, to apportion the taxes among

<small>Duties of assessors.</small>

said townships and wards, and said assessors shall thereupon proceed to apportion said school taxes as other taxes are apportioned, and to assess the same according to law.

<small>Assessment of state school tax when said tax has not been assessed at the regular time.
P. L. 1891, Chap. LXI, § 1.</small>

143. Whenever any borough or other taxing district in this state has refused or neglected, or shall hereafter refuse or neglect to elect or appoint an assessor to assess and levy, or a collector to collect the state school tax or other tax due to the state, it shall be the duty of the assessor and collector of the township from which the said borough or taxing district was originally carved or set off to assess, levy and collect all taxes due from such borough or taxing district, whether in arrears or otherwise, in the manner provided in the act to which this is a supplement, to wit, said supplement of April eleventh, one thousand eight hundred and sixty-six, and to pay over the same as by law they would be required to do if they had assessed, levied and collected the same under said act of April eleventh, one thousand eight hundred and sixty-six.

<small>Assessor to assess within thirty days after receiving notice
Ibid. § 2.</small>

144. It shall be the duty of such township assessor, within thirty days after written notice from the county collector of the amount of taxes due and unpaid from such borough or taxing district, to assess and levy upon the taxable property

---

*A mandamus will be allowed to compel townships to pay state and county taxes out of first tax moneys collected. *Veghte* v. *Township of Bernards*, 13 Vr. 338.

A peremptory mandamus will issue for the payment of state and county taxes by a city where it has collected sufficient moneys to pay such taxes. *Shields* v. *Paterson*, June Term, 1893.

of such borough or taxing district the taxes due and unpaid, and in giving such notice the county collector shall state the amount of taxes due or in arrears, and such statement and notice shall be a sufficient warrant to the assessor in assessing the same.

145. The said assessor upon receiving such notice shall proceed immediately to make such assessment, and as soon as the same is completed shall turn over his duplicate to the collector of said township, and such assessor shall be entitled to the same rate of compensation for assessing such taxes as he is now entitled to receive under the said act of April eleventh, one thousand eight hundred and sixty-six, or any act which amends or changes the provisions thereof. *Compensation of assessor. Ibid. § 3.*

146. The collector of said township shall, within two days after receiving the said duplicate, notify the commissioners of appeal of such township that the duplicate has been delivered to him, whereupon it shall be the duty of said commissioners of appeal, within ten days and upon giving not less than five days' notice of a time and place to be by them appointed, to hear all complaints relating to such assessment, and to correct and amend such assessment as fully and effectually as they are now empowered to correct assessments by said act of April eleventh, one thousand eight hundred and sixty-six, or any act which amends or changes the provisions thereof; and such commissioners of appeal shall be entitled to the same compensation for such service as they are now entitled to receive under said act of April eleventh, one thousand eight hundred and sixty-six, or any act which amends or changes said act. *Commissioners of appeal. Ibid. § 4.*

147. It shall be the duty of the collector of such township to proceed within two days after the meeting of said commissioners of appeal to collect the taxes assessed and levied by the assessor under this act; and in making such collections the said collector is hereby vested with all the powers conferred upon him for that purpose by any act of the legislature; and such collector shall be entitled to the same rate of compensation for collecting such taxes as he is now entitled to receive under any act of the legislature. *Collector to collect said tax. Ibid. § 5. Compensation.*

SCHOOL LAW.

County collector to pay to state treasurer.
Ibid. § 6.

[See sec. 143.]

148. It shall be the duty of the county collector of any county in which is located a borough or taxing district, such as is described in the first section of this act, to pay over to the state treasurer out of any moneys that may be in his hands belonging to the county and unappropriated, the amount of taxes due the state from said county, whether the full amount of the tax has been collected or not.

Freeholders to borrow in advance of such collection.
Ibid. § 7.

149. The board of chosen freeholders of the county shall have power to borrow the amount of any such taxes due the state, in anticipation of the collection of said taxes, upon such terms as they may deem proper, and issue proper obligations therefor signed and executed as bonds of said county are signed and executed, and pay said taxes to the state immediately.

Duties of county collectors.
P. L. 1871, Chap. DXXVII, § 3.
[See sec. 151.]

150. It shall be the duty of the county collectors of the several counties of this state to pay to the treasurer of this state the quotas due from their respective counties of the taxes imposed by this act, on or before the first day of January, annually, next ensuing the assessment thereof.

Collectors in counties of third and fourth classes may pay teachers' orders before settlement with county collector.
P. L. 1890, Chap. LXXIX, § 1.

151. Hereafter it shall be lawful for the collector of any town or township, school district or districts in counties of the third and fourth class, with the advice and consent of the county collector, to disburse and pay out for the salaries of teachers in the public schools any money received and collected by him for state school tax, pending settlement by him with the county collector of and for the amount due from the town or township to the county collector, and the amount due and coming through the hands of the county collector to the school district or districts as the apportionment of state school money, other than the state appropriation;

Proviso.

provided, that the amount of such disbursement shall not exceed seventy-five per centum of the amount of said apportionment of state school money; and all such payments so made, on presentation of warrants legally and regularly issued by the board of school trustees, shall be considered and credited as partial payments of the state school tax from the town or township to the county collector, and the warrants so paid shall be placed in his hands and retained by said county collector until final settlement be made by him with said township collector for the state school tax and state school apportionment for that current year, when the said warrants shall be returned, as part payment to the amount of their face value, of the apportionment of state school money due the town, township or school district or districts.

152. Ten per centum of the full amount of money annually raised by virtue of the seventy-seventh section of this act shall be known as a reserve fund, and shall be apportioned among the several counties of this state, by the state board of education, equitably and justly, according to their own discretion, on or before the fifteenth day of April subsequently to the aforesaid apportionment by the comptroller of the treasury; and it shall be the duty of the state superintendent of public instruction, on or before the tenth day of January next ensuing said apportionment, to draw orders on the comptroller of the treasury, and in favor of the county collectors, for the payment of ninety per centum of the amount of school tax paid by the counties respectively; and the said county collectors shall apply for and be entitled to receive the amount of said orders as soon as the same are received; and the said superintendent shall also draw his orders in favor of the respective county collectors, for such portion of the reserve fund as shall have been apportioned to the counties respectively, as aforesaid, which orders shall be payable when the said reserve fund has been paid by the several counties; *provided*, that no portion of said moneys shall be used for the support of sectarian schools.

State board of education shall apportion reserve fund among the counties. P. L 1881 Chap. CVI, § 3 [See sec. 141]

State superintendent to draw orders.

Proviso.

153. It shall be the duty of the county superintendent of each county, on or before the fifteenth day of May, to apportion annually to the districts of his county the state school moneys, together with the interest of the surplus revenue belonging to said county, in the following manner:

County superintendents shall apportion moneys. P L. 1894 Chap. CCCXXXVI, § 1.

I. He shall apportion to each district a sum equal to two hundred dollars for each teacher employed in the public schools in each district for the full time for which the schools in such districts were maintained during the year next preceding such apportionment;

II. He shall apportion to each district the remainder of the school moneys belonging to his county on the basis of the last published school census.

<small>State superintendent to give orders in favor of county collector. P. L. 1867, Chap. CLXXIX, § 74</small>

154. The state comptroller, annually, after having received from the state superintendent of public instruction a statement of the apportionment of the state's appropriation among the several counties, shall draw his warrant on the state treasurer in favor of the county collector of any county for the portions to which said county is entitled, whenever such county collector shall present an order for the same drawn by the state superintendent of public instruction in favor of such county.

<small>County superintendents to give orders in favor of township collectors. P. L. 1894, Chap. CCCXXXV, § 9.</small>

155. The county collector of each county shall receive and hold in trust that part of the state appropriation belonging to his county, and shall pay out the same to the collectors of the several townships and boroughs, and to the city treasurers of his county, only on the orders of the county superintendent.*

<small>Township collector to hold moneys in trust. Ibid § 10.</small>

156. It shall be the duty of the township collector to receive and hold in trust all school moneys belonging to the township whether received from the state appropriation,

---

* (1) A county collector is not required or permitted to exercise any discretion as to how much of the state appropriation the several township collectors in the county are entitled to receive from him. The question as between these officers is settled conclusively by the order of the county superintendent of public schools. (2) The notion that a county collector can, in any case, lawfully reduce the amount by setting up some counter-claim, whether in his own behalf or in behalf of his county, and whether against the township collector, personally, or against his township, is neither justified by the language nor consistent with the policy of our school laws. *State, Herder, &c.*, v. *Collector, &c.*, 7 Vr 363.

(1. The county collector of each county shall receive and hold in trust the state appropriation for public schools belonging to his county, and pay the same to the collectors of the several townships and to the city treasurers of the cities of his county only on the orders of the county superintendent, and is responsible for these moneys if otherwise expended. (2) School taxes are to be levied and applied for the fiscal year beginning September 1st, succeeding the assessment, and not for the preceding year. (3) A mandamus will be allowed for the payment of the county superintendent's order for the state appropriation for public schools, where the moneys have been applied for school purposes in the preceding year, beginning January 1st. *State ex rel. Board of Education, &c.*, v. *Sheridan, &c.*, 13 Vr 64

A mandamus will be granted against a county collector in favor of a township collector or city treasurer to compel the payment of school moneys, although the township collector or city treasurer may owe the county collector money for state or county taxes. *Board of Education* v. *Sheridan*, 16 Vr. 276.

The common council has no control over school funds, and a resolution directing the treasurer to retain a portion of the school fund and apply it to the payment of certain special assessments against school property, is a nullity. *Board of Education* v. *Town of Union*, 23 Vr. 69.

SCHOOL LAW. 53

from district tax or from other sources, and to pay out the same only on the orders of the district clerks, each of which orders shall specify the object for which it is given, and shall be signed by the president of the board of education and by the district clerk, and shall be made payable to the order of and be endorsed by the person entitled to receive it, and he shall pay over any balance of school funds remaining in his hands to his successor in office, and he shall, in the book provided for that purpose by the state superintendent, keep a record of the sums received and paid out by him, and he shall present his accounts to be examined and settled by the township committee at the close of the school year, a copy of which settlement, certified by the committee, showing the amounts received, the amounts expended by him for school purposes during the year, and the balance remaining in his hands; he shall transmit within ten days to the county superintendent and shall file another copy of the same with the district clerk; he shall also exhibit to the county superintendent, when requested so to do, his book of accounts and the vouchers in his hands, and as compensation for such service he shall be entitled to one and one-half per centum on all school funds paid out by him on the orders signed by the president and district clerk of the board of education, which compensation shall be paid by the township committee from the funds of the township; *provided,* that when the term of office of any township collector shall expire before the close of the school year, such township collector shall remain and continue to be the custodian of the school moneys and shall pay the orders legally issued as aforesaid until the close of the school year, and his bondsmen shall remain and be legally bound for the faithful performance of his duties until the final settlement of his accounts; *and provided further,* that where there is a borough situated in a township, and said borough is a separate and distinct school district, the borough collector shall be the legal custodian of the school moneys belonging to the borough, and shall perform the same duties and be entitled to the same compensation, to be paid from borough funds; but if such borough collector is paid a stated salary by the

[margin notes: To keep accounts of school moneys. Report to county superintendent and township committee. Compensation. Proviso. Proviso.]

borough for the performance of his duties as borough collector, then and in that case he shall not be paid any additional compensation for paying out the school moneys belonging to the borough.*

School orders to bear interest when collector has no funds to honor same. P. L. 1890, Chap. CXII, § 1.

157. Whenever any order for payment of teachers' salaries or the incidental expenses of public schools shall be drawn by any board of trustees on any township collector or other disbursing officer, which order there shall be no funds in the hands of such collector or other disbursing officer to meet, that then and in every such case such order shall bear legal interest until such time as said collector or other disbursing officer shall be prepared to honor the same, of which readiness he shall give public notice, whereupon said interest shall cease.

Sinking funds for schools P. L. 1882. Chap CXLIX. § 1.

158. The officer in every township whose duty it now is by law to receive and hold in trust the school moneys of the several school districts in such township (whether such officer be called collector of taxes, receiver of taxes, township treasurer, or by any other name), shall collect, receive and hold in trust and be accountable for all securities, funds and moneys of any school district in such township, which belong to any sinking fund or interest account, or to a fund provided for the redemption of any bonds or the payment of any debt of such district; and all payments and disbursements of money, whether for interest, for discharge of principal debt, or for investment, shall be made by and through such township financial officer, on school orders duly signed by the district trustees.

Trustees to pay and deliver moneys and securities to collector or other financial officer. Ibid. § 2.

159. It shall be the duty of the school trustees of any school district in this state, within thirty days after the passage of this act, to pay over and deliver to the township collector, receiver of taxes or other financial officer as aforesaid, of the township in which such district is situate, all

---

*1. A mandamus will be granted to compel a township collector to pay the balance of school moneys to his successor. *Meinzer* v. *Disbrow*, 13 Vr. 141.

2. An order of the district clerk, which specifies the object for which it was given without any designation of the yearly taxes out of which it shall be payable, is a sufficient voucher for the township collector. *Zimmerman* v. *Mathe*, 20 Vr. 45.

3. The township collector paying out school moneys on statutory orders is not responsible for the application the school trustees have made of the money. *Zimmerman* v. *Mathe*, 20 Vr. 45.

moneys and securities in their hands belonging or relating to any funded indebtedness of such district.

160. The bonds or other securities given and to be given for the faithful performance of duty by any such township collector, receiver of taxes or other financial officer of any township, into whose hands shall come the money and securities of any school district, shall be liable for and held to embrace the faithful performance of duty raised by this or any other act relating to the care of school funds and securities by such financial officer. *Bonds of collector, etc. Ibid. § 3.*

161. On or before the fifteenth day of September in each year, it shall be the duty of all township collectors, city treasurers and other persons who may be the custodians of moneys belonging to the several school districts in this state, to pay to the county collectors of their respective counties all balances derived from moneys apportioned to said districts by the county superintendents which may then be in their hands to the credit of said districts, and to report forthwith to the county superintendents of their respective counties the amount thus paid over; and it shall be the duty of each county collector, on or before the first day of October in each year, to report to the county superintendent of his county the amount of money received by him by virtue of the provisions of this act, and the county superintendent shall thereupon re apportion such amount among all the school districts in his county, except as hereinafter provided, and the sums thus re-apportioned shall immediately be returned to the several township collectors, city treasurers, and other persons entitled to the custody of the school moneys, on the orders of the county superintendent, and shall be available for the then current school year; and the sum thus re-apportioned to any district shall be in addition to and in excess of the sum apportioned to such district by the county superintendent for said school year; *provided*, that the county superintendent may, for good cause shown, allow the balance due any school district to remain in the hands of the custodian of the school funds of such district to the credit of such district, and such balance shall thereafter be used and expended by the trustees of such school district for the purpose of paying teachers' *Balances due districts to be paid to county collectors. P L. 1891. Chap. CLXV, § 1.* *County collector to report to county superintendent.* *County superintendent to re-apportion balances.* *Proviso.* *Balance used for improvements in certain cases.*

salaries and fuel bills, or, by and with a written consent of the county superintendent, in the improvement of the school house and grounds, the purchase of school furniture or apparatus, or for any other purpose connected with the schools of such district; *and provided also,* that in case the county superintendent shall allow any district to retain any such balance, the said district shall not be included in any such reapportionment nor entitled to any of the proceeds thereof.

<small>Proviso.</small>

<small>Board of education to have control of all school moneys.
P. L. 1894.
Chap. CCLXXXV, § 1.</small>

162. The board of education, or other body having control of the public schools in townships of this state having a population by the census of the United States taken in the year one thousand eight hundred and ninety, of ten thousand or more, or which may have such population by any census to be hereafter taken, shall have the expenditure of all moneys levied and raised, or appropriated or received from the state or any other source by any such townships for the support and maintenance of the public schools, or for the erection of public school buildings, and it shall be the duty of the township committee from time to time, upon the request of such board of education, to set apart moneys so received by them or lawfully levied by taxation, and hold the same subject to the order or warrant of such board of education or its duly authorized officers appointed for that purpose.

<small>School moneys to be used for no other purpose, and to be kept separate from other township moneys.
Ibid. § 2.</small>

163. It shall be the duty of the township committee to keep a separate account of all school moneys with such board of education, and credit such board in each year with the whole amount from time to time during the year as aforesaid of the money levied and ordered to be raised in each year by taxation for public schools; such moneys to be by such township committee, as in the first section hereof is provided, appropriated to and used by said board of education for school purposes, or for the objects for which the same may be specially raised or appropriated, and the treasurer or receiver of taxes or other financial officer of the town shall receive, and shall hold such school moneys when received, from whatever source the same shall arise, in a separate account to the credit of such board of education, and such funds shall not be used by the said township com-

mittee or by said disbursing officer for any other purpose or in any other manner than to meet the drafts or warrants of such board of education when presented.

DISTRICT TAX.

164. In addition to the moneys apportioned to it by the county superintendent, each school district may raise by tax such other sums of money as it may need for school purposes, in the following manner: The legal voters of such district are hereby authorized and required, at the meeting for the election of trustees, to determine what amount of school tax, if any, shall be levied upon the district, and in the notices calling said meeting* shall be inserted the amount of money desired to be raised; and the legal voters, so met, shall have power by a consent of a majority of those present, to authorize the board of education to purchase land** for school purposes† to build, enlarge or repair a school house or school houses, to borrow money therefor, or to sell or mortgage a school house or school houses, and to raise by taxation for these purposes, or to pay a debt of the district incurred for such purposes, and for the current expenses of the school or schools, such sum of money as a majority of the legal voters so assembled shall agree to; and in case any money shall be ordered to be raised by taxation, the district clerk shall make out and sign a certificate thereof‡ under oath or affirmation, that the same is correct and

Marginal notes: Districts may raise school tax. P. L. 1891, Chap. CCCXXXV, § 11. Annual meeting for ordering tax. Power of district meeting. Certificate of clerk.

---

* 1. When an assessment is ordered by the inhabitants of a school district called for that purpose, to sustain the assessment, proof must be clear that ten days' legal notice of the time, place and purposes of such meeting had been given. *State* v. *Van Winkle*, 1 Dutcher 73.

2. A notice indicating that the object of the meeting is to purchase a school house, will not warrant a resolution to pay for a house already built. *Lamb* v. *Hurff*, 9 Vr. 310.

**† The trustees must designate the place where the lands to be purchased lie, and the notices calling the district meeting must contain a description of the lands so designated. The district meeting cannot authorize the purchase of land not described in the notices. *Zabriskie* v. *School District 10, Bergen Co.*, 23 Vr. 104.

‡1. The sworn certificate of the clerk to the assessor must specify the amount to be raised for each purpose; that the notices were posted in "at least seven public places in said district," and all other facts necessary to show that the law has been complied with The affidavit must verify all the material facts set forth in the certificate. *State* v. *Hardcastle*, 11 Dutcher 143, 3 Dutcher 551; *Winsor* v. *Donahay*, 1 Vr. 404; *Banghart*

Assessment.

true, and deliver the same to the assessor, and shall send a duplicate of said certificate to the county superintendent, and the assessor shall assess on the inhabitants of the school district and their estates, and the taxable property therein, in the same manner as township taxes are assessed, such sum of money as shall have been ordered to be raised by the said meeting in the manner aforesaid; and said money shall be assessed, levied and collected; and it shall be the duty of the collector to collect and hold all taxes so assessed, and he shall pay out the same on orders signed by the president and district clerk of the board of education; *provided,* that whenever any meeting shall be held as aforesaid at the call of the trustees, as provided in the ninth and tenth division of the thirty-ninth section of this act, it shall not be lawful for such meeting to order a greater sum of money raised by a special tax than shall have been mentioned and designated in the notices of such meeting set up in the manner required by law. *

Collection.

Proviso.

Special school tax to be a separate item in tax levy.
P L. 1882,
Chap. CII, § 1.

165. In all cases where a tax shall be levied in any city, borough, town or township of this state, which tax shall include any moneys to be raised for school purposes, the

---

v. *Sullivan,* 7 Vr. 89; *Trustees* v. *Padden,* 15 Vr. 151; *Quaid* v. *Trustees, &c.,* 20 Vr. 607.

2. It is essential to the validity of the certificate of district clerk, that it set forth that due notice has been given of the amount of money proposed to be raised at the district meeting. *Slack* v. *Palmer,* 10 Vr. 250.

3. The certificate to the assessor must show how the money ordered to be raised is to be apportioned, and that the apportionment was made by the district meeting. *Duryea* v. *Greenleaf,* 5 Vr. 441; *Banghart* v. *Sullivan,* 7 Vr. 89; *Corrigan* v. *Duryea,* 11 Vr. 226; *Trustees* v. *Padden,* 15 Vr. 151.

4. The certificate to the assessor must state what the notice given of the meeting was, and when and where the notices were put up. *Quaid* v. *Trustees,* 20 Vr. 607.

* The resolution passed at the district meeting must direct the particular purpose, which must be one of the purposes in the act, and must be contained in the notice. If money is voted for more than one purpose, the resolution must specify the amount apportioned to each. *Cochrane* v. *Garrabrant,* 3 Vr. 444; *Banghart* v. *Sullivan,* 7 Vr. 89; *Corrigan* v. *Duryea,* 11 Vr. 266.

2. A resolution to raise money to build and furnish a school-house is not bad because the amount to be used for building and the amount for furnishing are not separately stated. *Stackhouse* v. *School Dist. No. 43, Sussex Co.,* 23 Vr. 291.

3. A resolution to sell an old school-house, passed at the same meeting that it was resolved to raise money to build a new house, is illegal if the notice calling the meeting does not state that it would be a subject for consideration. *Stackhouse* v. *School Dist. No. 43, Sussex Co.,* 23 Vr. 291.

4. It is essential that the purpose for which the tax is imposed shall be particularly designated " For incidentals " is not sufficient. *Schomp* v. *Cole,* 22 Vr. 277.

5. School taxes must be assessed upon the same property, and in the same manner as all other taxes. *Roll* v. *Perrine,* 5 Vr. 254.

amount of tax against any property, either real or personal, which shall be intended for such school purposes, shall be entered in the tax levy made against said property as a separate item; and all tax bills which shall be sent out or rendered by any city, borough, town or township of this state shall state the amount of said school tax in a separate item.

166. The several assessors and collectors of the townships and wards of this state shall be entitled to receive five cents, and no more, for each name for assesing, levying and collecting district school taxes. Compensation to assessors and collectors. P. L 1875, Chap. CCCXLVI, § 1.

167. Nothing in the act entitled "An Act to establish a system of public instruction" (Revision), approved March twenty-seventh, eighteen hundred and seventy-four, shall be construed to require the township collector to pay over to the county collector any school moneys received by him from special township or district school taxes raised under the eighty-sixth section of said act. Township and district taxes not to be paid to county collector. P. L. 1885, Chap. CXLI, § 1.
[See sec. 170]

168. At each annual or special school meeting held in any school district in this state, the legal voters thereof shall vote by ballot, and not otherwise, to raise money for any school purposes whatever. District meetings to vote only by ballot. P. L. 1889, Chap LXXXIV, § 2.

SCHOOL BONDS.

169. It shall and may be lawful for the legal voters, either at the annual meeting or at a special meeting called for that purpose, by the consent of a majority of those present, to authorize the board of education, for the purpose of purchasing land for school purposes or for the purpose of building a school house or school houses, or making additions, alterations, repairs or improvements in or upon such school house or school houses already erected, and the lands upon which the same are located, to issue bonds of the district in corporate name of the district in such sums and in such amounts, and payable at such times as the legal voters so met may direct, with interest at a rate not exceeding six per centum per annum, payable half yearly; which bonds shall be signed by the president of the board of education Districts may issue bonds. P. L. 1894, Chap CCCXXXV. § 19.

Rate of interest.

and attested by the district clerk, and shall bear the seal of the district, and said bonds shall have coupons attached for current payment of interest, which coupons shall be signed by the district clerk and shall be numbered to correspond to the bond to which they are attached; and any bonds so issued shall be numbered and a proper registry thereof kept by the district clerk; and such bonds may be sold at public or private sale for the best obtainable price, but not less than par; said bonds shall be a lien upon the real and personal estates of the inhabitants of the district, as well as the property of the districts, shall be liable for the payment of the same; and in all papers and proceedings authorizing the issue of bonds shall be submitted to the attorney general for his approval of the legality of the same, and duplicate copies of such papers and proceedings shall be sent to the state superintendent of public instruction.

Bonds a lien on districts,

Attorney general to approve proceedings.

Assessment for paying bonds. Ibid. § 20.

170. Whenever any district shall order and authorize the issue of bonds it shall be the duty of the district clerk, each and every year, to issue the warrant of the district, signed by the president of the board of education and attested by the district clerk, to the assessor of the township, directing him to assess upon the inhabitants of said township and their estates, and the taxable property therein, an amount sufficient to pay the bond or bonds maturing in such year, together with the interest accruing upon the whole issue of the unpaid bonds of such district, which warrant so issued as aforesaid shall be duly executed by him, and the moneys so assessed, levied and collected shall be held by the township collector, and said collector shall, upon the receipt of the orders of the board of education, signed by the president and attested by the district clerk (which orders shall state at what bank the said principal and interest is payable), deposit in such bank the sum of money necessary to pay the principal and interest as they become due and payable.

Renewal of school bonds. P. L. 1886, Chap. XV, § 1.

171. Whenever any bonds shall have been legally issued for the purpose of purchasing land and building school houses by any school district in this state, under authority of law, or any renewal or renewals thereof, and the same shall be due or unpaid or outstanding, and whenever it may

be desirable for the interests of the district that the same or any part thereof should be renewed by the execution of new bonds, the trustees or a majority of them of such district are hereby empowered to renew such outstanding bonds or any part thereof by the issuing of new bonds for that purpose in the name and under the seal of said district; *pro-* Proviso. *vided*, such renewal issue shall be authorized by said district at a meeting specially called to vote thereon, and such bonds shall be in the general form and manner of the bonds heretofore issued, signed by the trustees of said district or a majority of them, and attested by the clerk of the said district, which bonds shall be made payable at periods of time not exceeding fifteen years from the date of issuing the same, and they shall bear interest at a rate not exceeding six per Rate of interest. centum per annum and be issued in such sums of not less than one hundred dollars nor more than one thousand dollars, as the said trustees may determine, and which bonds shall have coupons attached for current payment of interest, which coupons shall be attested by the clerk of the district and bear its seal and shall be numbered to correspond with the bond to which they shall be respectively attached; and any bonds so issued shall be numbered and a proper registry thereof be kept by the said clerk; and such bonds may be sold at public or private sale for the best attainable price, but not less than par, and the money so realized shall be at once applied to the taking up and cancellation of such outstanding bonds; or said renewal bonds may be exchanged on an equal basis of principal and interest for such outstanding bonds; and the said bonds so redeemed shall be forthwith cancelled by the said trustees.

172. The bonds of the several school districts of this Bonds a lien on districts.
Ibid. § 2. state, so issued to renew bonds heretofore or hereafter legally issued for the purpose of purchasing land and building school houses, shall be a lien upon the real and personal estates of the inhabitants of the said districts as well as the property of the said districts; and the property of the inhabitants as well as the property of the districts shall be liable for the payment of the same; *provided*, that in all Proviso. cases copies of all resolutions, papers and proceedings author-

izing the issuing of such bonds shall be submitted to the attorney-general for his approval of the legality of the same, who shall receive such compensation for the examination thereof as shall be fixed by the trustees for the support of public schools, which sum shall be paid by the districts issuing such bonds.

Notice to Assessor. Ibid. § 3.

173. Whenever any district shall order and authorize the issue of bonds for the purpose aforesaid, it shall be the duty of the district clerk of such district, each and every year next before any such bond shall mature, to issue the warrant of the district, signed by the trustees and attested by the clerk under the seal of the district, to the assessor or assessors of the township or townships in which such district is situate, directing him or them to assess upon the inhabitants of said school district, and their estates and the taxable property therein, an amount sufficient to pay the bond or bonds of the district then next maturing, together with the interest accruing upon the whole issue of the unpaid bonds of such district, which warrant so issued as aforesaid shall be duly executed by him and the moneys be assessed, levied and collected; and the collector shall pay over, on the written order of the district clerk of said district, all money so collected by him.

Cancellation of old bonds. Ibid. § 4.

174. On the taking up of such outstanding bonds, or on the payment of any bonds of any school district, now issued or hereafter to be issued, the trustees of the district shall forthwith stamp and mark the same as canceled; and when so marked and canceled they shall be deposited in the office of the state superintendent of public instruction.

School fund may be invested in new bonds. Ibid. § 5

175. The treasurer of this state, under the direction of the trustees for the support of public schools, is authorized to invest the funds for the support of public schools in this state in such renewed bonds of the several school districts of this state, or to exchange therefor other bonds of the same district.

Cities may borrow money to build schoolhouses. P. L. 1889, Chap. CCXXII, § 1.

176. The board of education, board of school trustees, or other body having charge and control of the public schools in any school district in this state, acting under a special charter, or under the provisions contained in the charter of

any city, town, borough or other municipality, is hereby authorized and empowered, for the purpose of building or enlarging school houses, by and with the consent of the board having charge and control of the finances of such municipality, to borrow from the "trustees of the fund for the support of public schools" such sum or sums of money as may be necessary for that purpose; that the money thus borrowed shall be secured by bonds to be issued in the corporate name of said municipality or school district, to be known as district school bonds, which bonds shall bear interest at the rate of five per centum per annum, payable annually, and the said bonds shall and are hereby declared to be the first lien upon the school house and lot on which the same is erected, and for the erection or repair of which they shall have been issued; that no loan authorized by this act shall be less than five hundred dollars; that such loan may be paid at such times and in such amounts as the board of education, board of school trustees or other body borrowing money under the provisions of this act may direct; *provided*, that the first payment on any such loan shall become due and payable not later than five years from the date of said loan, and that the last payment on any such loan shall be made not later than ten years from the date thereof. *Money to be secured by bonds.*

Time of payment of bonds.

177. If any charter of any incorporated school district, city, town, borough or other municipality in this state shall limit the amount of indebtedness that may be incurred, or shall limit the amount of tax or the rate of taxation in any incorporated school district, city, town, borough or other municipality or by its terms prevent the carrying out of the provisions of this act, the same shall not hereafter be held to apply to the raising of money under the provisions of this act, and the powers herein conferred shall embrace every school district in the state, any public, local, special or other law to the contrary notwithstanding. *Charter limitations respecting indebtedness not to apply to money borrowed under this act. Ibid. § 2.*

178. The treasurer of this state, under the direction of the "trustees for the support of public schools," is hereby authorized to invest the fund for the support of public schools in this state in the bonds issued by virtue of this act; *provided, always,* that said trustees, before giving *Bonds may be taken by state school fund. Ibid. § 3.*

Proviso

such direction, shall be satisfied that the lot upon which the school house is proposed to be erected or repaired is free from all incumbrances, and that the said bonds, when issued, will become the first lien upon said lot with the improvements thereon, and that the city, town, borough or municipality applying for the loan has not defaulted in the payment of the principal or interest of any bonds theretofore issued within two years from the date of the application.

Proceedings to be approved by attorney general.
Ibid. § 4.

179. Copies of all papers and proceedings authorizing the issuing of such bonds shall be submitted to the attorney-general for his approval of the legality of the same, and that duplicate copies of such papers and proceedings shall be filed in the office of the state superintendent of public instruction.

Blanks to be prepared by state superintendent.
Ibid. § 5.

180. The state superintendent of public instruction shall prepare and furnish the necessary blanks and forms for all proceedings under this act.

Assessment for payment of bonds.
Ibid. § 6.

181. It shall be the duty of the officers or board charged with the raising, levying and assessing of taxes in any school district or municipality issuing bonds under the provisions of this act to assess upon the inhabitants thereof and their estates and the taxable property therein, an amount sufficient to pay the bond or bonds of the district maturing in such year, together with the interest accruing upon the whole issue of the unpaid bonds of such district or municipality, and the tax thus ordered shall be assessed, levied and collected in the same manner as other taxes for school purposes are assessed, levied and collected.

School bonds not taxable.
P. L. 1893, Chap CCLXXII, § 1.

182. All bonds, securities, improvement certificates, and other evidence of indebtedness heretofore or hereafter issued by this state, or by any county thereof, or by any city, town, township, borough, school district, or other municipality of this state, shall be exempt from taxation for any purposes.

Report of indebtedness to be sent to state superintendent.
Ibid. § 2.

183. The district clerk, or other persons performing the duties of a district clerk, in any district in which there is any interest-bearing school debt, shall, on or before the first day of September in each year, report to the state superintendent of public instruction the amount of such debt then remaining unpaid, together with the rate of interest, the date

SCHOOL LAW.

or dates on which the bonds, notes or other evidences of indebtedness were issued, and the date or dates on which they shall fall due.

SURPLUS REVENUE.

184. The several townships in this state are authorized and required to appropriate the interest of the surplus revenue received by them, and from other funds not raised by tax, such sums for the support of the public schools as they shall order and direct at their annual town meetings, in addition to the amount received from the state appropriation and the amount which they raise by tax. Interest on surplus revenue appropriated to schools. P. L. 1867, Chap. CLXXIX, § 77

SCHOOL LIBRARIES.

185. The treasurer of the school fund, upon the order of the state superintendent of education, is hereby authorized and directed to pay over the sum of twenty dollars out of the income of the school fund, to every public school for which there shall have been raised by subscription or entertainment a like sum for the same purpose, to establish in such school a school library, and to procure philosophical and chemical apparatus; and the further sum of ten dollars annually, upon a like order, to the said public school, upon condition that there shall have been raised by subscription or entertainment a like sum for such year, for the purposes aforesaid. Library appropriation. P. L. 1878, Chap. CCXLII, § 1. P. L. 1885, Chap. CLXIV, § 1, div. vii.

186. In all school districts where there are more than one school-house, it shall be lawful to receive from the state treasury, as in said bill directed, the sum prescribed to be paid to each school-house, and that such district shall have power to consolidate and establish a library in one place in said district as may be designated by the board of education or such other power as has control of the public schools in said district. Districts having more than one building may consolidate library P. L. 1891, Chap. CXCI, § 1.

187. The selection of books and apparatus shall be approved by the school trustees of such district. Selection of books. P. L. 1871, Chap DLVI, § 2.

188. The school trustees of each district shall make proper rules and regulations for the management, use and safe keeping of such libraries.

<small>Rules. Ibid, § 2.</small>

189. Whenever in any county in this state there shall have been raised by subscription a sum of money not less than one hundred dollars for the establishment of a library of pedagogical books for the use of the teachers of public schools in such county, the treasurer of the school fund, upon the order of the state superintendent of public instruction, is hereby authorized and directed to pay the sum of one hundred dollars out of the income of the school fund to the county superintendent of said county; and the further sum of fifty dollars annually thereafter, upon a like order upon conditions that there shall have been raised by subscription a like sum for such year for the purpose aforesaid.

<small>Teachers library, appropriation. P. L. 1891, Chap. XLIX, § 1.</small>

190. The county superintendent, and three teachers of public schools in such county appointed by him, shall constitute a committee for the selection of said books and the necessary apparatus, and the making of rules and regulations for the management, use and safe keeping of such libraries.

<small>Rules Ibid. § 2.</small>

191. The governor, the state comptroller and the state superintendent of public instruction be and they are hereby authorized, upon its publication, to purchase and pay for out of any funds not otherwise appropriated, as many copies of a political and legislative history of the state for the last twenty-five years, now being prepared by William Edgar Sackett, as they may deem proper for distribution among the public school libraries of this state.

<small>Certain books to be purchased for school libraries. P. L. 1894, Chap CLXX, § 1.</small>

ARBOR DAY AND HISTORICAL DAYS.

192. In order to secure the coöperation of the schools in carrying into effect the provisions of the joint resolution relative to the annual Arbor Day, it shall be the duty of the state superintendent of public instruction to prepare and issue such circulars of information and instruction as may be necessary.

<small>State superintendent to issue circulars of information, etc. P. L 1884, Chap. CIX, § 1.</small>

SCHOOL LAW.

193. On said annual Arbor Day appropriate exercises shall be introduced in all the schools of the state, and it shall be the duty of the several county and city superintendents to prepare a programme of the exercises used on such day in all the schools under their respective jurisdiction. Exercises
Ibid. § 2.

194. In all public schools of the state of New Jersey the last Friday preceding the following holidays, viz, Washington's Birthday, Decoration or Memorial Day, Fourth of July and Thanksgiving Day shall be devoted to the development and promotion of a higher spirit of patriotism by the observing of proper and appropriate exercises. Certain days to be observed in schools by special exercises.
P. L. 1894, Chap. XXVII, § 1

195. Such exercises shall consist of reading the Declaration of Independence, singing national and other patriotic songs, of select readings, declamations, essays, addresses and such other exercises of a public, non-sectarian and national character as the principal or teacher of the school may determine, or the school trustees, commissioners or city superintendent may direct. Nature of exercises.
Ibid. § 2

196. The school commissioners of the several counties, the city superintendents, the school trustees and boards of education of all the cities, towns and townships in the state of New Jersey are hereby charged with the duty of enforcing the provisions of this act, and are authorized and directed to cancel and revoke the certificate of license of any principal or teacher who refuses or neglects to provide for and conduct exercises as prescribed in the above sections. School officers to enforce
Ibid. § 3

Penalty.

PHYSIOLOGY AND HYGIENE.

197. The nature of alcoholic drinks and narcotics, and special instruction as to their effect upon the human system, in connection with the several divisions of the subject of physiology and hygiene, shall be included in the branches of study taught in the common or public schools, and shall be studied and taught as thoroughly and in the same manner as other like required branches, with adequate tests of the efficiency of the teaching by the use of graded text books in the hands of pupils where other branches are thus studied, and orally only in the case of pupils unable to read, and by Nature and effect of alcoholic drinks and narcotics to be taught.
P. L. 1894, Chap LXVII, § 1.

all pupils in all grades of all schools supported wholly or in part by public money.

*Text-books
Ibid. § 2.*

198. The space in the text books devoted to the consideration of the nature of alcoholic drinks and narcotics and their effects upon the human system shall be sufficient for a full and adequate treatment of the subject.

*Teachers to be examined.
Ibid. § 3.*

199. No certificate shall be granted to any person to teach in the public schools of New Jersey after January first next, who has not passed a satisfactory examination in physiology and hygiene, with special reference to the nature of alcoholic drinks and other narcotics and their effects upon the human system.

*Trustees to adopt text-books.
Ibid. § 4.*

200. In order to carry into effect the provisions of this supplement each district shall, in the manner now provided by law, on or before the first day of July next, adopt a graded series of text books in accordance with the provisions of this supplement.

*State superintendent to notify school officers of passage of law.
Ibid. § 5.*

201. The state superintendent of public instruction shall, immediately after the passage of this supplement, notify all boards of education, boards of school trustees, or other bodies having charge and control of public schools, of the provisions of this supplement, and particularly call their attention to their duty in enforcing the same.

*County and city superintendents to see that law is enforced.
Ibid. § 6.*

202. It shall be the duty of all city and county superintendents to report to the state superintendent of public instruction whether the provisions of this act have been complied with, as specified in the preceding sections; and any refusal thus reported, or otherwise satisfactorily proven, shall

Penalty for failure to carry law into effect.

be deemed sufficient cause for withholding the state appropriation of school money from such district or districts until such district or districts have fully complied with the provisions of this supplement.

*Law to apply to all districts.
Ibid. § 7.*

203. This act shall apply to all schools in this state supported wholly or in part by money received from the state, whether such schools are governed by the act to which this is a supplement or by any special law, or the provisions contained in the charter of any city, town, borough or other municipality, and that this act shall take effect at the beginning of the next school year.

COMPULSORY EDUCATION.

204. All parents and those who have the care of children, shall instruct them or cause them to be instructed in spelling, reading, writing, English grammar, geography and arithmetic, and every parent, guardian or other person having control and charge of any child or children between the ages of seven and twelve years, shall be required to send any such child or children to public day school for a period of at least twenty weeks in each year, eight weeks, at least, of which attendance shall be consecutive, unless such child or children are excused from such attendance by the board of the school district in which such parents or guardians reside, upon its being shown to their satisfaction that the bodily or mental condition of such child or children has been such as to prevent his, her or their attendance at school, or that such child or children are taught in a private school or at home by some qualified person or persons in such branches as are usually taught in primary schools. *Childred between 7 and 12 years of age to attend school 20 weeks each year. P. L. 1885, Chap XVII, § 1.*

205. No child under the age of fifteen years shall be employed by any person, company or corporation to labor in any business whatever, unless such child shall have attended within twelve months immediately preceding such employment some public day or night school, or some well recognized private school; such attendance to be for five days or evenings every week during a period of at least twelve consecutive weeks, which may be divided into two terms of six consecutive weeks each, so far as the arrangement of school terms will permit, and unless such child or his parents or guardians shall have complied with the provisions of the act approved March fifth, eighteen hundred and eighty-three, limiting the employment hours of the labor of children. *Children under 15 years of age not to be employed in any business unless they have attended school the preceding year. Ibid. § 2.*

206. Every parent, guardian or other person having charge or control of any child, from twelve to sixteen years of age, who has been temporarily discharged from employment in any business in order to be afforded an opportunity to receive instruction or schooling, shall send such child to some public or private day school for the period for which *Parents or guardians to comp'l children to attend school Ibid. § 3.*

such child shall have been discharged, unless such child shall have been excused from such attendance by the inspectors of factories and workshops, or by the board of the school district, for reasons as stated in section one hereof.

[See sec. 204]

Penalty for failure to comply with sections 200 and 201. Ibid. § 4.

207. In case any parent, guardian or other person shall fail to comply with the provisions of sections one and three of this act, such parent, guardian or other person shall be deemed guilty of a misdemeanor, and shall, on conviction, be liable to a fine of not less than ten dollars nor more than twenty-five dollars for each subsequent offense, or to imprisonment for not less than one month nor more than three; the said fines, when paid, to be added to the public school money of said school district in which the offense occurred.'

Juvenile disorderly persons. Ibid. § 5.

208. All children between the ages of seven and fifteen years, who are habitual truants from school, or who, while in attendance at any public school, are incorrigible, vicious or immoral in conduct, and all children between the said ages who absent themselves habitually from school, and habitually wander about streets and public places during school hours, having no business or lawful occupation, shall be deemed juvenile disorderly persons, and subject to the provisions of this act.

Truant officers. Ibid. § 6.

209. In cities having a duly organized police force, it shall be the duty of the police authority, at the request of the inspectors of factories and workshops, or of the school authority, to detail one or more members of said force to assist in the enforcement of this act, and in districts having no regular police force, subject to this act, it shall be the duty of the board of education, or the school district officers, to designate one or more constables of said city, township or village, whose duty it shall be to assist in the enforcement of this act, as occasion may require, and said board of education

Compensation.

shall fix and determine the compensation to be paid said police officer or constable for the performance of his duties under this act; members of any police force, or any constable designated to assist in the enforcement of this act, as provided in this section, shall be known as truant officers;

Proviso.

provided, that in districts where no constable resides the said board shall have power to appoint some other suitable person as truant officer.

210. It shall be the duty of any such truant officer or officers detailed to enforce the provisions of this act, to examine into all cases of truancy, when requested so to do by the inspectors of factories and workshops, or by the district school board, and to warn such truants, their parents or guardians, in writing, of the final consequences of truancy, if persisted in, and also to notify the parents, guardian or other person having the legal charge and control of any juvenile disorderly person, that the said person is not attending any school, and to require said parent, guardian or other person to cause the said child to attend some recognized school within five days from said notice; and it shall be the duty of said parent, guardian or other person having the legal charge and control of said child, to cause the attendance of said child at some recognized school; if said parent, guardian or other person having the legal charge and control of said child shall wilfully refuse, fail or neglect to cause said child to attend some recognized school, it shall be the duty of said officer to make, or cause to be made, a complaint against said parent, guardian or other person having the legal charge and control of said child, in any court of competent jurisdiction in the school district in which the offense occurred, for such refusal or neglect, and upon conviction thereof said parent, guardian or other person, as the case may be, shall be punished by a fine of not less than ten dollars nor more than twenty-five dollars; or the court may, in its discretion, require the person so convicted to give a bond in the penal sum of one hundred dollars, with one or more sureties, to be approved by said court, conditioned that said person so convicted shall cause the child or children under his or her legal charge or control to attend some recognized school within five days thereafter, and to remain at said school during the term prescribed by law; *provided*, that if said parent, guardian or other person in charge of said child shall prove inability to cause said child to attend said recognized school, then said parent, guardian or other person shall be discharged, and said court shall, upon com-

plaint of said truant officer or other person, that said child is a juvenile disorderly person within the meaning of this act, then said court shall thereupon sentence said child to a juvenile reformatory until such child shall arrive at the age of sixteen years, unless sooner discharged by the board of control of said juvenile reformatory; *provided, however*, that such sentence may be suspended, in the discretion of said court, for such time as the child shall regularly attend school and properly deport himself or herself; *it is further provided*, that if, for any cause, the parent or guardian or other person having charge of any juvenile disorderly person, as defined in this act, shall fail to cause such juvenile disorderly person to attend said recognized school, then complaint against such juvenile disorderly person may be made, heard, tried and determined in the same manner as is provided for in case the parent pleads inability to cause said juvenile disorderly person to attend said recognized school; *and it is further provided*, that no child under the age of nine years shall be sent to a juvenile reformatory under the provisions of this act.

<small>Proviso</small>

<small>Proviso.</small>

<small>Proviso.</small>

<small>Proceedings to be instituted against persons or corporations violating this act.
Ibid. § 8.</small>

211. It shall be the duty of the officers empowered, detailed or appointed under the provisions of this act to assist in the enforcement thereof, to institute or cause to be instituted, proceedings against any parent, guardian or other person having legal charge and control of any child, or any person, company or corporation violating any of the provisions of the sections of this act; *provided*, this law shall not be operative in those school districts of the state where there are not sufficient accommodations to seat the children compelled to attend school under the provisions of this act; and that no prosecution shall be instituted against any parent, guardian or child unless they have received due notification from an officer empowered under this act that they are acting in violation of the provisions of this act.

<small>Proviso.</small>

<small>Schools other than public schools to be approved by an inspector.
Ibid. § 9.</small>

212. When there is not within the distance of two miles from the factory or shop in which a child under the age of fifteen years is employed, or from the residence of the child, a recognized efficient school, attendance at a school temporarily approved by an inspector of factories and workshops shall,

for the purposes of this act, be deemed attendance at a recognized efficient school, and the inspector of factories shall immediately report to the educational department every case of the approval of a school by him under this section.

213. Two weeks' attendance of children between twelve and fifteen years of age, at a recognized half time or evening school, shall, for all purposes of this act, be counted as one week at a day school. *Attendance at half-time schools. Ibid. § 10.*

214. When any provisions of this act are violated by a corporation, proceedings may be had against any of the officers or agents of said corporation who in any way participate in or are cognizant of such violation by the corporation of which they are the officers or agents, and said officers or agents shall be subject to the same penalties as individuals similarly offending. *Corporations liable for violations of this act. Ibid § 11.*

CONDEMNATION OF LAND.

215. It shall be lawful for any school district of this state at their annual meeting or at any special meeting called for that purpose, upon legal notice, to vote and appropriate money for the purchase or acquirement of lands and the construction of a school house, or for the purchase or acquirement of additional lands to increase the present school grounds of said district, at such place in the said school district as the school trustees thereof may designate, and for that purpose the said school trustees may acquire the said land by purchase or condemnation; *provided*, a majority of the taxable voters of said school district shall be present at any meeting as aforesaid and shall vote on any proposition presented for the condemnation of land; and any money heretofore raised by tax for any of the purposes aforesaid in any school district, and not otherwise appropriated or expended, may be used for such purpose upon the order of the school trustees of such district. *Condemn land. P. L. 1888, Chap. LIX, § 2. Majority of taxable voters to vote on question of condemnation.*

216. It shall be lawful for such school trustees to enter upon any lands and make all such preliminary examinations, explorations, measurements and levelings as may be necessary and proper for their purposes, doing thereby as little damage as possible to the owner or owners thereof. *Trustees may make necessary surveys. P. L. 1880, Chap. CLVIII, § 2.*

SCHOOL LAW.

Supreme Co Justice may appoint commissioners. Ibid. ₴ 3.

217. In case said school trustees cannot agree with the owner or owners, or other persons interested in any lands which said school trustees may desire to take, use and occupy, or from which they may desire to take or divert, either in whole or in part, for the purposes of their building, or cannot agree with the owner or owners for the whole or any part of any lands as to the amount of compensation to be paid for such taking, use, diversion or occupation or interest, it shall be lawful for any justice of the supreme court of this state, upon application by

Notice to owners.

said school trustees, and upon two weeks' previous notice, served in person, or by leaving at the dwelling-house or usual place of abode of such owner or owners, or, in case of absence from the state or legal disability, published in a newspaper published nearest to the lands in question, to appoint three disinterested commissioners, residents of the county in which said lands are situated, to assess and ascertain the value of the lands so proposed to be taken, used

Meetings of commissioners.

and occupied, which commissioners shall appoint a time and place at which they shall meet to execute the duties of their appointment, and shall cause two weeks' notice thereof to be given to the parties interested therein, either by personal service or by publication in a newspaper published in the county where such lands may be, at which time and place the said commissioners shall meet and view the premises, and hear the parties interested, and take evidence, if any be offered, and for that purpose shall have power to administer oaths or affirmations, and to adjourn from day to day; and

Vacancy in commissioners.

in case of the refusal or failure of either or any of said commissioners to attend and perform their said duties, the said judge shall have power to appoint another or other disinterested person or persons as commissioners to act in the place of such absent commissioner or commissioners; and the said trustees shall make and exhibit to the said commissioners at their meeting aforesaid, for the use of the parties interested, a statement and description in writing, or by drawings or maps, or both, of the lands by them sought to be taken or diverted as aforesaid, and of the use, occupation of, and excavations upon any lands by them sought to be made;

and the said commissioners shall thereupon ascertain and assess the value and damages aforesaid, and shall execute under their hands and seals, or the hands and seals of a majority of them, an award to said trustees of the lands by them sought in the statements and description aforesaid, stating therein the amount of damages and compensation therefor by them assessed in favor of such owner or owners, which award shall be by them acknowledged and filed in the county clerk's office, and by him recorded; *provided, always*, that if any real estate, the owner or owners of which shall not have given his, her or their consent in writing to the diversion or to the taking of said land, shall not have been ascertained and paid pursuant to the directions of this act, shall be injured or damaged by the diversion or diminution of any said land, that the owner or owners thereof may have and maintain his, her or their action to recover damages for such injury which he, she or they may sustain by reason of anything done under this act, as if this act had not been passed. [See sec. 231.]

Proviso

218. Before taking possession of any such lands, or entering thereon for the purpose of making any excavation or occupation thereof, or taking any interest in land as aforesaid, the said trustees shall pay or tender to such owner or owners, or, in case of absence from the state or legal disability, shall deposit with the clerk of the circuit court of said county the value and damages so awarded; and the award of said commissioners and the payment or tender or deposit as aforesaid of the same, shall vest in said corporation the lands by them sought, described and set forth in said statement and description, in all respects the same as if the same had been conveyed to said trustees by said owner or owners under their hands and seals. Payment for land condemned Ibid. § 4.

219. If either party feel aggrieved by said assessment and award, such party may appeal to the next or second term of the circuit court of said county, by petition and notice thereof served upon the opposite party two weeks prior to such term, or publish a like space in a newspaper published nearest the lands in question, which petition and notice so served or published shall vest in said courts full power to Appeal to circuit court. Ibid. § 5.

[See secs. 232 and 233.]

hear and determine said appeal, and if required, they shall award a venire for a jury to come before them, who shall hear and finally determine the issue under the direction of the court, as in other trials by jury; and it shall be the duty of the said jury to assess the damages to the said lands as above mentioned, and the value of such lands as shall be absolutely taken; and said court shall have power to order a struck jury, or a jury of view, or both, to try any such appeal, and also to order any jury which may be empaneled and sworn to try any such appeal, to view the premises in question during said trial; and the right of said trustees to appeal from and dispute the correctness of any award shall not be waived or taken away by the paying or tendering the amount of the award and taking possession of the land, or exercising the rights covered by such award; and the right of any owner of such lands or rights in like manner to appeal, shall not be waived or lost by the acceptance of the amount so awarded, when tendered; and upon the final determination of any such appeal, the said court shall render such judgment in favor of the one party and against the other, as the right and justice of the case shall require, and shall award to the party substantially succeeding and prevailing in said appeal, his, her or their costs of said appeal against the opposite party, and shall have power to enforce the judgment so rendered by execution, as other judgments are enforced, and also by summary proceedings and attachments for non-payment thereof.

Trial by jury
[See secs. 232 and 233]

220. In case any school district of this state has purchased any lands in this state, or may hereafter purchase any lands, and has built, or may hereafter build thereon, any school house or school houses, the title to which said lands is in any way defective, it shall and may be lawful for any justice of the supreme court of this state, and the said justice is hereby directed, upon application by the trustees of said school district, upon two weeks' previous notice, served in person, or by leaving a copy thereof at the dwelling-house or usual place of abode of the owner or owners of said lands, or in case of the absence from the state or legal disability of the owner or owners, then the said notice shall be published in

Proceedings in case title to lands is defective.
P. L. 1888, Chap. XXXI, § 1.

Notice to owner.

the newspaper published in the county where said lands are situate, for two weeks prior to the time fixed for such application, to appoint three disinterested persons commissioners, which said commissioners shall be residents of the county where said lands are situate, to condemn and assess and ascertain the value of the lands so purchased as aforesaid, which commissioners shall appoint a time and place at which they shall meet and execute the duties of their appointment, and shall cause two weeks' notice thereof to be given to the owner or owners thereof, either by personal service or by leaving a copy thereof at the dwelling-house or usual place of abode of said owner or owners, or in case of the absence from the state or legal disability of said owner or owners, then said notice shall be published in a newspaper printed in the county where said lands are situate, for two weeks prior to the time of such meeting; at which time and place the said commissioners, or any two of them, shall meet and view the premises and lands, and hear all the parties interested, and take evidence, if any shall be offered, and for that purpose shall have power to administer oaths and affirmations, and to adjourn from time to time; and the said trustees of said school district shall make and exhibit to the said commissioners at their meeting aforesaid, a description of said lands purchased as aforesaid, either in writing or by maps or drawings or both; and the said commissioners, or any two of them, shall thereupon ascertain and assess the value of said lands, and shall execute under their hands and seals, or the hands and seals of any two of them, an award to said trustees of said school district of the lands by them sought in the description aforesaid, stating therein the amount of compensation therefor by them assessed in favor of said owner or owners, and a description of the said lands, which said award shall be acknowledged by the commissioners making the same and filed in the clerk's office of the county where said lands are situate, and recorded by the said clerk in the same manner and in the same books that deeds for real estate are now recorded.

Commissioners to meet.

Assess value of lands.

[See sec. 231.]

221. When the said commissioners, or any two of them, shall make their award and assess the value of the lands

Trustees to pay amounts assessed Ibid. § 2.

aforesaid, that it shall be the duty of the trustees of said school district to pay to the owner or owners of said land the amount so assessed by the said commissioners, and in case the said owner or owners refuse to receive the same, or reside out of this state, or are legally disqualified, or cannot be found, then the said trustees shall pay the said amount so assessed to the clerk of the circuit court of the county where said lands are situate.

<small>Title to vest in trustees. Ibid. § 3.</small>

222. The award of the commissioners aforesaid, or any two of them, and the payment of the money so assessed as aforesaid by the trustees of said school district in the manner aforesaid, shall vest in the trustees of said school district the lands and premises described in said award, the same estate that would have vested in them had the owner or owners thereof conveyed the same to the trustees of said school district under their hands and seals in fee simple.

<small>Proceedings in case of appeal. Ibid. § 4. [See secs. 232 and 233.]</small>

223. If the trustees of said district school or the owner or owners of said lands are not satisfied with the assessment of the said commissioners of the amount to be paid to the owner or owners of said lands, then and in that case either party may appeal to the next or second term thereafter of the circuit court of the county where said lands are situate, by filing a petition with the clerk of said circuit court and serving a notice of such appeal upon the opposite par'y, three weeks prior to such term, or by publication in a newspaper printed in the county where said lands are situate for four weeks prior to such term; which petition, when filed, and the notice served or published as aforesaid, shall vest in said court full power to hear and determine said appeal.

<small>Trial by jury. Ibid. § 5. [See secs. 232 and 233.]</small>

224. In all cases of appeal from the assessment of the commissioners it shall and may be lawful for either party to demand and have a trial by jury, and the assessment of the court or jury shall be final.

<small>Districts may vote money. Ibid. § 6.</small>

225. It shall and may be lawful for any school district in this state, at their annual meeting, to vote money to carry out the provisions of this act, as money is now voted for said school district under any existing law.

<small>Condemnation of land for school purposes in cities.</small>

226. Whenever, in the judgment of the board or body having control of the public schools, and the authority to

purchase lands therefor in any of the cities of this state, the price demanded by the owners of any lands or real estate which may be deemed by such board or body necessary for the use of the public schools of any such city, is exorbitant and more than the reasonable and fair market value thereof, it shall and may be lawful for such board or body, with the concurrence of the common council (whenever the concurrence of the common council or other governing body is necessary for the purchase of lands for public school purposes in any such city), to apply to a judge of the circuit court in and for the county in which such city is located, for the appointment of three commissioners to make an appraisement of the value of the lands and of the damages which the owner or owners may suffer by reason of the taking and condemnation thereof; such application shall be made upon petition, setting forth that the said board or body has been unable to agree with the owners for the purchase of such lands, and that the price demanded therefor is, in the judgment of the said board or body, exorbitant, and more than the market value thereof, and praying the same may be condemned, giving in the said petition a description of the lands which it is desired shall be condemned for the purposes aforesaid, and thereupon it shall be the duty of the said judge to appoint as commissioners three suitable persons (who shall be freeholders and residents of the county within which such application is made), to make an appraisement of the value of the lands so to be condemned, and of the damages which the owner or owners of such lands may suffer by reason of the taking thereof.

<small>P. L. 1889. Chap. CXXVI, § 1.</small>

<small>Appointment of commissioners.</small>

227. Such commissioners, appointed by the circuit court having taken an oath faithfully and impartially to execute the duties of their office, shall forthwith proceed to estimate and determine the fair value of the lands and real estate so to be taken and condemned as aforesaid, and of the damages which the owner or owners thereof will suffer by reason of the taking thereof, first having given at least ten days' notice in writing to the said owner or owners, either personally or by leaving the same at his or her place of abode, of the time and place when and where they may be heard

<small>Commissioners to take oath. Ibid. § 2</small>

<small>Notice to owners</small>

in relation to the matter; in case any owner shall be an infant, married woman, *non compos mentis* or absent from the city or place where such condemnation proceedings are taken, or be from any cause incapacitated to act in this behalf, then notice of the time and place and object of said

<small>Meetings of commissioners.</small>

meeting shall be advertised or other notice given, as the judge may direct, and said meeting or meetings may be adjourned from time to time at the discretion of said commissioners, and as soon as they shall have determined upon said valuation they shall make and sign a certificate

<small>[See sec. 231.</small>

thereof and file the same in the office of the city clerk of such city, or at such other place as the said judge

<small>Payment of award.</small>

may direct; and immediately upon the payment to said owner or owners of the amount of the said valuation, or in case he or they will not or cannot receive the same, upon deposit of the same in such bank or institution as the said court or judge may direct, the title to and right of possession of such property shall immediately become vested in such city or place; and any owner conceiving himself or herself aggrieved by the proceedings of

<small>Appeal from award of commissioners.</small>

said commissioners, may appeal therefrom to the supreme court of this state at any time within sixty days after the

<small>[See secs. 232 and 233.]</small>

filing of said certificate, and the said court shall thereupon order a trial by jury to assess the value of the said property and the said damages, which trial shall be conducted in all respects as in other cases of trial by jury, and the final judgment of the said court upon the verdict rendered therein shall be conclusive upon all parties as to the said valuation and damages, and the amount already paid or deposited as aforesaid shall be increased or diminished accordingly.

<small>Title to be in name of city. Ibid. § 3.</small>

228. All titles taken for the purposes mentioned in this act shall be in the name of the city in which the said lands are purchased or condemned by virtue of the provisions of this act.

<small>Compensation of commissioners. Ibid. § 4.</small>

229. The commissioners so to be appointed by the said judge of the circuit court shall receive such compensation for their services as the said judge shall order and direct, and the same, as well as the other expenses incident to the con-

demnation proceedings, shall be paid by the said city in which the lands are situate.

230. Any city in which such condemnation proceedings are taken shall provide the necessary funds to pay for the lands so condemned and the damages for the taking thereof, and such other expenses as may be incidental thereto, and for this purpose shall have power to raise money by taxation.

Expenses to be paid by city. Ibid. § 5.

231. All reports of commissioners hereafter appointed by any court or by any justice of the supreme court to appraise the damages for the taking of lands or other property for public use shall be made or filed on or before a day to be fixed in the order of appointment, unless the court of justice shall by order extend the time, in which case the report shall be made on or before the day limited by said court or justice, and every appeal from such report shall be taken within five days after the day thus fixed.

Reports of commissioners to appraise damages for taking lands for public use to be filed. P. L. 1893. Chap. LXXX, § 1.

232. Whenever an appeal shall be filed from an award of damages by commissioners heretofore or hereafter appointed in any proceeding for the taking of property for public use, notice in writing of such appeal shall be given by the party appealing to the other party within ten days after the filing of the petition of appeal, by service of such notice upon each person interested personally or by leaving at his residence if he resides in the state, or by service upon his attorney if any, who shall have appeared for him before the commissioners or any other attorney authorized to appear for him, and in case of a corporation, service may be made on such attorney or on any officer or agent upon whom a summons in an action at law against the company may be lawfully served; where it shall appear by affidavit that any person or corporation being a party to the proceedings is a non-resident of the state, or can not be found therein to be served, in such case notice shall be given in such manner as a judge of the court to which appeal is taken may direct; the said notice of appeal shall set forth that an appeal has been taken from the award of the commissioners, and shall specify the time and place when and where the appellant will apply to the court to which such appeal is taken or any judge thereof to frame the issue and to fix a day for the striking of the jury,

Proceedings when appeal filed from award of damages. Ibid. § 2.

and a day for the trial of the appeal, which time named for said application shall be not less than five nor more than ten days from the date of service of the notice, but the court or judge may by order change the time or place on the application of either party and direct what notice of such change shall be given to the other party.

Court shall fix day for trial of appeal.
Ibid. § 3.

233. After an appeal to any court from the award of commissioners appointed to assess the damages for the taking of lands or other property for public use by condemnation shall have been filed, and notice thereof shall have been given as above provided, the court to which such appeal is taken, or any judge thereof on application of either party shall fix a day for the trial of the appeal either during the term or vacation when such appeal shall be filed or during the following term or vacation, which day so fixed shall be not less than twenty nor more than forty days from the date of the order, and the court or judge shall also at the same time make an order framing the issue between the parties

Struck jury.

and directing a jury to be struck and a view of the premises and property to be had, and fixing a day and place for the striking of the jury for the trial of the appeal, which day shall be at least ten days before the day fixed for the trial of the appeal, and the filing of the order shall be notice to all parties of the day and place fixed thereby for the striking of the jury and of the trial, and the jury having been struck and the jurors summoned as required by law the cause shall be tried upon the day and at the place fixed unless for good cause shown the court shall adjourn the trial to another day which the court shall fix, in which case the court shall, in its discretion, either direct the same jurors to attend or order another jury to be struck and summoned in like manner, and all parties shall take notice of the day and place fixed for the adjourned trial.

Repealer.
Ibid. § 4.

234. All acts or provisions inconsistent with the provisions of this act shall be and are hereby repealed, and the practice prescribed by this act shall supersede the existing practice in all condemnation cases before commissioners or on appeal, so far as the provisions of this act shall extend, and the court shall make such further orders and take such

further proceedings as may be requisite according to the practice of the court and the several statutes regulating appeals and the trials thereof in condemnation cases and may permit such amendments of the proceedings and plans as may be reasonable and proper for the fair trial of the case or for the promotion of the public purposes for which the power to condemn was conferred.

MANUAL TRAINING.

235. Whenever any board of school trustees or board of education of any school district in this state shall certify to the state superintendent of public instruction that there has been raised by special district school tax, or by subscription, or both, a sum of money not less than five hundred dollars for the establishment in such district of a school or schools for manual training, or for the purpose of adding manual training to the course of study now pursued in the school or schools of such district, it shall be the duty of the said state superintendent of public instruction, with the approval of the governor, to draw his order on the comptroller and in favor of said district for the sum equal to that contributed by said school district as aforesaid for said object; and when such school or schools shall have been established, or manual training shall have been added to the course of study in any district, there shall be annually contributed by the state, in manner aforesaid, for the maintenance thereof, a sum of money equal to that raised each year in said district for such purpose; *provided*, that the course of manual training established or introduced under the provisions of this act shall be approved by the state board of education; *provided further*, that the moneys appropriated by the state as aforesaid to any school district shall not exceed in any one year the sum of five thousand dollars, and that all payments made in pursuance of the provisions of this act shall be paid on the warrant of the comptroller out of the income of the school fund. State appropriation for manual training. P. L. 1888, Chap XXXVIII, § 1.

Proviso.

Proviso.

236. The trustees of any school district in this state receiving an appropriation under the provisions of this cat Report to state superintendent. Ibid § 2.

shall annually, on or before the first day of September, make a special report to the state superintendent of public instruction of the progress of manual training in such district, and give such other information in connection therewith as he may require.

INDUSTRIAL EDUCATION.

<small>State appropriation for technical schools.
P. L. 1881, Chap. CXLIV, § 1.</small>

237. Whenever any board of education, school committee or other like body, of any city, town or township in this state shall certify to the governor that a sum of money not less than three thousand dollars has been contributed by voluntary subscriptions of citizens, or otherwise as hereinafter authorized, for the establishment in any such city, town or township, of a school or schools for industrial education, it shall be the duty of the said governor to cause to be drawn, by warrant of the comptroller, approved by himself, out of the income of the school fund, an amount equal to that contributed by the particular locality as aforesaid for the said object; and when any such school or schools shall have been established in any locality as aforesaid, there shall be annually contributed by the state, in manner aforesaid, for the maintenance and support thereof, a sum of money equal to that contributed each year in said locality for such purpose; *provided, however,* that the moneys contributed by the state, as aforesaid, to any locality, shall not exceed in any one year the sum of five thousand dollars.

<small>P. L. 1885, Chap. CLXIV, § 1, div. x.</small>

<small>Proviso</small>

<small>Money to be applied under direction of trustees.
P. L. 1881, Chap CXLIV, § 2.</small>

238. All money raised and contributed as aforesaid shall be applied under the direction of a board of trustees, organized as hereinafter provided, to the establishment and support of schools for the training and education of pupils in industrial pursuits (including agriculture), so as to enable them to perfect themselves in the several branches of industry which require technical instruction.

<small>Local tax.
Ibid. § 3</small>

239. Any city, town or township shall have power to appropriate and raise by tax for the support of any such school therein, such sum of money as they may deem expedient and just.

240. There shall be a board of trustees of each of such schools, which shall consist of the governor, *ex-officio*, who shall be president thereof; two persons selected by the state board of education; two by citizens and associations contributing; two by the board of education, school committee or other like body of the locality where such school is established; and one by the common council, township committee or other governing body thereof, if such city, town or township shall contribute to the maintenance of such school; the said board of trustees shall have control of the buildings and grounds owned and used by such schools, the application of the funds for the support thereof, the regulation of the tuition fees, the appointment and removal of teachers, the power to prescribe the studies and exercises of the school and rules for its management; to grant certificates of graduation, to appoint some suitable person treasurer of the board, and to frame and modify at pleasure such by-laws as they may deem necessary for their own government; they shall report annually to the state and local boards of education their own doings and the progress and condition of the schools.
Trustees. Ibid. § 4.

Powers.

Treasurer.

241. The board of trustees of the schools for industrial education, provided for and organized under the act to which this is a supplement, be and they are hereby created a body corporate under the name and style of "the board of trustees of schools for industrial education," with the right of perpetual succession, to sue and be sued, to purchase, lease and hold personal and real property, and to sell and mortgage the same, and with power to accept donations and bequests of money and property to be used for the purposes for which said boards are constituted and organized.
Trustees of industrial schools created bodies corporate. P. L. 1890, Chap. IX, § 1. [See sec. 240.]

242. The said trustees shall receive no compensation for their services, but the expenses necessarily incurred by them in the discharge of their duties shall be paid out of the income of the school fund upon the approval of the governor.
Compensation. P L 1881, Chap. CXLIV, § 5. P. L. 1885, Chap CLXIV, § 1, div x.

243. Whenever in any school district there shall have been raised by special school tax or by subscription, or both, a sum of money not less than five hundred dollars, for the establishment in such district of a school or schools for industrial education or for the purpose of adding industrial
State appropriation for industrial education. P. L. 1888, Chap CXIV, § 1.

education to the course of study now pursued in the school or schools of such district, there shall be appropriated by the state, out of the income of the school fund, an amount equal to that appropriated by the district as aforesaid ; and when such school or schools shall have been established in any district, or said industrial education has been introduced into the course of study in the school or schools of any district, there shall be appropriated by the state for the maintenance and support thereof a sum of money equal to that appropriated each year by the district for such purpose ; *provided*, that the moneys appropriated by the state as aforesaid to any school district shall not exceed in any one year the sum of five thousand dollars ; the treasurer of the city or the collector of the township, as the case may be, shall be the legal custodian of any and all funds subscribed, allotted or raised for the purpose of carrying out the instruction contemplated by this act, and he shall keep a separate and distinct account thereof, apart from all other moneys in his custody whatsoever, and shall disburse the fund on the properly authenticated drafts of the trustees of the school district, or other persons or board having charge of public schools in such district ; any unexpended balance to the credit of this fund in any township or city at the end of any fiscal year, shall not be covered into the treasury of the city or township, but shall be at the disposal of the school trustees or other persons or board having charge of public schools in the district, for the purpose of aiding industrial education in the succeeding year or years ; *provided*, that any such unexpended balance shall not be included in the report of the amount raised in any succeeding year for the purpose of procuring state funds as above provided.

244. The trustees or other persons or board having charge of public schools of any district in [this] state receiving an appropriation under the provisions of this act shall annually, on or before the first day of September, make a special report to the superintendent of public instruction of the progress of industrial education in such district and such other information in connection therewith as he may require.

245. It shall be lawful for the trustees or other persons or board having charge of public schools of any school district to associate with themselves in the management of this fund a number of citizens not exceeding ten representing the donors, in case the sum or any part thereof necessary to obtain the state appropriation shall have been raised by private subscription. Who may be trustees. Ibid. § 3.

246. Whenever in any school district, city or township, in which industrial education has heretofore been established, or where industrial education has been added to the course of study in the school or schools of such district, city or township, for which moneys have been raised, subscribed or appropriated under the act to which this is a supplement, and such industrial education so established or added to the course of study in any such district, city or township has been or may hereafter be discontinued or abandoned, and there now is or hereafter may be any moneys or unexpended balances of such fund in the treasury of the city or in the hands of the collector of the township, or other legal custodian of such funds, and which are or may be kept in a separate and distinct account apart from all other moneys in his custody, and not now or hereafter covered into the treasury of such city or township; that one-half of such moneys or unexpended balance in the treasury of the city or collector of the township in which such industrial education has been discontinued or abandoned shall, and may be, by the order or direction of the persons or board having charge of public schools in such district, city or township, returned to the state treasurer to be credited to the account of state school fund, and the remaining one-half used for any other public school purpose, as such persons or board may designate, and the said moneys or unexpended balance, after the payment of the one-half thereof as aforesaid to the state treasurer, shall be transferred by the city treasurer or collector of any such city or township either to the general school fund or appropriations of such city or township, or to any particular fund or appropriation for public school education or instruction as directed by such persons or board. District to refund to state when industrial education has been abandoned. P. L. 1894, Chap. CXI, § 1.

District may dispose of apparatus when industrial education is abandoned.
Ibid. § 2.

247. The implements or articles purchased and used in connection with industrial education which has been or may hereafter be discontinued or abandoned in any district, city or township, may be disposed of by the persons or board having charge of public schools in such district, city or township, and the proceeds thereof paid to the city treasurer or to the collector of such city or township, and one-half thereof paid to the state treasurer, to be credited to the account of the state school fund, and the remaining one-half placed to the credit of the public school funds or appropriations in such city or township, for any purpose of public schools, education or instruction.

MANUAL TRAINING SCHOOL AT BORDENTOWN.

Students may be appointed from assembly districts.
P. L. 1894, Chap. CCCXLIX, § 1.

248. For the purpose of carrying out and putting in force the true intent of the supplement to an act of congress of August thirtieth, one thousand eight hundred and ninety, chapter eight hundred and forty-one, section one, acts of congress one thousand eight hundred and seventy-four to one thousand eight hundred and ninety-one, pages seven hundred and ninety-seven and seven hundred and ninety-eight, revised statutes of the United States and the several acts of the legislature of New Jersey respecting industrial education and manual training schools; that for the purpose of carrying more fully into effect the true intent of these acts, the manual training and industrial school at Bordentown, New Jersey, Burlington county, be and the same is hereby designated as a branch institution for the education of such students as may be appointed from the several assembly districts and counties of this state, as hereinafter provided; that the said school shall be managed and controlled by a board of trustees consisting of the following persons and their successors in office: The governor of the state, who shall be president ex-officio; the state superintendent of public instruction, the president of the senate, the speaker of the assembly, the chairman of the committee on education of the senate, the chairman of the committee on education of the house, the president of the state agricul-

Board of trustees.

tural college, the trustees of school district number fifteen, Burlington county; the principal of the state normal school, the principal of the Farnum preparatory school at Beverly, New Jersey; two persons selected by the state board of education and the county superintendent of Burlington county; these trustees shall have all the power and responsibilities given by the laws of this state to trustees of public and manual training schools.

249. All laws applying to and governing industrial and manual training schools now in force in this state shall apply to this school. Manual training laws to apply to this school. Ibid. § 2.

250. When the trustees of said school are ready to receive students, one student from each county in the state to be selected by the senator thereof and one student from each assembly district to be selected by the assemblymen thereof and be approved of by the trustees and faculty of the school, shall be entitled to free scholarships in said school. Manner of appointing students. Ibid. § 3.

251. The state superintendent of public instruction is hereby authorized and required to make an examination of the books and records of the colored industrial education association of New Jersey, with a view of ascertaining what amount of subscriptions have been given said association for industrial and manual training under the several acts of the legislature of this state, and the value of the assets that they have come into possession of by reason of the act of the legislatue of May twenty-first, one thousand eight hundred and ninety, and the value of all donations and subscriptions and assets held by said association from the tenth day of November, one thousand eight hundred and eighty-nine, to the present time, and to draw his warrant on the comptroller for a like sum in favor of the board of trustees created by this act for the maintenance of said school, in accordance with the provisions of the act of the legislature of March twenty-fourth, one thousand eight hundred and eighty-one, and the act of the legislature of one thousand eight hundred and eighty-eight, known as the manual training act; *provided*, that the sum for which said warrant shall be drawn shall not exceed in the aggregate the sum allowed by said acts of the legislature for each year. State superintendent to determine value of apparatus, etc. Ibid. § 4.

Association to transfer property to new board of trustees. Ibid. ₰ 5.	252. The colored industrial educational association of New Jersey and the trustees of school district number fifteen, Burlington county, be and they are hereby authorized to turn over to the trustees created by this act all moneys, real estate and personal property which they hold for industrial education in said district.
Appropriation. Ibid. ₰ 6.	253. In lieu of all claims, rights and titles which the branch institution designated by this act has, or may hereafter have, upon the annual appropriation coming to this state from congress, under the provision of the supplement to the act of congress of August thirtieth, one thousand eight hundred and ninety; three thousand dollars is hereby annually appropriated for the maintenance of said school out of any money in the state treasury not otherwise appropriated.

CHILDREN IN FACTORIES.

Age of children in factories. P. L., 1883, Chap. LVII, ₰ 1.	254. No boy under the age twelve years, nor any girl under fourteen years of age, shall be employed in any factory, workshop, mine or establishment where the manufacture of any goods whatever is carried on.
Children between ages of twelve and fifteen must attend school before employment in factory, etc. Ibid. ₰ 2.	255. On and after the first day of July, one thousand eight hundred and eighty-four, no child between the ages of twelve and fifteen years shall be employed in any factory, workshop, mine or establishment where the manufacture of any kinds of goods whatever is carried on, unless such child shall have attended, within twelve months immediately preceding such employment, some public day or night school, or some well recognized private school; such attendance to be for five days or evenings every week during a period of at least twelve consecutive weeks, which may be divided into two terms of six consecutive weeks each, so far as the arrangement of school terms will permit, and unless such child, or his parents or guardian shall have presented to the manufacturer, merchant or other employer seeking to employ such child, a certificate giving the name of his parents or guardian, the name and number of the schools attended, and the number of weeks in attendance, such certificate to be

signed by the teacher or teachers of such child; *provided,* that in case the age of the child be not known, such teacher shall certify that the age given is the true age, to the best of his or her knowledge and belief; *provided,* that in case of orphan children, where necessity may seem to require, the guardian or others having charge of the same, may, upon application to the inspector provided for in this act, receive from him a permit for the employment of such child or children, under such regulations as the said inspector may prescribe. *Proviso. Proviso.*

256. No child or children under the age of fourteen years shall be employed in any factory, workshop, mill or establishment where the manufacture of any kind of goods is carried on, for a longer period than an average of ten hours in a day, or sixty hours in a week. *Children under fourteen not to be employed more than ten hours a day. Ibid. § 3.*

257. Every manufacturer, merchant or other employer employing any person contrary to the provisions of this act, or who shall be guilty of any violation hereof, shall be liable to a penalty of fifty dollars for each offense, to be recovered in an action of debt in any district court in any city, or before any justice of the peace having jurisdiction, and that any parent or guardian who knowingly permits the employment of any such child or children, shall be liable in any like action to a penalty of not more than fifty dollars, as the court shall fix; that such action shall be prosecuted in the name of the inspector; the trial shall proceed as other actions of debt, and the first process shall be a summons returnable in not less than five days or more than ten after issue, and it shall not be necessary to indorse the same as *qui tam* actions, the finding of the court shall be that the defendant has or has not, as the case may be, incurred the penalty claimed in the demand of the plaintiff, and judgment shall be given accordingly; in case an execution shall issue and be returned unsatisfied, the court, on application, after notice to the defendant, may award an execution to take the body of the defendant, and in case such defendant is committed under such an execution, he shall not be discharged under the insolvent laws of the state, but shall only be discharged by the court making the order for the body *Penalty for violation of act. P. L. 1884, Chap. CXXXVII, § 5.*

execution, or one of the justices of the supreme court, when such court of justice shall be satisfied that further confinement will not accomplish the payment of the judgment and costs; an affidavit of the age of any minor, made by its parent or guardian at the time of its employment, shall be conclusive evidence of the age of such minor upon any trial against a manufacturer or employer for a violation of this act, but any parent or guardian that shall knowingly swear falsely in such affidavit shall be guilty of perjury, and the inspector or deputy inspector shall be authorized, in case they shall find any minor employed under any false affidavit given as aforesaid, to order and compel such minor to desist from work; the provisions of this act in relation to the hours of employment shall not apply to or affect any person engaged in preserving perishable goods in fruit canning establishments.

Inspector of factories.

258. The governor shall, immediately after the passage of this bill, appoint, with the advice and consent of the senate, some suitable person, who shall be a resident and citizen of this state, as inspector, at a salary of twelve hundred dollars per year, to be paid monthly, whose term of office shall be for three years; the said inspector shall be empowered to visit and inspect, at all reasonable hours, and as often as practicable, the factories, workshops, mines and other establishments in the state where the manufacture or sale of any kind of goods is carried on, and to report to the governor of this state on or before the thirty-first day of October in each year; it shall also be the duty of said inspector to enforce the provisions of this act, and prosecute all violations of the same in any recorders' courts of cities, and justices of the peace or other courts of competent jurisdiction in the state.

Salary and term of office.
P. L. 1883,
Chap. LVII, § 5.

Expenses.
P. L. 1884,
Chap CXXXVII, § 6.

259. All necessary expenses incurred by said inspector in the discharge of his duty shall be paid from the funds of the state, upon the presentation of proper vouchers of the same; *provided*, that not more than one thousand dollars shall be expended by him in any one year.

Proviso.

Fines.
P. L. 1883,
Chap. LVII, § 7.

260. All fines collected under this act shall enure to the benefit of the school fund of the district where the offense has been committed.

AGRICULTURAL COLLEGE.

261. It shall be the duty of the county superintendent, at such time and place as the state superintendent may appoint, to examine such candidates for state scholarships at the agricultural college as may present themselves, and the candidates shall be subjected to such examination as the faculty of the said college and the state superintendent shall prescribe; and the candidates who shall receive certificates of appointment to the agricultural college in any one county shall be those who obtain, on such examination, the highest average for scholarship; and the number of certificates thus granted shall in no case exceed the number of state scholarships to which such county is entitled.* <small>Appointment of student for agricultural college. P. L. 1867, Chap. CLXXIX, § 27.</small>

262. In order that students in all schools in all parts of the state may receive the stimulus afforded by the opportunity to pursue the courses of study in the state agricultural college, and in order to enable said state agricultural college to furnish instruction gratuitously to students, residents of this state, in its several courses of study, as special courses of advanced study in the public school system of this state, there shall be sent to the said college students to the number of one each year from each assembly district of this state, to be selected and designated as hereinafter provided, who shall receive gratuitous instruction in any or all of the prescribed branches of study in any of the courses of study of said state college, under the general powers of supervision and control possessed by the board of visitors of said state college; said students so received shall be residents of this state and shall be admitted into said state college upon the terms and subject to the rules and discipline which shall apply to all the free students of said state college, and if there should be more than one suitably prepared applicant from the same assembly district in the same year, such additional applicant may, in the discretion of the board of visitors of the said state agricultural college, be received upon any vacant scholarships of any other assembly districts until <small>Additional free scholarships P. L. 1890, Chap. CVIII, § 1. Students from each assembly district. Students may be received on vacant scholarships.</small>

---

*Each county is entitled to as many students as it has representatives in the Legislature. P. L. 1864, Chap. CCCLXIX, § 10.

such district shall require such scholarships, after notice has been served upon the superintendent of education of the county in which such vacant assembly districts are situated.

<small>Examination for scholarships. Ibid § 2.</small>

263. Said students shall be selected as follows: a competitive examination under the direction of the city superintendents and the county superintendent of education in each county, shall be held at the county court house in each county of the state, upon the first Saturday in June in each year, and the necessary traveling expenses of said examiners, not otherwise provided for by law, on the approval of the president and secretary of the board of visitors of said state agricultural college, shall be paid by said state college; students who apply for examination shall be examined upon such subjects as may be designated by the faculty of said college, and the state board of education, and the said city and county superintendents shall report to the president of said college and the state superintendent of public instruction the names of all such students examined as in their opinion are suitably prepared to enter said college, with their estimate of the order of excellence in scholarship shown by said students at such preliminary examina-

<small>Certificates, by whom issued.</small>

tion; certificates of appointment to the state agricultural college shall be issued by the state superintendent of public instruction to all such students as are so found to be qualified to enter said college, and in case the vacant scholarships shall not be sufficient to receive all successful candidates, preference to appointing to vacant scholarships shall be given to successful candidates in the order of the excellence of their examination as certified by said superintendents, and in general the regulations and provisions governing the conduct of such examinations and the appointment of said students to scholarships shall be subject to the control of said board of visitors of said college.

<small>Students appointed to hold state scholarships. Ibid. § 3.</small>

264. Each student so appointed and admitted to said college shall be regarded as holding a state scholarship, and for each scholarship so held there shall be paid as hereinafter provided, on the first day of November in each year,

<small>Appropriation from income of state school fund.</small>

to the treasurer of said college, the same sum of money as the said college is entitled to receive for each scholarship established in said college under the existing state agricultural college fund; *provided*, that such payment shall be made only out of the income of the fund for the support of public free schools remaining after appropriations heretofore made payable out of said income are met. Proviso

265. In order to ascertain the number of scholarships for which payment shall be made as aforesaid, the president of said college shall, in the month of October, in each year, make his certificate in writing, setting forth the names of the students so as aforesaid appointed and then in attendance at said college, the assembly districts from which they were appointed and the classes in college in which they belong, or the special courses of study which they are pursuing, which certificate, when approved by the president of the board of visitors of the state agricuctural college, shall be plenary evidence of the number of scholarships for which payment shall be made, and on filing the same with the comptroller of the state he shall draw his warrant upon the treasurer of the school fund for the sum of money to which the said college may accordingly be entitled, and the said treasurer shall thereupon pay the same as aforesaid. President of college to certify number of students. Ibid. § 4.
Certificate filed, with state comptroller.

GENERAL LAWS APPLYING TO ALL CITIES.

266. In any city in this state where the board of education is authorized by law to determine the amount required for the current expenses of such board, without the concurrence of any other board, it shall be lawful for such board of education to incur expenditures for such purposes in excess of and beyond any limit now fixed by law; *provided*, that such expenditures shall not exceed in any one year the average enrollment of pupils in the public schools in such city during the next preceding year; *provided*, that this act shall not be construed so as to decrease the limit of expenditure for the purposes aforesaid in any city where by present law the limit is more than fifteen dollars or where there is no limit. Boards of education in certain cities to incur expenditures in excess of limit. P. L. 1890, Chap. CLXXIX, § 1.
Proviso.
Proviso.

267. It shall be lawful for the board of education of any city, with the concurrence of the board of aldermen or other

body having charge of the finances of such city, to appropriate and expend such sum and sums of money as in the judgment of such boards shall be needed from time to time for the current expenses of the public schools of such city, or for the improving or increasing the school accommodations of such city, by the erection or alteration of school houses or otherwise, in excess of and notwithstanding any limitation upon any such expenditure in this or any other law of this state, general, special or local, contained.

May appropriate money for current expenses for buildings, &c. Ibid § 2.

268. It shall be lawful for any city in this state to raise by taxation, and expend for the purposes of current expenses of the department of public instruction for any fiscal year, an amount which, together with the state appropriation for schools, shall equal fifteen dollars per scholar on the average number reported as enrolled in the public schools of such city in the last preceding year; *provided*, that this act shall not be construed so as to decrease the limit of expenditure for the purposes aforesaid in any city where by present law the limit is more than fifteen dollars or where there is no limit.

Limit of expenditures in cities. P. L. 1886, Chap. CLXXII, § 1.

Proviso.

269. The municipal board in any city authorized to determine annually what amount of tax shall be required for school purposes, shall have power to determine an amount not to exceed one-half of one per cent. of the taxable valuation of the real and personal property in any city, in addition to the state school tax levied for that year; and such amount of tax so determined shall be assessed and collected at the same time and in the same manner with the taxes of the city assessed and collected for other city purposes; *provided*, that this act shall not take away from any city any power now existing to raise a larger amount of taxes for school purposes; *and further provided*, that this act shall not take effect in any city until the same shall have been first submitted to a vote of the qualified voters at any annual municipal election, and shall have received the approval of a majority of those voting at such election.

City tax for schools. P. L. 1885, Chap. CCXXII, § 1.

Proviso.

Proviso.

270. All special charters and acts limiting the amount to be raised for school taxes in any such city, and all other acts or parts of acts inconsistent herewith be and the same are hereby repealed.

Repealer. Ibid. § 2.

SCHOOL LAW.

271. The amount of money raised in any one year by tax in any city, by order of the board of aldermen, for the current expenses of public schools, shall not be greater than the entire amount received from the state for school purposes during the preceding fiscal year; *provided*, that a special additional appropriation may be made at any time by a three-fourths vote of all the members of the board of aldermen.

<small>Special city school tax not to exceed amount received from state. P. L. 1878, Chap CXXXIV, § 11. Proviso.</small>

272. It shall be lawful for any board of education of any incorporated city of this state, from time to time, to modify the several appropriations made by the board, to be expended under the direction of the several committees during any fiscal year; *provided however*, that said modifications shall not authorize any expenditure in excess of the sum appropriated for the current expenses of the department of public instruction at the time when such appropriation shall have been originally made.

<small>Boards of education may modify appropriations. P. L. 1877, Chap. CXII, § 1. Proviso.</small>

273. The amount appropriated by the board of aldermen or other body charged with the duty of making appropriations for defraying the current expenses of the department of public instruction in any city of this state, for each successive year, shall thereby become appropriated to defray such current expenses and shall be used for no other purpose whatever.

<small>Appropriations for current expenses not to be used for other purposes. Ibid. § 2.</small>

274. Whenever it has become or may become necessary in any of the cities of this state to use the whole or any part of the appropriation annually made by the state for the support of public schools therein, before the same has been actually paid over by the state to such city, it shall and may be lawful for such city to borrow, on temporary loans, in anticipation of such receipt, the whole or any part thereof; *provided*, the amount so borrowed shall not exceed in any one year the amount so apportioned.

<small>Cities may borrow for school purposes on temporary loans. P. L 1889, Chap. LXXXII, § 1. [See sec. 319.] Proviso.</small>

275. It shall be the duty of such city to pay off and discharge all such loans outstanding when such money so anticipated is received.

<small>Payment of temporary loans. Ibid. § 2.</small>

276. Whenever, in the opinion of the board of education of any city in this state, it shall become necessary for the proper maintenance and continuance of the schools in such

<small>State school moneys may be used for calendar year instead of school year. P. L. 1886, Chap. XXIV, § 1.</small>

city, to use and expend the money appropriated by the state for school purposes, it shall be lawful for the said board to use and expend the same at any time during the calendar year, and without regard to the state school year; *provided,* that the said board shall not use or expend the same for any purpose inconsistent with or other than those specified in the act to which this is a supplement.

Proviso.

Purchase supplies without advertising.
P. L. 1878, Chap LXXXVI, § 1.

277. Boards of education now prohibited by law from purchasing any article necessary for the schools under their control without advertising for the same, are hereby authorized to purchase, without advertising, to the extent of twenty-five dollars for any one article; *provided,* the same be sanctioned by a majority of the board.

Proviso.

Appropriations for relief and education of indigent children in cities.
P. L. 1883, Chap. CLXII, § 1.

278. In addition to its yearly appropriations for school purposes, it shall be lawful for the body having control of the finances of any city in this state to raise, in its annual tax levy, a sum of money not exceeding one thousand dollars, which, together with any moneys obtained therefor by voluntary contributions, shall be expended for the relief and primary education of such indigent, homeless or deserted children of said cities, by reason of their age, their inability to obtain suitable clothing, their necessary occupations or otherwise, are unable to attend the public schools; *provided, however,* that the moneys thus appropriated shall be expended under the direction of the mayor of said city.

Proviso.

Salary of president of boards of education.
P. L. 1880, Chap. CCVII, § 1.

279. In cities of this state where the office of president of the board of education, or board of directors of education, exists or is created by any general or special law, such president shall hereafter receive no salary or compensation whatever for performing the duties of such office, but nothing herein contained shall be deemed or taken to affect or take away the salary of the present incumbent of any such office.

Bonds for school houses in cities not to exceed $50,000.
P. L. 1882, Chap. CXIII, § 1
Proviso.

280. It shall and may be lawful for any city in this state, from time to time, to purchase lands for the purpose of erecting school houses thereon, and to raise the money required for such purpose by loan on the credit of such city; *provided,* that the total amount of bonds outstanding and unpaid,

issued for such purpose, shall not exceed at any one time the sum of fifty thousand dollars; and further, that said bonds shall not bear more than the legal rate of interest, and said bonds shall not be sold at less than par value.

281. All such loans shall be authorized by an ordinance of the common council or board of aldermen of such city, which ordinance shall distinctly specify and provide the ways and means, exclusive of loans, to pay the principal of said loans and the interest on the same annually, and also the time within which the said bonds shall be paid, which ordinance shall be irrepealable until such debt is paid. *Bonds to be authorized by common council. Ibid. § 2.*

282. When, in any city of this state, loans have heretofore been made for the purpose of purchasing lands and erecting school houses thereon, and the bonds issued for such purpose are still outstanding and unpaid, the amount of the bonds so issued shall be included within the amount authorized to be issued by this act, and nothing in this act shall be taken or construed as authorizing the issuing of bonds to a greater amount, at any one time, than the sum of fifty thousand dollars, for the purposes aforesaid. *Bonds already issued to be included in the amount authorized by this act. Ibid. § 3.*

283. It shall be lawful for the corporate authorities of the cities of this state, upon request by the board of education or other body having the charge of the public schools in such city, to purchase lands and erect school houses thereon, and to furnish the same, from time to time, as the increase of population in any such city may demand; *provided, however*, that the expense incurred in any one instance shall not exceed forty thousand dollars; *provided, further*, that where the charter of any city, or any supplement or supplements thereto provides a limit of annual expenditure for permanent improvements, nothing in this act shall authorize expenditure in excess of such limit. *School houses authorized to be built. P. L. 1882, Chap CLXXIX, § 1. Proviso. Proviso.*

284. To raise the fund for the purposes aforesaid the corporate authorities of such city shall have power to raise money by temporary loans for a term not exceeding three years, and to meet such loan they shall include in the next annual tax levy one-third, at least, of the amount of such temporary loan, with interest thereon, and in the second succeeding annual tax levy they shall include at least one- *Loans to be paid in three installments. Ibid. § 2.*

third of such amount, with interest thereon, and in the third succeeding tax levy they shall raise any balance unpaid, with interest; and as fast as such moneys shall come into the treasury of such city they shall be applied to pay such temporary loan; and such loan shall be so obtained that it can be paid by installments, with interest, semi-annually.

Security for loan. Ibid. § 3

285. To secure such temporary loan the corporate authorities may authorize the issue of temporary loan bonds or scrip, which shall bear such interest as may be agreed upon, not exceeding the legal rate, to an amount not exceeding the expenditure to be incurred in any one instance; *provided, however*, that no bonds shall be issued in excess of ten per centum of the assessed valuation of such city.

Proviso.

Loans taken by sinking fund. Ibid § 4.

286. Such temporary bonds or scrip may be taken for the sinking fund of any such city, if the authorities having charge of such sinking fund shall so elect, and if such bonds can be so taken it shall be the duty of such authorities to so take them, and the money raised by taxation for payment of the principal and interest shall then be paid into the sinking fund.

Mortgage school property to build school houses P. L. 1882, Chap CLXXXI, § 1.

287. If, in the judgment of any board of education of any city in this state, or other body having control of the public schools in any city of this state, it shall at any time be deemed necessary and expedient to provide additional school accommodations in such city for the benefit of those entitled to attend the public schools in such city, it shall be lawful for the mayor and common council or other governing body in such city to authorize money to be borrowed for the purpose of purchasing land and the erection of suitable school buildings and providing such school buildings with suitable school appliances and conveniences and to secure the payment of the money borrowed as aforesaid by mortgage bearing annual interest at a per cent. not greater than the legal rate on the land purchased and the building or buildings to be erected thereon in pursuance of this act; or if the city own suitable land, rendering a purchase of land unnecessary, on such land and the building or buildings to be erected thereon; and in case the title to lands on which public

school buildings are now erected in any city is vested by law in a board of education or other body having control of the public schools in such city, such board of education or other body having the control of public schools in such city, and not the mayor and common council or other governing body of such city, shall have the power to borrow money as aforesaid, and to secure the payment of the same by mortgage as aforesaid; *provided*, that not more than one school building, with the necessary appliances and conveniences, shall be authorized to be erected in any city in any one year in pursuance of the powers conferred by this act. Proviso.

288. Any mortgage to be given in pursuance of this act shall be payable in less than ten years from the time of giving the same except at the option of the city, board of education, or other body giving the same, who are authorized to renew such mortgage; and money to pay the annual interest accruing on any such mortgage shall be raised in the same manner as the money to pay the current expenses of the public schools is raised in any city in which the property on such mortgage shall be given is situate; any money may be raised for a sinking fund to pay such mortgage in the same manner; *provided, however*, that nothing in this act shall be held to permit the authorities of any city in this state to exceed any limit of expenditures for such purposes now fixed by any city charter or any supplement thereto, nor to exceed the limit of indebtedness fixed by any such charter. Mortgage to be payable in ten years Ibid. § 2

Proviso.

289 That the common council or other legislative body of any city of this state shall have power to borrow any sum or sums of money, not exceeding in the aggregate the sum of thirty thousand dollars, to be used for the purchase of land and the erection, furnishing and fitting up of a building or buildings for public school purposes in said city; and that the said common council or other legislative body of said city may secure the repayment of the said sum or sums so borrowed, together with interest thereon at a rate not to exceed five per centum per annum, in such manner and upon such terms as to the said common council or other legislative body may seem proper, by the issuing of bonds Cities may borrow money to erect school houses. P. L. 1887, Chap. CXXXV, § 1.

Issue bonds

in the corporate name of said city, to be signed by the mayor or other chief executive officer of said city and countersigned by the city clerk or other person performing the duties of recording officer for the said common council or other legislative body, as the case may be, and sealed with the common seal of said city; *provided*, that in cities having a board of education or other board having control of the public schools than the common council, the purchase of land, erection, furnishing and fitting up of a school house or school houses with the money so borrowed shall be made in the same manner as heretofore provided by law for the city borrowing money by virtue of this act.

Proviso.

290. It shall not be lawful for any board of education in any city of this state to borrow money, issue bonds or incur indebtedness in excess of five thousand dollars for the purpose of purchasing lands or erecting any school building, without the concurrence and approval first obtained of the common council, board of aldermen or other governing body of said city, *provided, however*, that the provisions of this act shall not apply to any school district wherein moneys for school purposes are raised at an annual meeting of the voters thereof. And, *provided, further*, that this act shall not apply to or affect any board of education the boundary lines of whose school district extend beyond the boundary lines of the town or city in which the school houses are located, into any adjoining township outside of the limits of such town or city.

Boards of education not to borrow without consent of governing body of city.
P. L. 1894.
Chap. CCCXXIV, § 1.

Proviso.

Proviso.

FIRST CLASS CITIES.

Common council in cities of the first class may provide manner of paying teachers
P. L. 1893,
Chap. X, § 1.

291. It shall be lawful for the common council or other governing body in any city of the first class of this state to provide by ordinance for the manner in which payments shall be made to teachers of the public schools in such cities, and for the form and manner in which warrants upon the public treasury of any such city shall be drawn and signed for this purpose; and all payments and disbursements made, and all warrants drawn in accordance with the terms of an ordinance duly passed for that purpose, in any such city shall be deemed and taken to be in all respects regular and lawful.

292. All moneys received from any source by municipal boards or departments established in cities of the first class in this state shall be paid by such boards or departments to the treasurer or other person charged with the custody of the funds of such city. And where the power to borrow money in anticipation of estimated receipts has heretofore been vested in any board in such city such power shall be and is hereby transferred to and vested in the mayor and common council or other body having control of the finances of such city. <small>Treasurers in cities of the first. class to be custodians of all moneys received by municipal boards. P. L. 1894, Chap. CCCII, § 1.

Common council only body authorized to borrow.</small>

293. All moneys expended by such boards or departments shall be by warrant on the treasurer or other persons charged with the custody of the funds of such city issued, countersigned and audited as warrants of the board of police and fire commissioners in such cities are now required to be issued, countersigned and audited. <small>All payments by municipal boards to be by warrant on city treasurer. Ibid. § 2.</small>

294. The board of education, or other board having charge of the public school department in cities of the first class in this state, shall have the entire control and management of the buildings owned or leased by such city and used in connection with the school department thereof; that such board shall keep and maintain all the buildings of said department in good order and repair, and make such alterations and additions thereto as may be necessary from time to time; that said board of education shall also be charged with the duty of furnishing and refurnishing said school buildings. <small>Boards of education in cities of the first class to have entire control of all school buildings. P. L. 1894, Chap. CCXCII, § 1.</small>

295. All unexpended appropriations heretofore made to any other board or department in said city for the alteration, addition, furnishing or repair or any of them, of such school buildings, shall forthwith be transferred upon the books of the city to the credit of said board of education. <small>Unexpended balances to be transferred to credit of board of education. Ibid. § 2.</small>

296. Nothing in this act contained shall affect existing contracts made by such city for the repair of buildings for school purposes, and that the expenditures by said board of education for any purpose herein authorized shall comply with the provisions of law now or hereafter in force fixing and limiting appropriations and their disposition. <small>Existing contracts not affected by this act. Ibid. § 3.</small>

297. All laws now in force in such city relative to the alteration, addition, furnishing and repair of public school <small>Laws now in force to apply to board of education. Ibid. § 4.</small>

buildings therein shall apply to and bind said board of education.

<small>Authorities in cities of the first class to purchase land and erect school houses.
P. L. 1884, Chap. CXXIX, § 1.</small>

298. The corporate authorities of the cities of the first class of this state, upon request by the board of education or other body having the charge of the public schools in such city of the first class, shall purchase lands and shall erect school houses thereon, and shall furnish the same from time to time, as the increase of population in any part of such city of the first class having the least school accommodations

<small>Proviso.</small>

may demand; *provided, however,* that the expenses incurred in each year shall not exceed forty thousand dollars; *and*

<small>Proviso.</small>

provided further, that such expenditures shall be concurred in by the city board authorized by law to make appropriations for the expenses of the city government.

<small>May raise funds for building school houses by temporary loans.
Ibid. § 2.</small>

299. To raise the funds for the purpose aforesaid, the corporate authorities of such city of the first class shall have power to raise money by temporary loans for a term not exceeding three years, and to meet such loan they shall include in the next annual tax levy one-third at least of the amount of such temporary loan, with interest thereon, and in the second succeeding annual tax levy they shall include at least one-third of such amount with interest thereon, and in the third succeeding tax levy they shall raise any balance unpaid with interest, and as fast as such moneys shall come into the treasury of such city of the first class, they shall be applied to pay such temporary loan, and such loan shall be so obtained that it can be paid by installments with interest payable semi-annually.

<small>May issue bonds or scrip to secure loan.
Ibid. § 3.</small>

300. To secure such temporary loan, the corporate authorities may authorize the issue of temporary loan bonds or scrip, which shall bear such interest as may be agreed upon, not exceeding the legal rate, to an amount not exceeding the expenditure to be incurred in each year.

<small>City sinking fund may invest in bonds.
Ibid. § 4.</small>

301. Such temporary loan bonds or scrip may be taken for the sinking fund of any such city of the first class, if the authorities having charge of such sinking fund shall so select, and if such bonds can be so taken, it shall be the duty of such authorities to so take them, and the money raised by

taxation, for the payment of the principal and interest, shall then be paid into the sinking fund.

SECOND CLASS CITIES.

302. There shall be established in every city of the second class of this state, whose population now exceeds or may hereafter exceed fifty thousand, a board of education, which shall be composed of and managed and controlled by eight commissioners, to be known as commissioners of public instruction, and not more than one-half of the said commissioners shall be of the same political party; the said commissioners shall be appointed by the mayor of such cities for the term of two years; not more than one commissioner shall be appointed from the same ward, except in such cities where there are less than eight wards; the first appointment of commissioners shall be four for one year, and the remainder of the board for two years, so that they shall be divided into classes, one class going out each year; and thereafter there shall be appointed every year an equal number to fill the places of those whose terms expire in that year, and in case of a vacancy in any such office the appointment to fill the same shall be for the unexpired term only and shall be made by the mayor; and the mayor of such cities shall be a member ex-officio of said board and shall be entitled to vote therein in case of a tie; the said commissioners appointed under this act shall perform their duties without pay.

Commission of public instruction in cities of the second class having population exceeding 50,000. P. L., 1892, Chap. XLIX, § 1.

Term.

Mayor is, ex-officio, a member.

303. The commissioners of public instruction appointed under this act shall be and they are hereby invested with and shall possess and exercise all the same powers which by law are now vested in and exercised by the department of public instruction, boards of education, school trustees, commissioners of public instruction, or other such body, by whatever name called, having the management and control of the public schools in any such cities of the second class in this state, and the said commissioners shall perform the same duties now required of or imposed by law upon any such department, boards, trustees or commissioners in any such cities; they shall also adopt such rules and regulations as to

Powers and duties. Ibid. § 2.

[See sec. 315.]

the appointment, control, duties, dismissals and salaries of their officers, teachers or other employees as to them shall seem expedient, and may alter the same at pleasure, except where the term of office or salaries of such officers or employees is now fixed by law; no such officer or employee shall be a member of such commission; and the salaries of the officers, teachers and other employees of such board, and all other moneys necessary for the use of said board, shall be obtained and paid in the same manner as is now provided by law in any such cities; *provided,* that none of the powers and privileges conferred in this act shall be so exercised as to nullify or conflict with the rules and regulations of the state board of education.

Proviso.

304. The said commissioners of public instruction, appointed under this act, shall take or subscribe an oath or affirmation before the police justice of such cities or any other officer qualified to administer oaths, faithfully and impartially to perform the duties of such office, and on the third Monday in April next after this act takes effect, at ten o'clock in the forenoon, and annually thereafter, shall proceed to organize said board by the election of one of the said commissioners as president for the term of one year.

Oath of commissioners. Ibid. § 3.

Time of organization of commission.

305. The said commissioners of public instruction hereby established in such cities of the second class, shall be instead, and shall take the place of, and be in lieu of, any and all other boards of education, departments of public instruction, commissioners of public instruction, school trustees, or by whatever name such offices, officers, departments or boards may be called in such cities, and the offices and terms of office of any and all other commissioners of public instruction, school trustees, or boards of education, or departments of public instruction, except those appointed and recognized by this act, shall be and they are hereby abolished, terminated and ended at ten o'clock in the forenoon on the third Monday in April next after this act takes effect.

Former boards abolished. Ibid. § 4.

306. The board of aldermen, common council or other governing body, by whatever name called in such cities, where the said commissioners of public instruction are

Governing body of city to provide rooms, etc. Ibid. § 5.

appointed under this act, shall provide suitable rooms for the transaction of the business of the said board of education and shall procure suitable furniture therefor.

307. The corporate name of such commission shall be known as "The Commissioners of Public Instruction of the City of (here insert the name of the city)." Corporate name
Ibid. § 6.

308. Any board of education of cities of the second class in this state shall have power to appoint a person of suitable attainments to be city superintendent of schools, define his duties and fix his term of office, not to exceed three years, and his compensation, which shall not be changed during his term of office. Superintendents in cities of the second class.
P. L. 1891, Chap. XXVI, § 1.
[See sec. 303.]

309. The city superintendent of schools shall hold office for the said term and until his successor is appointed, subject to removal by the board of education on complaint for cause stated. Term of office.
Ibid. § 2.

310. It shall and may be lawful for any city of the second class in this state, from time to time, to purchase lands for school purposes and to erect school houses thereon and to raise the money required for such purposes on the credit of the city by the sale of its bonds; *provided*, that the total amount of outstanding and unpaid bonds issued by any such city for school purposes, under any general, public, special or local law or laws whatever, shall not at any one time exceed the sum of fifteen dollars for each child between five and eighteen years of age within such city, as shown by the last school census of such city. Cities of the second class may issue bonds to build school houses.
P. L. 1890, Chap. CXXXVII, § 1.
Proviso.

311. Said bonds shall bear interest at a rate not exceeding five per centum per annum, shall not be sold below their par value, and shall be made payable in not more than twenty years. Rate of interest.
Ibid. § 2

312. Before any moneys shall be raised under the provisions of this act, authority therefor shall be given by an ordinance of the common council, board of aldermen or other governing body of the city desiring to raise moneys for the purposes aforesaid, which shall distinctly specify and provide the ways and means of paying the principal of said bonds and the interest thereon, and also the time within Common council to authorize the issue of bonds.
Ibid. § 3.

which said principal shall be paid and when the interest thereon shall be paid.

Cities of the second class may issue bonds to reconstruct school houses.
P. L. 1891, Chap. CXCIX, § 1.

313. Hereafter it shall be lawful for the common council, board of aldermen or other governing body of any city of the second class in this state in which a public school house shall be in a dilapidated, unsanitary, unsafe or unsatisfactory condition for school purposes, to purchase additional ground, either adjoining such school house or elsewhere, as may seem best for school purposes, and reconstruct such school house on a larger scale and with better and more modern appointments, at an expense not to exceed one hundred thousand dollars.

Bonds not to exceed $100,000
Ibid. § 2.

314. For the purposes aforesaid, it shall be lawful for said common council, board of aldermen or other governing body to issue bonds of such city for the payment of such expenditure, not to exceed the said sum of one hundred thousand dollars, payable in not less than twenty years, at a rate not to exceed five per centum, pledging the faith and credit of such city for the payment thereof, which bonds shall be sold to the highest bidder, after having first advertised the same for sale in two newspapers of the county for at least two weeks.

Cities of the second class may borrow to erect school houses.
P. L. 1893, Chap. CXLV, § 1.

315. The common council or other legislative body of any city of the second class of this state shall have power to borrow any sum or sums of money, not exceeding in the aggregate the sum of fifty thousand dollars, to be used for the purchase of lands and the erecting, furnishing and fitting up of a building or buildings for public school purposes in said city; and that the said common council or other legislative body of said city may secure the repayment of the said sum or sums so borrowed, together with interest thereon at a rate not to exceed five per centum per annum, in such manner and upon such terms as to the said common council or other legislative body may seem proper, by the issuing of bonds in the corporate name of said city, to be signed by the mayor or other chief executive officer of said city and countersigned by the city clerk or other person performing the duties of recording officer for the said common council or other legislative body, as the case may be, and sealed with

the common seal of said city; *provided*, that in cities having a board of education or other board having control of the public schools than the common council, the purchase of land, erecting, furnishing and fitting up of a school house or school houses with the money so borrowed shall be made in the same manner as heretofore provided by law for the city borrowing money by virtue of this act. _{Proviso.}

316. It shall be lawful for the commissioners of public instruction or other body having the control of public schools in any city of the second-class of this state, to provide by resolution for the manner in which payments shall be made to teachers of the public schools in such cities, and receipts taken therefor; and all payments made and receipts taken therefor by the city treasurer, in the manner prescribed by such resolution or resolutions, shall release and discharge the treasurer of any city from all further liability and responsibility on account thereof, and shall be deemed and taken to be in all respects regular and lawful. _{Board may provide by resolution manner of payment to teachers. P. L. 1894, Chap. CCXL, § 1.}

THIRD CLASS CITIES.

317. In all cities of the third class the term of office of members of the board of education shall be for as many years as there are members of such board of education elected from each ward; and that at each annual municipal election after the next succeeding election each ward shall elect one member of such board of education. _{Term of office of members of boards of education in cities of third class. P. L. 1883, Chap. XXXI, § 1.}

318. At the next succeeding municipal election the members of the board of education shall be elected as heretofore, and at the first meeting of such board of education then elected, the members from each ward shall, by lot, divide themselves into classes, so that the term of office of one member from each ward shall expire in each succeeding year. _{Shall divide into classes. Ibid § 2.}

TOWNSHIPS, TOWNS, BOROUGHS AND SPECIAL CHARTERS.

319. The board of education, board of school trustees or other body having charge and control of the public schools

110 SCHOOL LAW.

Incorporated places may borrow to pay teachers' salaries.
P. L. 1894, Chap CCXXX, § 1.

in any school district in this state, acting under a special charter or under the provisions contained in the charter of any city, town, borough or other municipality, may in any year borrow a sum of money not exceeding four-tenths of the amount apportioned to such district from the state school moneys for such year for the purpose of paying teachers' salaries falling due within said year; and that the said district may pay the amount so borrowed, together with interest thereon at a rate not exceeding six per centum per annum, out of the state school moneys apportioned to said district for the then current school year as soon as the same have been received by the city treasurer or other person designated by law as the custodian of the school moneys belonging to such district.

District acting under special charter may borrow, although charter does not grant that power.
P. L 1894, Chap. XCII, § 1

320. Any school district in this state acting under a special charter, and which has no power under such charter to issue bonds for the purpose of purchasing land for school purposes, or for the erection or enlargment of a school house or school houses, may issue bonds for such purpose or purposes in the manner provided for the issuing of bonds by districts organized under the provisions of the act to which this is a supplement;

Proviso.

provided, that this act shall not apply to any district until such district shall decide to accept the same by a vote of the majority of the legal voters present at any regular annual meeting of the district.

Act shall not be operative without vote of district.
Ibid § 2.

321. Any district voting to accept this act, may order the issue of bonds as provided in section one, either at the annual meeting or at a special meeting, which special meeting shall be called in the same manner as is provided by the charter of such district for calling the annual meeting.

Inhabitants of towns, boroughs or townships may incorporate.
P. L. 1888, Chap CCCXXV, § 1.

322. The inhabitants of any town or borough or any township having a special charter, or of any township which has or hereafter may have a population exceeding six thousand inhabitants, may become a body politic and corporate in fact and in law, by the name and title of "the town of   , in the county of   ," whenever, at a special election, to be called for that purpose as hereafter provided, it may be so decided by a majority of the electors of said proposed town who shall vote at such special election.

323. The town and ward officers of the town shall be a * * * * town treasurer, * * * * a board of education, consisting of three members from each ward. _{Board of education. Ibid. ₴ 9.}

324. At the annual town election held under this act one member of the board of education for each ward shall be elected for one year, and one member for two years, and one member for three years; and the electors voting at such election shall designate on their ballots the terms for which the several candidates for such offices shall be elected; and thereafter, annually, a member of the board of education shall be chosen for three years. _{Election of members of board of education. P. L. 1892 Chap. LIX, ₴ 6.}

325. No person shall be eligible to any office under this act unless he shall have resided in the town for the period of at least one year, and no person shall be eligible to any ward office unless he shall be an actual resident of the ward; no person shall be eligible to any office unless he is a citizen of the United States. _{Who are eligible as members of board of education. P. L. 1888, Chap. CCCXXV, ₴ 17.}

326. In case any vacancy shall occur in the board of education, said board of education may fill such vacancy by appointment until the next town election, when the vacancy shall be filled by the electors of the town; *provided*, that if at any town election there shall be a vacancy in any office to be filled, and at the same time an election for the full term of such office, the term for which each person shall be voted for shall be designated on each ballot cast therefor. _{Vacancy, how filled. Ibid. ₴ 18. Proviso.}

327. The town treasurer shall receive, safely keep and disburse all moneys raised and received for public school purposes; he shall keep separate accounts thereof and pay the same out only on warrant signed by the chairman and clerk of the board of education, and no warrant for any such purpose shall be drawn on the treasurer except in pursuance of an order or resolution passed at a stated meeting and entered in their minutes and the provisions of the last preceding section of this act relative to warrants on the treasurer by the town council shall apply to the warrants of the board of education; and the said treasurer shall do and perform all acts and duties enjoined upon township collectors by the school laws of the state. _{Treasurer to hold school moneys. Ibid. ₴ 30.}

SCHOOL LAW.

Council may appropriate money for schools.
Ibid § 52, div. xi.

328. The council shall have power to pass ordinances appropriating and providing for raising by taxation moneys for the support of public schools.

School districts in towns incorporated under this act to be consolidated.
P. L. 1892, Chap. LIX, § 8.

329. All the property, real and personal, of the several school districts existing within the limits of any town, borough or township, before its incorporation under the provisions of this act, shall, upon such incorporation, become and be the property of such incorporated town, and shall be held in its corporate name, and the several obligations, contracts and debts of said previously existing school district shall be assumed by and shall become and be the obligations, contracts and debts of said incorporated town; and that the board of education shall possess and exercise all the powers and perform all the duties by law vested in or imposed upon the trustees of school districts; they shall organize annually by choosing a chairman and a clerk, and may establish schools and provide for their government, and shall keep all school property in good repair;

Powers of board of education.

they shall define and fix the duties and compensation of their clerk, who shall also perform all duties enjoined by law on district clerks;

Proviso.

provided, that no property shall be bought or building erected by the said board unless a majority of the voters of the town voting at an annual town meeting shall have voted an appropriation for that purpose; in case any appropriation for the purchase of land and the erection of a school building shall be voted by the electors of the town at any town election, the council shall

May issue bonds

issue bonds in the corporate name of the town for the amount of such appropriation in such denominations as they shall deem proper; such bonds shall be designated "school bonds," shall bear interest at not exceeding the rate of six per centum per annum, and shall not be sold for less than their par value; they shall be made payable in such manner that at the expiration of three years three-fifteenths thereof shall become due and payable, and thereafter one-fifteenth thereof shall become due and payable annually; the council shall provide for raising by taxation annually, the interest thereon and one-fifteenth of the principal thereof; the proceeds of the sale of said bonds shall be held by the town treasurer, and shall be paid out by him on the warrants of the board of education; at any time after an appropriation is voted as aforesaid, the board of education may purchase the necessary land and enter into contract for the erection of a school building thereon, the title to which property shall be vested in the town by its corporate name.

330. That in all municipalities where a consolidated school district has been formed from two or more individual districts, by reason of the incorporation of such municipality, any subsequent division of such municipality shall not create a division of said consolidated school district. *Consolidated school districts. P. L. 1887, Chap. XXXII, § 1.*

331. That for the better government and representation of such consolidated districts, the original individual districts of which such consolidated district is formed shall be known as sub-district number one, two, three, four, and so on, of school district number ——, of —— county, and that in such consolidated district the elective members of the board of trustees or board of education shall consist of two members elected from each original individual district, whose term of office shall be equal in length to the number of original districts from which the consolidated district was formed, but that both of said trustees from said sub-district shall not be elected in one year. *Districts, how known. Ibid. § 2. Trustees to be elected from sub-districts.*

332. That before the first annual election after the passage of this act, the existing board of trustees or board of education of such consolidated district shall meet and so distribute the representation by trustees; that at the coming annual election two trustees shall be elected to represent the sub-districts in which there may have been no trustees heretofore elected and shall so divide the time for which said trustees or members of the board of education shall be elected, that a portion of the board shall be elected each year, but no two from any sub district shall be elected in any one year after the first election; that notice of such distribution and the length of time for which said members shall be elected shall be published by the district clerk in his notice of the annual election of school trustees; *provided*, that all trustees or members of the board of education now in office shall *Term of trustees. Ibid. § 3. One trustee from each sub-district. District clerk to give notice of term. Proviso.*

remain in office until the time for which they have been elected has expired.

Act not to apply. Ibid. § 4.

333 That this act shall take effect immediately, but shall not apply to districts that are governed by the charters of any chartered municipality.

Township committee to build school houses. P. L. 1885, Chap CCXXI, § 1.

334. The board of township committee, or other legislative body of any township in this state, upon written notice duly served upon them by the board of education, or other body having charge of the school affairs of such township, that in their judgment it is necessary to build an addition to any school house in said township, or to construct a new school house therein, in order to provide proper accommodation for the children of school age in said township, may proceed and cause said addition to said school house to be built, or may purchase lands and construct a new school house thereon, and shall furnish the same from time to time.

Township bonds Ibid. § 2.

335. To raise the funds required for the purposes aforesaid the said board of township committee, or other legislative body of any township of this state, are hereby authorized and empowered to issue in the corporate name of such township either coupon or registered bonds, bearing interest not exceeding six per centum per annum, payable semi-annually; the principal of the whole number of bonds issued for any of the purposes aforesaid shall be payable in ten annual payments from the date of the issue thereof; said bonds shall be signed by the president or chairman of said committee, and countersigned and registered where registered bonds are issued by the township clerk, and sold at public or private sale at not less than the par or face value thereof.

Payment of bonds. Ibid. § 3.

336. It shall be the duty of the said board of township committee, or other legislative body of any township of this state, to place in the annual tax levy of each year a sum sufficient to pay the interest and extinguish the principal of said bonds as the same shall become due and payable, and apply the same to the purposes of this act, and to no other purpose whatever.

337. Whenever in the school districts of this state, except school districts in cities and towns of five thousand inhabi-

tants and upwards, which said cities and towns have a common council, there may exist a board of education or trustees holding their charters by special act of the legislature and independent of any city charter, the district clerk shall be secretary of the board, and in addition to the duties as laid down in sections thirty-five and thirty-six of the act to which this is a supplement, he shall conduct the correspondence of the board, keeping copies of such letters as he may write, in some suitable manner, and filing all such letters and papers as the board may direct at their stated meetings; also, he shall notify the assessor of the amount of special tax to be assessed and collected in each and every year for the payment of the principal and interest of school bonds that may have been issued in such districts, also the amount of special tax to be assessed and collected to defray the incidental expenses of such schools during the year; and at the close of each year he shall present at the annual meeting for the appropriation of moneys for such district, a report of the general financial state of the district, the condition of the school property, the school work during the year, the requirements for the year to come, and such other matters as may be needful to an intelligent understanding of the present state or which is desirable for the future promotion of public education in the district; and for such services he shall receive such compensation as the board of education may allow. *[In school districts having special charters the district clerk shall act as secretary. P. L. 1882, Chap. LXXVI, § 1. [See secs. 58 and 59.] Duties of district clerk.]*

338. At the annual election of officers of such board a treasurer may be elected from the members of the board, who shall receive from the collector of the township or townships in which such district is situated all moneys due said district, from whatever source, within ten days from the time when such moneys shall come into such collector's hands; and said treasurer shall disburse the same in the way and manner provided in section eighty-four of the act to which this is a supplement, and, within ten days after his election, he shall give such bonds for the faithful discharge of his duty as shall be acceptable to the township committee of the township in which the school house is situated, for double the amount that may come into his hands during any one *[Treasurer to hold school moneys. P. L. 1878, Chap CCLXII, § 2. [See sec. 156.] Treasurer to give bonds.]*

Report of treasurer.

year, and every year at the annual meeting for the election of trustees he shall present an itemized statement of the receipts and the expenditures of the year then closing; which statement, in conjunction with the annual report of the secretary, shall be published in the newspaper printed nearest to said district, or in such other manner as may be deemed best for the public good; and for his services he shall be entitled to receive the amount provided for the town col-

[See sec. 156.]

lector for such disbursements in section eighty-four of the act to which this is a supplement.

Election of trustees.
P. L. 1882,
Chap.
LXXVI, § 2.

339. The election of trustees or members of such boards of education shall be held in each district on the Tuesday of the week following the annual town meeting in each and every year; the terms of service of those then elected to begin immediately; and the term of any trustee which would expire on the first Monday of July following such election shall expire on the Tuesday of the week following the annual town meeting; and that five days' notice of said meeting for election of trustees shall be set up by the secretary in five of the most prominent places of the district;

Proviso.

provided, however, that in all cases where the trustees of any district are elected at any municipal election, by virtue of any independent charter, the election for such trustees in such district shall be held in the manner and at the same time as heretofore, and the beginning and length of their terms of office shall remain as before the passage of this act.

Term of office.
P. L. 1878,
Chap.
CCLXII, § 4.

340. In all boards of education or trustees hereafter elected, of which all the members are now elected annually, and to which this supplement applies, the principle of classification provided for trustees elected under the general school law shall govern, so that at least two members of the board shall remain in office from each previous year.

Number of trustees.
Ibid. § 5.

341. Where the present number of trustees or members of the board of education of any district to which this supplement is applicable may be such as to embarrass a proper classification of the term of service of the members of the board, it shall be lawful for the legal voters of such district, by a majority vote at an annual meeting of the district, to make such change as may be desired in the number of trus-

tees or members of the board of education; *provided*, that by such change the whole number shall not exceed six; *and provided further*, that public notice be given of such contemplated change by the district secretary in his notice for the annual meeting. Proviso.
Proviso.

342. Each member elect of such boards of education, before entering upon the duties of his office, shall take the following oath or affirmation before some person duly authorized to administer an oath, to wit: "I, A. B., having been duly elected a member of the board of education of school district number C, D county, New Jersey, do solemnly swear (or affirm) that I will faithfully execute the trust reposed in me as a member of said board. Trustees to take oath. Ibid. § 6.

"Dated ———, A. D. ———. (Signed) ———."

343. The provisions of this act shall not apply to boards of education in any city or borough of this state nor to any county in this state containing less than twenty-five thousand inhabitants. Act not to apply to counties having less than 25,000 inhabitants. Ibid § 7

MISCELLANEOUS.

344. In case any school district shall use any of the school money received by it, except such as may be raised within the district, for any other purpose than the payment of teachers' salaries and fuel bills, such district shall forfeit out of the next annual appropriation a sum equal to twice the amount thus used, and it shall be the duty of the county superintendent to re-apportion the money thus forfeited among the other districts of his county; *provided*, the state superintendent may remit such penalty for cause. Moneys received from state to be used only for teachers' salaries and fuel. P. L. 1894, Chap. CCCXXXV, § 12.
Penalty. [See sec. 161.]
Proviso.

345. In any district as now constituted, where there has been ordered a special district tax, which tax has not yet been collected, such tax shall be assessed, levied and collected on the district as now constituted, and that the moneys collected from such tax shall be expended by the board of education solely for the benefit of the school or schools for which it was ordered to be raised, and for no other purpose whatsoever. District taxes for 1894 to be used only for districts where ordered. Ibid. § 26.

346. The school houses, lands, apparatus and other property owned by the school districts hereby abolished, shall,

SCHOOL LAW.

Value of property of districts to be appraised. Ibid. ₴ 27.

immediately after the passage of this act, be appraised by the assessors of the several townships; in making said appraisement, the amount of debt incurred by any district for the purchase of lands, apparatus and other property, or for the erection of a school house or school houses, which debt is unpaid at the time of making such appraisement, shall be deducted from the appraised value of such property;

Copies of appraisement to be filed.

one copy of said appraisement shall be filed with the county superintendent, one copy with the district clerk of the consolidated district and one copy with the township collector, and at each assessment for special school tax thereafter (until the whole amount is remitted) there shall be remitted to the tax-

Value to be remitted to taxpayers in installments.

payers of each of said districts one-tenth of the said appraised value of the property of the school district in which such taxpayers reside or own property;

Proviso.

provided, that in case any such district is situated in two or more townships, the assessors of said townships shall jointly make said appraisement, and shall determine the part thereof belonging to each of said townships, and each township shall remit to the taxpayers in its part of such district the part so determined, in the same manner as in case of districts wholly within a single township; *and provided further*, that in case any such district is situated in two or more boroughs, or partly in a borough and partly in a township, said appraisement shall be made by the several borough assessors or by the borough and township assesors (as the case may be) in the manner aforesaid.

Districts to purchase flags. P. L. 1894, Chap. XXXIV, ₴ 1.

347. The board of education or the board of school trustees in the several cities, towns, townships, boroughs, villages and school districts of this state shall purchase a United States flag, flag-staff and the necessary appliances therefor, and shall display said flag upon or near the public school building during school hours, and at such other times as to the said boards may seem proper; and that the necessary funds to defray the expenses to be incurred herein shall be assessed and collected in the same manner as moneys for public school purposes are now raised by law.

348. From and after the passage of this act any officer of public instruction of this state, being intrusted with the

funds of any school board, and not directed by law to give security for the same, shall enter into such security as any school board under whom he may serve shall direct, before entering on the duties assigned to him by said board.

<small>School officer to give bonds. P. L. 1882, Chap. XLIII, § 1.</small>

349. Hereafter there shall not be assessed upon any inhabitant of this state more than one poll-tax in any one year.

<small>Not more than one poll tax to be assessed in any year. P. L 1891, Chap. CCLXX § 1.</small>

350. Any person who shall enter the buildings or go upon the lands belonging to any public school district of this state, or used and occupied for school purposes by any public school in this state, and shall break, injure or deface such building or any part thereof, or the fences or outhouses belonging to or connected with such building or lands, or shall disturb the exercises of such public school, or molest or give annoyance to the children attending such school, or any teacher therein, shall be deemed and adjudged to be a disorderly person, and may be apprehended in the manner hereafter prescribed in this act, and taken before any justice of the peace of the county where such person may be apprehended; and it shall be the duty of the said justice to commit such disorderly person, when convicted before him by the confession of the offender, or by the oath or affirmation of one or more witness or witnesses, to the county jail of such county, there to be kept at hard labor for any term not exceeding thirty days.

<small>Injury to school property or disturbing schools. P. L. 1871, Chap. CXVII</small>

351. Any person who shall directly or indirectly give, or receive, or promise; contract or agree to give or receive, any sum or sums of money, or any goods, chattels, gift, lands or real estate, or any other thing, bribe, present or reward whatsoever, for, or to obtain, or for giving out the printing of blanks, notices, advertisements, or any other printing, or for, or to obtain, or for giving out any other work or thing, connected with, or in or appertaining to, any office or department of this state, or any office or department in any county, city, town, township, borough or other place in this state, shall be guilty of a misdemeanor, and on conviction thereof shall, for every such offence, be liable to a fine not exceeding three hundred dollars, or suffer imprisonment at hard labor

<small>Penalty for bribery. P. L 1879, Chap. CXLIII, § 1.</small>

not exceeding one year, or both, at the discretion of the court.

Penalty for exceeding appropriations. P. L. 1876. Chap. III, § 1.

352. If any board of chosen freeholders or any township committee, or any board of aldermen or common councilmen, or any board of education, or any board of commissioners of any county, township, city, town or borough in this state, or any committee or member of any such board or commission, shall disburse, order or vote for the disbursement of public moneys, in excess of the appropriation respectively to any such board or committee, or shall incur obligations in excess of the appropriation and limit of expenditure provided by law for the purpose respectively of any such board or committee, the members thereof, and each member thereof thus disbursing, ordering or voting for the disbursement and expenditure of public moneys, or thus incurring obligations in excess of the amount appropriated and limit of expenditure as now or hereafter appropriated and limited by law, shall be severally deemed guilty of malfeasance in office, and, on being thereof convicted, shall be punished by fine not exceeding one thousand dollars, or imprisonment at hard labor for any term not exceeding three years, or both, at the discretion of the court.

Penalty for officers having an interest in furnishing supplies. P. L. 1876, Chap. CXXXIV, § 1.

353. If any employee or person or persons having the control or management of any institution, the moneys for the support of which are drawn in whole or in part from the treasury of the state, shall be directly or indirectly interested in furnishing any goods, chattels, supplies or property of any kind whatsoever, to or for the use of any such institution, which may be in whole or in part supported by appropriations paid out of the treasury of the state, such person, officer or employee shall be deemed guilty of a misdemeanor, and, on conviction thereof, shall be punished by a fine not exceeding one thousand dollars, or imprisonment at hard labor for any term not exceeding one year, or both, at the discretion of the court.

Penalty for bribery. P. L. 1879, Chap LXXIV, § 1.

354. If any member of any state, county or city government, or any member of any public board, association or commission, shall hereafter solicit or receive, either directly or indirectly, any money or valuable consideration for his

vote in the appointment of any person or persons to any position in any department of any public body aforesaid, the person or persons so offending shall be deemed and taken to be guilty of a misdemeanor, and on conviction thereof be punished by fine or imprisonment, or both; said fine not to exceed one thousand dollars, nor such imprisonment one year, and be forever thereafter debarred from holding any office of profit, trust or emolument in this state.

355. If any member of any board of chosen freeholders, or of any township committee, or of any board of aldermen or common councilmen, or any board of education or school trustees in any city, or any board of commissioners of any county, township, city, town, borough or school district in this state, shall be directly or indirectly concerned in any agreement or contract for the construction of any bridge or building of any kind whatsoever, or any improvement whatever to be constructed or made for the public use or at public expense, or shall be a party to any contract or agreement, either as principal or surety, between the county, township, city, town, borough or school district, as the case may be, and any other party, or shall be directly or indirectly interested in furnishing any goods, chattels, supplies or property of any kind whatsoever, to or for the county, township, city, town, borough or school district, the contract or agreement for which is made, or the expense or consideration of which is paid, by the board, council or committee of which such member is a part, shall be deemed guilty of a misdemeanor, and, on being thereof convicted, shall be punished by fine not exceeding one thousand dollars, or imprisonment at hard labor for any term not exceeding three years, or both, at the discretion of the court. *Penalty for public officer being concerned in any public contract. P. L. 1888, Chap. CCCXXVIII, ₴ 1.*

356. All acts and parts of acts of a general character on the subject of public schools, and of the normal school and its appropriations, passed before the twenty-first day of March, one thousand eight hundred and sixty-seven, are hereby declared to be repealed. *Repealer. P. L. 1867, Chap. CLXXIX, ₴ 82.*

357. This act shall apply to all districts in this state receiving any portion of the state school moneys; *provided*, that in any district acting under a special charter, or under *Act to apply to all districts. P. L. 1894, Chap. CCCXXXV, ₴ 23. Proviso.*

the provisions contained in the charter of any city, town, borough or other municipality, this act shall apply only so far as it is consistent with the provisions of such charter, and that all such charters shall remain and be in full force and effect the same as if this act had not been passed.

Rules and Regulations

Prescribed by the

State Board of Education.

(123)

Rules for State and County Examinations.

Prescribed by the State Board of Education in Conformity with the Act Entitled "An Act to Establish a System of Public Instruction," Section 2, Clause 1.

I. GENERAL INSTRUCTIONS RELATING TO BOTH STATE AND COUNTY CERTIFICATES.

1. No person shall be employed as a teacher by any Board of Trustees unless he holds a regular teacher's certificate in full force and effect at the time that the engagement is made. Any person accepting a position as a teacher in any school in this State shall, before taking charge of such school, exhibit his or her certificate to the County Superintendent of the county in which such school is situated; and any contract entered into between any teacher and any Board of Trustees shall not be valid until the requirements of this rule are complied with. It shall be the duty of the County Superintendents to keep a record of such certificates.

2. Any person desiring to obtain a position as a teacher in any school in this State between the dates of the regular examinations, and who is not in possession of a regular certificate in full force and effect, may obtain from the State or County Board of Examiners a provisional certificate, good until the next regular examination; *provided*, that such provisional certificate shall not be renewed or extended.

3. No certificate shall be issued to a teacher whose average in any subject covered by the examination falls below 70.

4. All candidates are required to furnish testimonials as to their moral character, and as to the times and places in which they may have taught, and their success in teaching. Such testimonials shall be retained by the Board of Examiners and form part of their permanent records.

5. Any certificate may be revoked for cause, either by the Board which issued it or by the State Board of Examiners. Every such case shall be reported to the State Board of Education in writing.

6. Every Board of Examiners shall keep a full and correct list of all certificates issued, together with the names and addresses of the holders. Such list shall be transmitted to the State Superintendent within ten days after every examination, and shall be printed as part of the annual report of that officer.

7. In all examinations for teachers' certificates the diploma of a college in good standing shall be accepted in lieu of an examination in the academic subjects prescribed.

8. The State Board of Examiners may endorse the diploma of any Normal School or Training College or the permanent certificate issued by a State Superintendent, or Board of Examiners, of another State, when the course of study of such normal School or Training College, or the requirements for such certificates, are, in the judgment of the State Board of Examiners, equivalent to those required for similar diplomas or certificates in this State; and when so endorsed, such diploma or certificate shall have full force and effect as if issued in this State.

9. With the exception of Reading, Elocution, Music, School Gymnastics, Drawing and Manual Training, all examinations are to be conducted in writing.

10. A special average will be given for correctness in Orthography and Composition and for neatness and order in the general appearance of the examination papers. Special credit marks will be given for ability to teach Elocution, Music, School Gymnastics, Drawing and Manual Training.

11. Any Board of Examiners shall accept from any applicant for a Second or First Grade County Certificate, or for any State Certificate, any certificate of any grade, in lieu of further examination in the academic subjects covered by said certificate ; *provided,* that the applicant shall have attained a general average of 85 per cent.; and shall present satisfactory evidence of having been a teacher in good standing during the time subsequent to the granting of said certificate.

12. Applicants for employment as special teachers to give instruction in any subject not prescribed in the certificates granted by the State or County Boards of Examiners, may be examined by the Board of Examiners in such subject, and when satisfied of the fitness of the

applicant to teach any of the branches referred to, said Board of Examiners may issue a special certificate to said applicant. Such certificates shall remain in force three years, and shall be valid as licenses to teach the subjects for which they are issued, within the jurisdiction of the Board of Examiners granting the certificates.

II. COUNTY EXAMINATIONS.

13. The County Superintendent, together with those persons whom he may appoint as County Examiners, shall hold three stated meetings during each year for the examination of teachers, in such places in the county as are most convenient of access to the teachers. The first examination shall be held on the first Friday and Saturday in October; the second on the first Friday and Saturday in February, and the third on the first Friday and Saturday in May; *provided*, that when any of these days falls upon a legal holiday, the examination shall be postponed one week. The October and February examinations shall be for Second and Third Grade Certificates, and the May examination for First, Second and Third Grade Certificates. At all examinations the day and order in which subjects required for a certificate of any grade may be taken shall be determined by the State Superintendent.

14. The County Superintendent will issue certificates of the three grades, to be known respectively as the First, Second and Third Grade County Certificates. No County Certificates issued after March 15th, 1893, shall be valid outside of the county in and for which it is issued.

15. Candidates for the *Third Grade County Certificate* are to be not less than eighteen years old. No experience in teaching will be required. Applicants for a Third Grade Certificate will be examined in Orthography, Reading, Penmanship, Geography, Arithmetic, English Grammar, and the Theory and Practice of Teaching. The certificate will continue in force for one year from date, and will be valid as a license to teach in an ungraded school or in a primary school or department. After October 6th, 1891, Third Grade County Certificates shall not be issued to the same person more than twice.

16. Candidates for the *Second Grade County Certificate* are to be not less than nineteen years old, with an experience in teaching of not less than one year. The examination will be the same as that for the

Third Grade Certificate, with the addition of English Composition, Physiology, the History of the United States, and Book-keeping. The certificate will continue in force for three years from date, and will be valid as a license to teach in any school or department not above the grade of a grammar school.

17. Candidates for the *First Grade County Certificate* are to be not less than twenty years old, with an experience in teaching of not less than two years. The examination will be the same as that for the Second Grade Certificate, with the addition of Algebra, Physics, History of Education, the Constitution of the United States, and the School Law of New Jersey. The certificate will remain in force for five years from date, and will be valid as a license to teach in any school or department in the county. A First Grade County Certificate may be renewed without a re-examination.

18. An ungraded school is defined as one in which but a single teacher is employed. A graded school is one in which more than a single teacher is employed, and which is divided into at least two departments. A primary school or department is defined as one having the first four years of the usual school curriculum, consisting of studies similar to those prescribed in the primary department of the State Model School. A grammar school or department is defined as one having the second four years of the usual school curriculum, consisting of studies similar to those prescribed in the grammar department of the State Model School. A high school is defined as a school, the curriculum of which includes more advanced instruction than that of a grammar school, as herein defined.

19. A new set of questions shall be prepared for each county examination under the direction of the State Superintendent of Public Instruction, and ten questions will be given in each study. No special examination shall be held unless the consent of the State Superintendent of Public Instruction has been first obtained, and no questions shall be used at any regular or special examination except those issued or approved by the State Superintendent. County Superintendents, on granting certificates at special examinations, may grant them in the usual form; or if they deem it advisable, they may grant them to be good only until the next regular examination.

20. Upon each County Certificate shall be written the special average in each study gained by the holder, and his or her general average, each marked as a percentage upon the scale of 100.

III. STATE EXAMINATIONS.

21. The State Board of Examiners will grant certificates of three grades, to be called respectively First, Second and Third Grade State Certificates, the third or lowest grade ranking one degree above the highest grade issued by a County Board of Examiners. Two examinations for State Certificates, and only two, shall be held each year, in the city of Trenton, beginning on the first Thursdays of June and December respectively. These examinations shall be public, and the questions used shall be approved formally by each member of the Board of Examiners.

22. Candidates for the *Third Grade State Certificate* are to be not less than twenty years old. No experience in teaching will be required. They will be examined in all the subjects required for a First Grade County Certificate, together with Psychology, Plane and Solid Geometry, Chemistry, Geology, Botany and Free-hand Drawing. The certificate will remain in force for seven years from date, and will be valid as a license to teach in any school in the State. It may be renewed without re-examination.

23. Candidates for the *Second Grade State Certificate* are to be not less than twenty-one years of age, with an experience in teaching of not less than two years. The examination will be the same as that required for a Third Grade State Certificate, together with the Philosophy of Education and the Principles of Manual Training and Physical Culture. The license will remain in force for ten years from date, and will be valid as a license to teach in any school in the State. It may be renewed without re-examination.

24. Candidates for the *First Grade State Certificate* are to be not less than twenty-five years old, with an experience in teaching of not less than five years. Candidates will be required to present satisfactory evidence that their teaching has been in every way successful. The examination will be the same as that required for the Second Grade Certificate. The certificate will remain in force during the life of the holder, unless revoked for cause (see Rule 5), and will be valid as a license to teach in any school in the State.

25. Graduates of the State Normal School who have completed the three years' course shall be entitled to a Second Grade State Certificate;

provided, that five years after graduation from the State Normal School, any holder of a Second Grade State Certificate is entitled to have said certificate renewed for life, without examination, by the State Board of Examiners, on presentation of satisfactory evidence to that Board that the holder has been continuously and successfully engaged in the profession of teaching during the five years next preceding the date of the application.

IV. COUNTY SUPERINTENDENTS

26. It shall be the duty of each County Superintendent to visit the Schools in his county as often as may be necessary; *provided*, that he shall visit every school under his jurisdiction at least once in each year; *and provided further*, that the total number of visits made during the year shall equal at least twice the number of schools under his jurisdiction; the additional visits to be made to such districts as, in his judgment, most need his encouragement and advice.

27. He shall note at such visits, in a book provided for the purpose, to be designated "The Superintendent's Visiting Book," the condition of the school buildings and out-houses, the appearance and correctness of the records kept in the School Registers, the efficiency of the teachers, the character, record and standing of the pupils, the methods of instruction, the branches taught, the text-books used, and the discipline, government and general condition of each school; and from the notes thus taken he shall ascertain and report the relative grade of merit of each school.

28. He shall labor in every practicable way to elevate the standard of teaching and to improve the condition of the schools in his county; shall give such directions in the science, art and methods of teaching as he may deem expedient, and shall be the official adviser and constant assistant of the school officers of his county.

29. He shall distribute promptly all reports, forms, laws, circulars and instructions which he may receive from the State Superintendent or the State Board of Education, and in accordance with their directions.

30. He shall take care that the decisions of the State Superintendent or the State Board of Education, upon controversies relating to the school laws of the State, or to the rules and regulations pre-

scribed by the State Board of Education, be complied with by the parties concerned; and in case such decisions are not complied with, he shall inform the State Superintendent thereof, and state the circumstances connected therewith.

31. He shall carefully preserve all reports of school officers and teachers, and all examination papers of teachers examined by the County Board of Examiners, and, generally, shall carry out the provisons of the law "Establishing a System of Public Instruction," and the rules and regulations prescribed by the State Board of Education, and at the close of his official term shall deliver to his successor all records, books, documents, papers and property belonging to the office.

32. No County Superintendent shall act as agent for any author, publisher or bookseller, nor directly or indirectly receive any gift, emolument or reward for his influence in recommending or procuring the use of any book, or school apparatus, or furniture of any kind whatever in any public school; and any one who shall violate this provision shall be subject to removal from office.

33. He shall meet each Township Board of Trustees at least twice each year, which meetings shall be held at such times and places as he may appoint.

34. He shall ascertain from the Township Collectors, within five days after the annual town meetings, the amount of school tax ordered to be assessed in each township, and on or before the first day of May of each year, he shall apportion, according to law, to the several townships and school districts of his county, all the school moneys to which they are entitled for the following year, whether received by State appropriation or ordered to be assessed as township school tax.

35. It shall be the duty of the District Clerk of any school district to deposit with the Township Collector, or other legal custodian, all moneys received by the Board of Trustees from tuition, loans, proceeds from the sale of bonds or other school property, or from any other source, and disburse the same only by orders upon the Collector of the township in which said school-house is located; and in case of the refusal of a District Clerk to comply with the above, it shall be the duty of the County Superintendent to serve the Collector with a written notice forbidding him to honor any drafts against the State moneys until the provisions of this rule be complied with.

36. Every County Superintendent shall encourage and assist in the organization and management of County Institutes, as the Committee on Education may direct, and be present at and preside over the same.

37. He shall inquire and ascertain whether the boundaries of the school districts in his county are definitely and plainly described, and shall keep in his office a full and correct map, showing such boundaries and the location of the various school-houses, a copy of which he shall furnish to the State Superintendent of Public Instruction. No changes in the boundaries of school districts shall be valid without the approval of the State Superintendent.

38. No changes in the boundaries of districts, in which district taxes have been ordered, shall be made between the times of ordering and assessing the same.

39. At the close of their official terms, or on the vacation of their office, by resignation or otherwise, should the same occur during the scholastic year, all County Superintendents shall report to the State Superintendent for the portion of the year that may have expired, as provided for in the 47th section of the School law, with reference to their annual reports; and no order shall be given for their last quarter's salary until such reports are received in a manner satisfactory to the State Superintendent.

40. That in case of the failure of any County Superintendent to make his report to the State Superintendent on the first day of September, as required by law, the State Superintendent shall not give to such County Superintendent any order for the payment of salary for the quarter next succeeding such delinquency, except by special resolution of the State Board of Education for this purpose.

41. All teachers are required to attend the annual Institute held for the county in which they are teaching; and no deduction shall be made by Trustees from the salary of any teacher for the time he or she is in attendance upon said Institute.

42. When it is within the knowledge of the State Superintendent that a County Superintendent is not attending to the duties of his office, he shall withhold from such County Superintendent orders for his quarterly salary until the Board shall direct such orders to be drawn.

43. No allowance shall be made for office rent in the expenses of the County Superintendents.

44. Whenever there is a vacancy in the office of County Superintendent, the State Superintendent is hereby authorized to appoint a suitable person as County Superintendent *pro tempore;* said appointment to be approved by the President of the State Board of Education.

Decisions

By State Superintendent.

Decisions by State Superintendent.

No. 1.—The State School Moneys Intended Only for the School Year beginning July 1st next after the Apportionment is made.

As the amount of the State School Tax for any one year is determined by the number of children of school age as contained in the next preceding school census, and as the apportionment of the State school moneys is made upon the basis of the number of such children in the respective school districts, it is the evident intention of the statute that these school moneys should be applied for the maintenance of the school during the school year beginning July 1st next after the apportionment is made.

In the case of the Board of Education of Elizabeth vs. Patrick Sheridan, Collector, tried in the November Term of the Supreme Court in 1879, Justice Scudder held that the "School Taxes are to be levied and applied for the fiscal year succeeding the assessments, and not for the preceding year."

The same rule will prevent the application of these taxes to a *succeeding* year.

In each year a large number of children pass beyond the school age, and a large number of children just enter it, so that each year has a school generation of its own. It is the generation of each year that is to be benefited by the school tax of that year, and not a future generation.

No. 2.—Official Acts of Trustees.

For any act of a district clerk which requires the sanction of the school trustees, it is not sufficient that the said trustees individually consent. The trustees of the school district are municipal officers. All of their official acts must be performed in their corporate capacity at a regularly convened meeting, of which all should have notice and in which all have opportunity to participate.

No. 3.—Suspension of Pupils.

Section 81 of the School Law, so far as it relates to the suspension of pupils, does not confer that power upon assistant teachers in graded schools.

As such a construction would tend to interfere with the proper supervision of the school by the principal, I decide that, in a graded school which is under the general supervision of a principal, the section is restricted, in its application to the principal, and does not give the right of suspending pupils to assistant teachers.

No. 4.—Salaries of City Superintendents not to be paid from the State School Moneys.

As the State provides supervision by County Superintendents, who are not paid out of the State school moneys, and, as City Superintendents take their places, and do their work in cities, I think that City Superintendents should not be paid out of the State school moneys.

No. 5.—Proceedings in Bonding a District.

1. The notices calling a district meeting to authorize the trustees to issue district bonds must be ordered at a regularly called meeting of the board of education, and must be signed by the president and district clerk. The board must decide for what purpose or purposes the district meeting shall be called. Full and accurate minutes of the meeting of the board must be kept.

2. The notice calling the district meeting must state all the purposes of said meeting, as decided upon at the meeting of the board, and must be posted not less than ten days, in at least seven public places in the district, one being posted on each school-house.

3. The district meeting must decide the amount of money to be appropriated to each object for which money is ordered to be raised,

and the total amount voted must not exceed the amount stated as thought to be necessary in the notices. A majority of the taxable voters of the district must be present and vote on any proposition for the condemnation of land.

On all other questions a majority vote of the legal voters present at the meeting is all that is required.

The district meeting must decide the number of bonds to be issued, the denomination of the bonds, and the time or times of payment.

All proceedings must be approved by the Attorney-General before the bonds are issued. One copy of each of the following papers must be sent to the Attorney-General and one copy to the State Superintendent, viz.:

1. Minutes of the meeting of the Board of Education at which the posting of the notice was ordered.

2. The notice calling the district meeting.

3. Minutes of the district meeting.

These papers must be verified by an affidavit showing that they are true copies, and that the notices were posted according to law.

If the school meeting has voted on any proposition for the condemnation of land, there must also be an affidavit showing that a majority of the taxable voters were present and voted thereon.

On any question to raise money for any school purpose the vote must be taken by ballot.

The minutes of the Board of Education meeting and the notice of the district meeting should be sworn to by the District Clerk. The minutes of the district meeting should be sworn to by the secretary of said meeting.

No. 6—School Residence of Children.

The fact of a child's name being included in the census of any particular district does not give such child a right to attend school in that district after he has lost his residence there. The school census is taken simply to determine the amount of money to be raised for school purposes, and to enable the Superintendent to apportion the money among the several districts according to their needs.

A child has the right to attend the school in the district in which he is actually living and in no other district. The fact that he comes into the district on Monday morning and remains until Friday, simply for the purpose of attending the school, does not give him such a right. The residence of a child is generally to be determined by the residence of its parents or guardians. There are, however, exceptions to this rule; for instance, if a child is working and living with the person for whom he works, or boarding away from his parents in order that he may be nearer his work, such a child would have the right to attend the school in the district in which he was at work; also if a child were living with his grandparents or other relatives, not merely for the purpose of going to school, but a *bona fide* residence, such a child would also have the right to attend the school in the district in which he was actually living.

No. 7.—Collectors to Return to Districts the Exact Amounts Ordered to be Raised by District Tax.

A School District may order to be raised, by District Tax, the exact amount required to enable it to fulfill its contracts and obligations. When the tax is collected, the Collector must place the sum to the credit of the District, or be held responsible for his failure to do so.

No. 8.—Fees of Assessors and Collectors Not to be Taken Out of the School Moneys.

Assessors and Collectors are township officers and must be paid out of township moneys provided for that purpose. Their fees cannot be taken from the school moneys, whether such school moneys are raised by tax or are derived from other sources.

No. 9.—Who are Legal Custodians of the School Moneys.

Our School Law nowhere provides that Boards of Education or District Clerks shall have the custody of any school moneys belonging to the Districts. It is, on the contrary, clearly the intention of the law that such district officers shall not, in any case, have such moneys in their custody, but that the moneys shall be held by some one else, subject to their order, and that they shall be paid out by the custodian only on orders signed by the President and District Clerk.

The Township Collectors are made the custodians of *all* school moneys belonging to the Townships.

In cities, the City Treasurer is made the legal custodian of the school moneys.

In boroughs, the Borough Collector is the legal custodian of all school moneys.

No. 10.—Incompatible Offices.

There is no statute in this State that I know of, nor is there any decision that I can find, bearing upon the question as to whether a person may act as District Clerk and as Township Assessor at the same time. In giving my opinion, the only guide that I have is the Common Law principle that a person cannot hold two offices that are incompatible; or, where the duties of the one interfere with or are inconsistent with the duties of the other. For instance, a person cannot be at the same time employer and employee; or, holding one office, take another where his duties will be to fix, or help to fix, his own salary, or determine his duties in his other office; or hold two offices where one is designed as a check upon the other, or where the duties of the one are such as to interfere with or prevent his performance of the duties of the other.

Now, let us see whether the offices of District Clerk and Township Assessor come within this principle. The duties of a District Clerk are such that he need not neglect them to do the work of an assessor, and *vice versa*, neither office is intended to be, nor is it, in fact, a check upon the other. The only official business relation between the two officers is when the District Clerk is required to certify to the Assessor the amount of money voted to be raised by district taxation. The only purpose of this notice is to give to the proper tax officer the necessary information. I cannot see that the duties of either office are incompatible with the duties of the other, and, therefore, my opinion is that one person can legally hold both.

No. 11.—School Holidays.

No teacher shall be required to teach on January 1st, February 22d, May 30th, July 4th, the first Monday in September (Labor Day), Thanksgiving Day, December 25th, nor on any day on which a general election is held (an election for State officers) or any day set apart by proclamation of the Governor of this State, or the President of the United States, for the purpose of public observance, nor upon the Monday following when any of the above-named days fall on a Sunday.

If any of the above days fall on a Saturday, it is not to be counted as a school day in making up the teacher's time or the school term. If it falls on a Sunday, the Monday following is to be counted as a school day, though no school be held. If it falls on any other day in the week, it is to be counted as a school day, as though the school had been held.

Teachers cannot be required to make up any time lost by not teaching on any of the above days.

No. 12.—Collection of Delinquent Taxes.

In case of a failure to collect a school tax, the property liable for the tax may be sold and the tax recovered in the same manner as township taxes are recovered.

When a Collector sells property for the taxes in pursuance of a writ from the Township Committee, he shall retain the amount belonging to the School district and pay the balance of the proceeds over to the Township Treasurer.

If the Township purchases the property sold for taxes, it should pay over to the Township Collector the amount belonging to the School District, as any other purchaser would have to do. In no case should the Township Treasurer retain in his custody money belonging to the School District. He is only authorized to hold such moneys as are subject to the orders of the Township Committee, and the proceeds of a School tax are not subject to their order.

Such a course is absolutely necessary to the carrying out of the School Law. The citizens of a School District are authorized by law to vote taxes for certain purposes. Having notified the Assessor of such vote, they may make their contracts for the year based upon the amount of tax voted. The duty of levying and collecting the tax rests with the Township, which is vested with ample powers. If the taxing officers fail to collect the tax voted, the powers of the incorporated School District are destroyed, and the duties which the law imposes upon its officers and people cannot be performed.

The School Law is not perfect in itself in the matter of taxation, because it does not provide for the collection of delinquent taxes; for this purpose it relies on the general tax laws. But these are not perfect so far as relates to the schools, because they require the moneys received for delinquent taxes to be paid to the Township Treasurer, and do not require that they shall be returned to or paid over to the Township Collector to be placed to the credit of the Board of Education. But law never contemplates its own defeat, nor can it justify injustice or misapplication of money, and we cannot shield ourselves with one law while violating another. We must take the tax acts and the school acts together, and carry out the spirit as well as the letter of both.

No. 13.—Meetings for the Election of President and District Clerk.

The School Law provides that Boards of Education shall meet for the election of a President and District Clerk within ten days of the annual election for members of the Board. Neither the time nor the place is definitely fixed. The law is silent as to who shall call the meeting and fix the time and place. The Trustees may do it themselves at a previous meeting, or a majority of them may agree upon and sign a call to be duly sent to the minority. If this is not done by the Trustees, or a majority of them, it is plainly the duty of the clerical officer of the District, viz., the District Clerk, to call such meeting, and name the time and place.

Blanks and Forms

For School Officers

(145)

Blanks and Forms for School Officers.

The following Forms have been prepared for the use of all officers having duties to discharge under the School Law. Their use will secure uniformity and correctness in the transaction of financial and general school business. The *literal* use of these Forms is in no case *essential* to the validity of a school instrument. Any form may be used which clearly expresses the objects designed, or the intention of the parties interested, and conforms in all respects to the requirements of the law, but as those annexed have been prepared with strict reference to these necessary conditions, their use is recommended. The blank spaces are to be filled to meet the varying circumstances in each case. These forms have been submitted to and approved by the State Board of Education.

ADDISON B. POLAND,
State Superintendent of Public Instruction.

Forms for County Superintendents.

Form No. 1.—Notice of Institute.

..........., N. J., ..., 18......

The Teachers' Institute for .... County will be held at ...., commencing .... 18..., and closing ... . 18......

...., *County Superintendent.*

RULE PRESCRIBED BY THE STATE BOARD OF EDUCATION.—"All Teachers are required to attend the Annual Institute, held for the county in which they are teaching, and no deduction shall be made by Trustees from the salary of any Teacher for the time he or she is in attendance upon said Institute."

Form No. 2.—Certificate of Teacher's Attendance at Institute.

..........., N. J., ..., 18......

To the Trustees of School District No. ......:

I hereby certify that .... has been in attendance at the Annual Institute of the County, just closed, ... days.

...., *County Superintendent.*

Form No. 3.—Statement of Expenses.

..........., N. J., ..., 18......

To the State Board of Education :

I herewith submit a statement, by items, of the expenses I have incurred in the performance of my official duties as County Superintendent of .... County, for the six months ending ...., 18......

OFFICE EXPENSES.

Postage, ...
Expressage, ...
Stationery, ...
Printing, ...

MISCELLANEOUS EXPENSES.

. . . .
. . . .

EXPENSES INCURRED IN VISITING SCHOOLS.

Week ending........., visited Schools Nos...... . . . .
Week ending ...., visited Schools Nos...... . . . .

SUMMARY.

Office expenses, ...
Miscellaneous expenses, ...
Expenses incurred in visiting schools, ...
    Total, ...
Total number of districts in the County, ...
Total number visited during the six months ending.........,
    18....., ...

STATE OF NEW JERSEY, }
    .... COUNTY. } ss.

On this...... ......day of...... ......, 18......, before me personally appeared ...., County Superintendent of .... County, who, on his oath, saith that the within statement is true, and that, to the best of his knowledge and belief, he has, during the time for which this statement is made, faithfully performed all the duties imposed by the School Law and by the regulations of the State Board of Education.

Sworn and subscribed before me }
  this.........day of.........., 18... }   ....

Form No. 4.—Order on County Collector for the $100,000 Appropriation.

OFFICE OF COUNTY SUPERINTENDENT,
........., N. J.,............, 18.... }

To the Collector of.........County :

Pay to the order of the Collector of .... Township, ... $\frac{}{100}$ Dollars, being the amount apportioned out of the State Appropriation of $100,000 for the support of Public Schools in said Township, for the School Year beginning July 1st, 18..., $..........

$.......... ...., *County Superintendent.*

Form No. 5.—Order on the County Collector for the State School Tax.

OFFICE OF COUNTY SUPERINTENDENT,
........., N. J., ..., 18.... }

To the Collector of .... County :

Pay to the order of the Collector of .... Township, ... $\frac{}{100}$ Dollars, being the amount apportioned out of the State School Tax for the support of Public Schools in said Township, for the School Year beginning July 1st, 18......

$ ...., *County Superintendent.*

Form No. 6.—Order on the County Collector for the Interest of Surplus Revenue.

OFFICE OF COUNTY SUPERINTENDENT,
........., N. J., ..., 18.... }

To the Collector of .... County :

Pay to the order of the Collector of .... Township, ... $\frac{}{100}$ Dollars, being the amount apportioned out of the Interest of the Surplus Revenue for the support of Public Schools, for the School Year beginning July 1st, 18......

$ ...., *County Superintendent.*

Form No. 7.—Order on County Collector for Balances.

OFFICE OF COUNTY SUPERINTENDENT,
.... , N. J., ..., 18.... }

To the Collector of .... County:

Pay to the order of the Collector of .... Township, ... $\frac{}{100}$Dollars, being the amount of balance of the State appropriation re-apportioned to said Township for the support of Public Schools, for the School Year beginning July 1st, 18......

$......... ...., *County Superintendent.*

Form No. 8.—Order on the County Collector for Examiner's Salary.

No. ....   OFFICE OF COUNTY SUPERINTENDENT,
.... N. J., ..., 18...... }

To the Collector of .... County:

Pay to the order of ...., County Examiner, ... $\frac{}{100}$ Dollars, being the amount due him for services and traveling expenses at the ...., 18. ...., session of the Board of County Examiners.

$......... ...., *County Superintendent.*

Form No. 9.—Appointment to Fill a Vacancy in a Board of Education.

To ....:

The office of one of the Board of Education of the Township of ...., in the County of ...., having become vacant through failure of the District to elect according to law [*or for any other reason*], you are hereby appointed to fill such vacancy, until the next annual meeting for the election of Trustees in said District.

Dated this .... day of ...., 18......

...., *County Superintendent.*

Form No. 10.—Appointment of a District Clerk.

To .... :

The office of District Clerk of the Township of ...., in the County of ...., being vacant through failure of the Trustees to elect according to law [*or for any other reason*], you are hereby appointed to fill such vacancy until the next annual meeting for the election of Trustees in said District.

Dated this .... day of ...., 18......

...., *County Superintendent.*

Form No. 11.—Notice to Township Collector, directing him to withhold School Moneys from a Teacher.

To the Township Collector of.........Township :

SIR :—You are hereby directed to withhold all further payment of salary to......... ...., a teacher now employed in School No........., situated in your Township, said Teacher not being in possession of a certificate [*or not having kept the School Register*], as is required by the School Law.

Dated this.........day of........., 18......

...., *County Superintendent.*

Form No. 12.—Notice to Township Collector, Directing Him to Withhold School Moneys from a District.

To the Township Collector of.........Township :

SIR :—You are hereby directed to withhold [*here state the amount in words*] from the school moneys apportioned to your Township [*here state the reason why the money is withheld*].

Dated this.........day of........., 18......

...., *County Superintendent.*

Form No. 13.—Notice of Meeting for Examination of Teachers.

Notice is hereby given that there will be a meeting of the County Board of Examiners of ...., County, for the examination of candidates for teachers' certificates at .... , on ...., the ....instant. Each applicant for a certificate should be present as early as............ o'clock A. M.

...., *County Superintendent.*

...., 18......

Form No. 14 —Notice to Teacher Revoking His Certificate.

To .... :

Sir :—The certificate of qualification held by you as a Public School teacher in the County of ...., issued on the ...... day of........., 18......, is hereby revoked, for the reason that [*here state reason why certificate is revoked*].

Dated this .... day of ...., 18......

...., *County Superintendent.*

See Rule 5 of the State Board of Education.

Form No. 15.—Notice to District Clerk informing him of the Revocation of Teacher's Certificate.

To..... ...., District Clerk of the Township of ...., of the County of .... :

Sir :—You are hereby notified that on the .... day of......... 18......, I revoked the certificate of qualification held by ...., a teacher in your Township, for the reason that, in my opinion, the said...... .... does not possess the requisite qualifications as a teacher in respect to [*moral character, learning or ability to teach, as the case may be*].

Dated this .... day of ...., 18......

...., *County Superintendent.*

Note.—When a teacher's certificate is revoked, a notice similar to the above should also be sent the Collector of the Township in which the Teacher has been engaged.

Form No. 16.—Notice to Township Collector of Apportionment of Balances.

OFFICE OF COUNTY SUPERINTENDENT, }
............, ..., N. J., ..., 18...... }

To the Collector of .... Township :

The amount of balances of the State Appropriation due your Township, under the act of 1887, is $ ....

...., *County Superintendent.*

Form No. 17.—Notice to District Clerk of Apportionment of Balances.

OFFICE OF COUNTY SUPERINTENDENT, }
...., N. J., ..., 18...... }

..............., D. C., District No......

I have this day apportioned to your District, from the Balances of the State Appropriation, the sum of $......... for the school year beginning July 1st, 18...

...., *County Superintendent.*

Form No. 18.—Certificate of County Superintendent in Appeals.

OFFICE OF COUNTY SUPERINTENDENT, }
....N. J., ..., 18... }

To ...., State Superintendent of Public Instruction :

SIR :—I transmit, herewith, a full and correct statement of the facts and documentary evidence presented to me in the case of .... *vs.* ...., together with my decision thereon, from which appeal has been taken to the State Department.

I certify that the accompanying statement is correct to the best of my knowledge and belief.

...., *County Superintendent for* .... *County.*

NOTE.—The above certificate should be furnished by the County Superintendent in cases of appeal, when requested by the State Superintendent.

Form No. 19.—Form of Certificate Condemning a School-House.

This is to certify that I, the undersigned, have this day condemned public school-house No. ......, in the Township of .... and County of ...., as being, in its present condition, unfit for use.

Dated this ...... day of ...., 18......

........., ..., *County Superintendent.*

NOTE.—This certificate is held by the County Superintendent, and the school-house remains condemned until repaired or rebuilt.

Forms for City Superintendents.

Form No. 20.—School-House Bond for Use in Incorported Cities.

STATE OF NEW JERSEY.

DISTRICT SCHOOL BOND.

No. ...... $.........

School District No. ......, ... County.

Know all men by these presents, that ...., in the County of ...., which municipality is also designated and known as School District No. ......, in the County of ...., is justly indebted unto " The Trustees for the Support of Public Schools of the State of New Jersey " in the sum of .... dollars, lawful money of the United States of America, to be paid to the said " The Trustees for the Support of Public Schools of the State of New Jersey " on the ...... day of ...., eighteen hundred and ...., at the .... Bank, at ...., with interest therefor from the date hereof, at the rate of five per centum per annum, payable annually on the ...... day of .... in every year, at the .... Bank, at ...., on the presentation of the annexed coupons as they severally become due.

This is one of a series of coupon bonds, amounting in the aggregate to the sum of .... dollars, numbered from ...... to ......, both inclusive. And all of said bonds have been issued for money borrowed by the said .... for the purpose of building a school-house in said municipality or School District, pursuant to the statute entitled "A further supplement to an act entitled 'An act to establish a system of public instruction' (Revision), approved March twenty-seventh, one thousand eight hundred and seventy-four," which said supplement was approved May sixth, one thousand eight hundred and eighty-nine, and by and with the consent of the .... of said municipality lawfully given, on the .... day of . ..., in the year one thousand eight hundred and ...., said .... being the body having charge and control of the finances of said municipality; and this bond, by virtue of the provisions of said statute, is made a first lien upon the lot of land upon which the school-house which shall be erected with the proceeds of the sale of said bonds, and also a first lien upon said school-house and all other improvements, of whatever nature, that are now on or that may hereafter be placed on said lot.

In witness whereof, on this .... day of ...., in the year one thousand eight hundred and ...., this bond is signed by the President and Secretary of the .... of said School District, and attested by the Secretary under the seal of the District.

...., *President.*
...., *Secretary of the Board*
Attest: *of .... of the ....*
  ...., *Secretary.*

DISTRICT SCHOOL BOND COUPON.

$.........

Interest warrant for .... dollars, payable at the .... Bank, at ...., New Jersey, to the Trustees for the support of Public Schools of the State of New Jersey, ..., 18......, for twelve months' interest on Bond No. ......

....,
Secretary.

The within bond having been issued by and with the consent of the .... of the........., the payment of the same is hereby guaranteed by ....

In witness whereof on this .... day of ...., in the year one thousand eight hundred and ...., the .... of said municipality have hereunto signed their names and affixed the corporate seal of said municipality.

                                                                                  ....

Attest:
                                                                                  ....

    ....

For forms for Application for State Aid to School Libraries, Application for State Aid for Manual Training, Application for Loan from State School Fund, and Report of School Debt, see under heading " DISTRICT CLERKS."

Forms for District Clerks

Form No. 21.—Report of District Clerk to County Superintendent of the Amount of District School Tax Ordered to be Raised.

To ...., County Superintendent of .... County:

    The legal voters of the School District of the Township of........., in the County of ...., met at ...., a convenient public place within the District, on the ...... day of ...., 18......, and notice thereof, setting forth the time, place and object of said meeting, specifying ...... dollars as the amount of money thought necessary to be raised, was given by the District Clerk, and set up at seven public places within the District ten days before the meeting, and the said legal voters, so met, by the consent of a majority of those present, authorized the Board of Education of said District ...., and ordered, by a like vote, ... dollars for the purpose of ...., and .... dollars for the purpose of ...., amounting in all to .... dollars, which sum is not in excess of the amount thought to be necessary as set forth in the notices.

    Dated this ...... day of ...., 18......

                                                     .... *District Clerk.*

STATE OF NEW JERSEY, } ss.
COUNTY OF ....

...., being duly sworn, on his oath saith that he is the District Clerk of the Township of ...., in the County of ...., and that the above statement is correct and true.

Sworn and subscribed before me this .... day of .,....... 18......

....

Form No. 22.--Certificate of the amount of School Tax voted to be raised in a School District, to be delivered by the District Clerk to the Township Assessor.

To........., Assessor of .... Township, ... County, State of New Jersey:

The legal voters of the School District of the Township of ...., in the County of ...., met at ...., a convenient public place within the District, on the ...., day of ...., 18......, a notice thereof, setting forth the time, place and object of said meeting, and specifying .... dollars as the amount of money thought necessary to be raised, was given by the District Clerk, and set up in at least seven places within the District, ten days before the meeting; and the said legal voters, so met, by the consent of a majority of those present, authorized the Trustees of said District [*to purchase lands, etc., as the case may be*], and ordered by a like vote .... dollars for the purpose of [*as purchasing land*], and .... dollars for the purpose of [*as building a school house*], etc., amounting in all to .... dollars, which sum is not in excess of the amount thought to be necessary, as set forth in the notices, and you are therefore directed to assess the said sum of .... dollars on the inhabitants of said Township, and their estates, and the taxable property therein, pursuant to the statute in such case made and provided.

Dated this .... day of ...., 18......

...., *District Clerk.*

STATE OF NEW JERSEY, } ss.
COUNTY OF ....

........., being duly sworn, on his oath saith that he is the District Clerk of the Township of ...., in the County of ...., and that the above statement by him is correct and true.

Sworn and subscribed before me, this ... . day of ...., 18......

....

NOTES TO FORM No. 22.—The certificate must state which of the object or objects specified in Section 164, for which the money is raised. 3 Vr. 444. If more than one object is specified, the amount of money apportioned to each must be stated. 7 Vr. 89.

A district tax ordered for the purpose of "maintaining a school" is illegal. The express purpose for which the money is to be used must be stated and voted upon.

The law requires that notice of the above action should also be sent to the County Superintendent.

Form No. 23.—Order on Township Collector for Teacher's Salary.

No. ...., N. J., ..., 18......
To ...., Township Collector for the Township of ......,
   County of ...., State of New Jersey:
Pay to the order of ...., Teacher, ... $\tfrac{\ \ }{100}$ Dollars, being the amount of salary due .... for teaching in Public School No. ...., from ...., 18......, to ...., 18......

...., *President.*   } Board of Education of
...., *District Clerk.* } the Township of ....

I hereby certify that ...., the Teacher in whose favor this order is drawn, is in possession of a Teacher's Certificate, in full force and effect, and that .... has properly kept the School Register, as required by law, and that I have certified thereto in said Register.

...., *District Clerk.*

NOTE.—Money raised by district tax can be used for such school purposes as are specified at the meeting at which the money is ordered. All other school money, except twenty dollars annually, which the law allows for incidental expenses, must be reserved for the payment of teacher's salary and fuel bills.

Payments can only be made for the support of those schools that conform in all respects to the provisions of the School Law, and to those teachers only who possess certificates in full force and effect, covering the time for which salary is demanded, and who have kept the School Register in the manner prescribed.

The collector should invariably refuse to pay orders until he is satisfied that all these conditions have been complied with.

Form No. 24.—Order on Township Collector for District School Tax Raised for Other Purposes than the Payment of Teacher's Salary.

To ...., Township Collector for the Township of ....,
County of ...., State of New Jersey:

Pay to the order of ...., ... $\frac{}{100}$ Dollars, for [*here state for what the money is to be paid*], out of the funds raised by District School Tax in our District, now in your hands.

...., *President.* } Board of Education of the
...., *District Clerk.* } Township of............

Form No. 25.—Notice by District Clerk to County Superintendent of the Election of Trustees.

To ...., County Superintendent:

SIR:—You are hereby notified that at the annual school meeting in the Township of ...., in the County of ...., held on the ...... day of.........., 18......, ..., was elected Trustee in the place of ...., whose term had expired.

The Board of Education now consists of—

Mr. ...., whose term expires 18......
" ...., " " " 18......
" ...., " " " 18......
" ...., " " " 18......
" ...., " " " 18......
" ...., " " " 18......
" ...., " " " 18......
" ...., " " " 18......

The Trustees have elected Mr. ...., President, and Mr. ...., District Clerk, whose post office addresses are ....
...., *Secretary of School Meeting.*

NOTE.—This notice should be sent to the County Superintendent as soon after the election as possible. It may be sent by the District Clerk or the Secretary.

Form No. 26.—Application for State Aid to Establish a School Library.

..............., N. J., ..., 18....
To the State Superintendent of Public Instruction:

SIR:—We, the undersigned, Trustees of School District of the Township of ...., County of ...., State of New Jersey, do hereby certify that there has been raised in our District, by subscription, [or entertainment, as the case may be,] the sum of ....Dollars, for the purpose of establishing a School Library in School No. ...., in accordance with the provisions of Section 185 of the revised School Law. And we, therefore, request you to send an order for the amount due us from the State in accordance with the further provisions of said act.

...., *President.*
...., *District Clerk.*

STATE OF NEW JERSEY, } ss.
.........County.

........., District Clerk, of the Township of ...., in the County of ...., being duly sworn, on his oath saith that the within statement is true.

Sworn and subscribed before me, this
......day of........., A.D. 18...
....
....

NOTE.—The first appropriation is twenty dollars, and subsequent ones ten dollars.

Form No. 27.—Report of Purchases Made for School Library.

..............., 18......

To the State Superintendent of Public Instruction :

I hereby report that the following purchases have been made for our School, with the amount raised in the District, and the appropriation received from the State.

........................., *District Clerk.*

N. B.—This report must be made in order that the District may be entitled to future payments. It should give the names and prices of the several articles purchased.

Form No. 28.—Application for State Aid for Manual Training.

To the State Superintendent of Public Instruction :

SIR :—We hereby certify that for the school year beginning September 1st, 18......, there has been raised by.........in the township of........., in the county of.........., the sum of.........dollars, for the purpose of.........course of Manual Training pursued in the Schools of the Township, and that said amount has been appropriated for such purpose.

This application is made in accordance with the provisions of the act of the Legislature of the State of New Jersey, entitled "An act for the promotion of manual training," approved February 15th, 1888, and we do hereby make application for a State appropriation equal to the sum of money so raised and appropriated as aforesaid.

........................., *President.*

Attest :

..................., *District Clerk.*

Form No. 29—Report of Proceedings Authorizing the Issue of Bonds.

MINUTES OF BOARD OF EDUCATION MEETING.

Pursuant to notice given to each member, the Board of Education of the Township of........., in the County of........., met at ...., on

the .... day of ...., 18......, at .... o'clock, in the............
There were present Messrs. .... On motion of Mr. .... it was resolved that the District Clerk is hereby directed to post notices calling a meeting of the legal voters of the district, said meeting to be held at ...., on the......... day of ...., at .... o'clock in the........., and that in said notices he state the following items of business to be acted upon at said meeting:

....
....

...., *District Clerk.*

STATE OF NEW JERSEY, } ss.
 COUNTY OF............

........., being duly sworn, on his oath saith that he is the District Clerk of the Township of .... , in the County of ...., and that the foregoing is a true copy of the proceedings and resolutions adopted by the Board of Education of said School District at a meeting held on the ...... day of ...., 18.....

Sworn and subscribed before }
me this .... day of .... }
. 18..... }

....

....
....

NOTICE.

Notice is hereby given to the legal voters of the Township of ...., in the County of ...., that a .... school meeting will be held at ...., on the .... day of ...., 18......, at .... o'clock in the ...., at which meeting will be submitted the following propositions:

....
....

The amount of money thought to be necessary for the foregoing is .... dollars.

To authorize the Board of Education to borrow the money ordered to be raised by issuing the bonds of the District.

Dated........., 18......

....D. C., } *Trustees of*
.... } *School District*
.... } *No. ......*

STATE OF NEW JERSEY, } ss.
COUNTY OF ....:

.........., being duly sworn, on his oath saith that he is the District Clerk of the Township of ...., in the County of ...., and that he posted ...... copies of a notice, of which the foregoing is a true copy, on the ...... day of ...., 18......, in public places in said District, one of which was the school-house, and that the said notices were posted in all respects according to law.

Sworn and subscribed before
me, this .... day of.........., } ....
18......

....
....

DISTRICT MEETING.

The legal voters of the Township of ...., in the County of .... met at ...., on the .... day of ...., 18......, at .... o'clock in the ...., pursuant to legal notice, a copy of which notice is hereto appended. Mr. .... was elected Chairman, and Mr. .... Secretary of the meeting. The Secretary read the notice calling the meeting.

The following resolutions were adopted:

Resolved, That the Board of Education be authorized to purchase, as a lot on which to build a school-house, the plot of land situated as follows :

....
....

The cost of said lot not to exceed the sum of .... dollars.

The vote on this resolution was by ballot—Ayes ...., Nays ....

Resolved, That the Board of Education be authorized to erect and furnish a school-house on said plot of land, said school-house to be built of .... and to contain .... rooms, and to cost not more than .... dollars.

The vote on this resolution was by ballot—Ayes ...., Nays ....

Resolved, That for the purpose of securing the money needed to purchase said lot and to erect and furnish said school-house the sum of .... dollars be raised by issuing bonds of the District, in the corporate name of the District, in the denomination of .... each.

The vote on this resolution was by ballot—Ayes ...., Nays ....

Resolved, That one bond shall be issued for .... year, one for .... years, one for .... years, one for .... years.

And that each year until the last bond is paid a tax shall be levied, according to law, on the property and the inhabitants of the District sufficient to pay the bond maturing, together with the accrued interest on those then outstanding.

The vote on this resolution was by ballot—Ayes ...., Nays ....

...., S·cretary.

STATE OF NEW JERSEY, }
COUNTY OF .... } ss.

........., being duly sworn, on his oath saith that he was the Secretary of the meeting of the legal voters of the Township of ...., in the County of ...., and that the foregoing is a true copy of the proceedings and resolutions adopted at said meeting, and that all votes taken at said meeting were by ballot.

Sworn and subscribed before }
me, this .... day of........., }   ....
18...... }

....
....

Form No. 30.--Application for Loan from State School Fund.

To the Trustees for the Support of Public Schools for the State of New Jersey:

The Board of Education of the Township of ......, in the County of ...., in the State of New Jersey, ask to borrow of the Trustees for the support of Public Schools the sum of .... dollars, for the purpose of purchashing land and building a school-house in the aforesaid Township, and offer as security for said loan the coupon bonds of the School District to the amount at par of said loan. Said loan and bonds were authorized by the inhabitants of said District when met, upon due and legal notice, for that purpose, upon the ....

day of ...., 18...... The principal of said loan is to be paid in installments of .... dollars; the first installment to be paid on the .... day of ...., 18...... ; the second installment to be paid on the .... day of ......, 18...... ....
....
with interest from date at the rate of five per centum per annum, according to the terms aforesaid; principal and interest payable at the .... bank at ...., and the bonds hereby offered are of the denomination of $...... each, and are numbered from ...... to........, both inclusive.

We submit herewith a copy of the proceedings had at said meeting of said inhabitants, a copy of the minutes of the meeting of the Board of Education of said District at which the posting of the notices calling said meeting of the inhabitants was ordered, a copy of the notices calling said meeting duly verified by affidavit, and the approval of the Attorney-General as to the legality of said proceedings.

Dated........., N. J., ..., 18......

...., *President,*
...., *District Clerk.*

Form No. 31.—Directions for Bonding a District.

1. There must be a regularly-called meeting of the Board of Education, of which meeting all the members must have had notice. At that meeting the Board must decide on the amount of money thought to be necessary. If land is to be purchased, the Board must decide upon the site or sites they think suitable. They must also decide upon the time for holding the District meeting, and the form of the resolutions to be inserted in the notices to be posted by the District Clerk. Full minutes of the meeting must be kept.

2. The District Clerk must post the notices ordered by the Board at least ten days before the date of the meeting of the legal voters; the day the notices are posted must not be counted in the ten days. The notices must state the time and place of the District Meeting, and all business that is to be acted upon. It must state

if land is to be purchased, and, if so, must describe the plot or plots thought to be suitable by the Board. The Board may submit more than one site, if they think best, in which case all the plots must be described in the notices. The notices must also state the amount of money thought to be necessary. It is not necessary to divide the amount among the several objects in the notices. The notices must also state that the question of authorizing the Board to issue bonds will be submitted. Not less than seven notices must be posted, one of which notices must be posted on each school-house in the township.

3. The district meeting must decide the amount of money to be raised, and also decide what portion of the money so ordered shall be used for the purchase of land, and what portion for building and furnishing the school-house. The aggregate amount ordered raised must not exceed the sum named in the notices. The District Meeting must also decide how many bonds shall be issued, the denomination of each bond, and the time of its payment. It must also select a site from among those offered by the Board in the notices. The meeting may, however, reject all the sites offered. All votes in the District Meeting must be by ballot. Full minutes of the meeting must be kept.

4. Two copies of the minutes of the meeting of the Board, attested by the District Clerk; two copies of the notices posted, attested by said Clerk, and two copies of the minutes of the District Meeting, attested by the Secretary of the meeting, must be sent to the State Superintendent, one copy to be approved by the Attorney-General, and the other to be filed in his office. When it is intended to borrow the money from the State School Fund, an application must accompany the copies of the proceedings sent to the State Superintendent. Blank forms to be used for the copies of the proceedings to be sent to the State Superintendent may be obtained from the County Superintendent. In making reports, only such business as relates to the purchase of land, building the school-house and bonding the district need be inserted in the copies of the meetings of the Board and legal voters. In the blank for the report of the proceedings of the District Meeting, a resolution is inserted for the purchase of land; when land is not ordered to be purchased, this resolution should be crossed out in making the report, also in the application for the loan from the State School Fund.

5. The approval of the Attorney-General must be secured before bonds can be legally issued, whether the money is to be borrowed from the State School Fund or from private parties.

6. When district bonds have been issued, it is the duty of the District Clerk, when any bond is paid and canceled, to forward said canceled bond to the State Superintendent, to be filed as required by law.

7. Blank bonds will be furnished by the State Superintendent.

Form No. 32.—Bond to be Issued for Loan.

No. ......   Bond of School District of the Township of ....
$.........   .... County, N. J.

Know all men by these presents, that "The Board of Education of the ...., in the County of ....," in the State of New Jersey, are justly indebted unto ...., or bearer, in the sum of .... dollars, lawful money of the United States of America, to be paid to the said .... or bearer, on the .... day of ...., 18....., at the .... Bank, ..., N. J., with interest therefor from the date hereof, at the rate of .... per cent. per annum, payable semi-annually, on the .... days of .... and .... in every year, at the bank aforesaid, on the presentation of the annexed coupons, as they severally become due.

This is one of a series of coupon bonds of .... dollars each, issued by the Board of Education of said Township, amounting in the aggregate to .... dollars, numbered from ...... to ......, both inclusive; and the said bonds are issued for money borrowed by said Board of Education for the purpose of building a school-house in said School District, pursuant to the statute entitled "An Act to Establish a System of Public Instruction," approved March 27th, 1874, and by the consent of the inhabitants of said District lawfully given, at a meeting lawfully held on ...., 18......

In witness whereof, on the .... day of ...., in the year eighteen hundred and ...., this bond is signed by the President of the Board of Education of said District, and attested by the Clerk, under the seal of said District.   ....,

Attest : ...., *District Clerk.*   *President.*

[*Form of Coupon to be attached to the above Bond.*]

School District of the Township of ...., County of ...., N. J.

SCHOOL-HOUSE LOAN.

Interest warrant for ...... dollars, payable at the .... Bank, ..., N. J., to bearer, ..., for six months' interest on Bond No. ....

...., *D. C.*

Form No. 33.—Notice for Annual Meeting for the Election of Members of the Board of Education.

Notice is hereby given to the legal voters of the Township of ...., in the County of ...., that the annual school meeting for the election of members of the Board of Education will be held at ...., on Tuesday, the .... day of ...., 18 ......, at .... o'clock ..... M.

Dated this .... day of ...., 18......

...., *District Clerk.*

Note.—The above notice must be posted in at least seven public places in the District, one copy being posted on each school-building at least ten days previous to the time of the meeting. The notice must also be published in all papers in the county authorized to print the laws, in the last issue of said papers prior to the election. The election must be held on the Third Tuesday of March.

Form No. 34.—Notice for a Meeting of the District Board of Education.

To ....

You are hereby notified that there will be a meeting of the Board of Education of the Township of ...., on .... evening, ..., 18......, at .... o'clock, in the school-house.

[*Date*].

...., *District Clerk.*

Form No. 35.—Notice for the Annual District Meeting for Determining what District School Tax shall be Assessed.

Notice is hereby given to the legal voters of the Township of ...., in the County of .... that the annual school meeting will be held at .... , on the third Tuesday in March, being the .... day of March, 18......, at .... o'clock in the .... noon, at which meeting will be submitted the question of voting a tax to maintain a free Public School the coming year [*or to build a school-house, etc.*]

The amount thought to be necessary for this purpose is .... dollars.

Dated this ...... day of ...., 18......

...., *District Clerk.*

NOTE.—In the above notice must be particularly specified each item of business to be acted upon.

Form No. 36.—Notice for a Special District Meeting for Determining what District School Tax Shall be Assessed.

Notice is hereby given to the legal voters of the Township of ...., in the county of ...., that a special school meeting will be held at ...., on the ...... day of ...., 18......, at ...... o'clock in the ......noon, at which meeting will be submitted the question of ordering a District School Tax [*here particularly specify each item of business to be acted upon.*]

The amount thought to be necessary for this purpose is .... dollars.

...., *President.*
...., *District Clerk.*

Form No. 47.—Various Specifications of Business to be Transacted that may be Inserted in any Notice for District Meeting, as they may be needed.

To authorize the Board of Education to purchase land and to erect a school-house thereon ;

To see if the District will take measures for the repair, alteration, enlarging or furnishing of the present school-house;

To appoint a committee to prepare and report a plan for such erection or repair, with the probable expense of the same;

To raise money by district tax to defray the expenses of such erection, alteration or repair;

To authorize the Board to borrow money to defray the expenses of such erection, alteration or repair, and to provide for the payment of the same by ordering a district tax [or by bonding the District, as the case may be];

To see if the District will vote a sufficient district tax to defray the expenses of maintaining a free School during the ensuing year, or during .... months of the ensuing year; or the issuing of bonds;

To order a district tax for the payment of a debt of .... dollars, now resting upon the school-house property;

To order the sale of the present school-house property, and to decide what disposition shall be made of the proceeds;

To authorize the Board to condemn land for school purposes;

To authorize the Board to renew outstanding bonds;

To do any other business within the scope of the foregoing propositions.

Form No. 38.—Order of Business at a District School Meeting.

1. Choose a Chairman, Secretary and Tellers.
2. Read the notice calling the meeting.
3. Report of District Clerk.
4. Transaction of the business for which the meeting was called, as set forth in the notices.
5. Miscellaneous business.
6. Adjournment.

Form No. 39.—Affidavit to Bills Presented to a Board of Education.

STATE OF NEW JERSEY, } ss.
.... COUNTY.

...., of full age, being duly sworn, on his oath saith that the goods or services itemized in the annexed bill have been delivered or rendered; that no bonus has been given or received by any person or persons in connection with the same; that the same is correct and true, and the amount therein stated is justly due and owing as set forth.

Sworn and subscribed before me }
this .... day of ...., 18 ..... }
...., D. C. }

....

Form No. 40.—Notice to County Superintendent of a Vacancy in Board of Trustees.

To ...., County Superintendent:

SIR:—You are hereby notified that a vacancy now exists in the Board of Education of the Township of ...., through [*here state the cause of the vacancy*], which you are requested to fill by appointment.

Dated this .... day of ...., 18......

...., *District Clerk.*

NOTE.—The above notice should be sent to the County Superintendent as soon as the vacancy exists. If the office of District Clerk is vacant, the notice should be sent by one of the other members of the Board.

Form No. 41.—Notice to be given by the Secretary of a District School Meeting, to the Officers-elect.

To .... :

You are hereby notified that at the annual school meeting in the Township of ...., in the County of ...., held on the .... day of ...., 18......, you were elected a member of the Board of Education in said township.

Dated this .... day of .... , 18......

...., *Secretary of said Meeting.*

Form No. 42.—Form of Contract Between District and Teacher.

It is hereby agreed between "The Board of Education of the Township of ...., in the County of ...." and ...., a qualified teacher, possessing a license in full force and effect, that the said ...., is to teach the public schools of said District for a term [*here insert the time*], for the sum of ....dollars per month, commencing on the.........day of .... 18......, and for such services, properly rendered, the said Board of Education is to pay the said........., monthly, the amount that may be due, according to this contract.

Dated this ....day of .... 18.......

      ...., *President.*
      ...., *District Clerk.*
      ...., *Teacher.*

NOTE.—In case the Teacher is employed in a Graded School, the particular department for which he is engaged should be specified in the contract.

Form No. 43.—Form of a Lease.

Know all men by these presents, that A. B., of the Township of........., in the County of ...., in the State of New Jersey, of the first part, for the consideration herein mentioned, does hereby lease unto "The Board of Education of the Township of........., in the County of ....," in the State aforesaid, party of the second part, and their assigns, the following described parcel of land :

[*Here insert description of land.*]

Together with all the privileges and appurtenances thereunto belonging : To have and to hold the same for and during the term of......... years from the.........day of........., A.D. 18......; and the said party of the second part, for themselves and assigns, do covenant and agree to pay the said party of the first part, for said premises, the annual rent of ....dollars.

In testimony whereof, the said parties have hereunto set their hands and seals, this .... day of ...., 18......

          A. B., *Lessor.*

...., *President.*
...., *District Clerk*

Form No. 44.—Form of a Deed of a School-House Site.

Know all men by these presents, that A. B. [*and C. B., his wife, if married*], in the Township of ...., in the County of ...., in the State of New Jersey, party of the first part, for and in consideration of the sum of .... dollars, to them in hand paid by "The Board of Education of the Township of ...., in the County of ....," and State aforesaid, party of the second part, the receipt whereof is hereby acknowledged, do hereby grant, bargain, sell and convey to the said party of the second part, and their assigns, the following described piece of land, namely:

[*Here insert description of land.*]

Together with all the privileges and appurtenances thereunto belonging: To have and to hold the same to the said party of the second part and their assigns forever; and the said party of the first part, for themselves, their heirs, executors and administrators, do covenant, bargain and agree, to and with the said party of the second part, and their assigns, that at the time of the ensealing and delivery of these presents, they are well seized of the premises above conveyed, as of a good, sure, perfect, absolute and indefeasible estate of inheritance in the law in fee simple, and that the said lands and premises are free from all incumbrances whatsoever; and that the above bargained premises, in the quiet and peaceable possession of the said party of the second part, and their assigns, against all and every person or persons lawfully claiming or to claim, the whole or any part thereof, the said party of the first part will forever warrant and defend.

In witness whereof the said A. B. and C. B., his wife, party of the first part, have hereunto set their hands and seals, this .... day of ...., A. D. 18......

SIGNED, SEALED AND DELIVERED }   A. B. [SEAL.]
    IN PRESENCE OF   }   C. B. [SEAL.]
      E. F.

NOTE.—Such deeds should be duly acknowledged before a judge, commissioner of deeds, master in chancery, or other officer authorized by law to take such acknowledgment, and recorded in the office of the County Clerk. The bond and mortgage given by the Trustees to secure payment of part of purchase money may be in the usual forms, and for the execution of deeds, mortgages and bonds each District should have a corporate seal. Notes given for borrowed money should be in the name of the District and signed by the President and District Clerk.

Form No. 45.—Contract for Building a School-House.

Contract made and entered into between A. B., of the County of ...., State of New Jersey, and "The Board of Education of the Township of ...., No. ...., in the County of ....," State of New Jersey.

In consideration of the sum of one dollar in hand paid, the receipt whereof is hereby acknowledged, and of the further sum of .... dollars, to be paid as hereinafter specified, the said A. B. agrees to build a frame school-house and to furnish the materials therefor, according to the plans and specifications for the erection of said house hereto appended, at such point in said District as the said Board may designate. The said house is to be built of the best material, in a substantial, workmanlike manner; and is to be completed and delivered to said Board, or their successors in office, free from any lien for work done or materials furnished, by the .... day of ...., 18......; and in case the said house is not finished in the time herein specified, the said A. B. shall forfeit and pay to the said Board, or their successors in office, for the use of said District, the sum of .... dollars, and shall also be liable for all damages that may result to said District in consequence of such failure, and said Board may finish the building and charge the cost of the same to the said A. B.

The said Board, or their successors in office, in behalf of said District, hereby agree to pay the said A. B. the sum of .... dollars when the foundation of said house is finished; and the further sum of .... dollars when the building is ready for the roof; and the remaining sum of .... dollars when the said house is finished and delivered, as herein stipulated.

It is further agreed that this contract shall not be sub-let, transferred or assigned without the consent of both parties.

Witness our hands this .... day of ...., 18......
A. B., *Contractor*.

...., *President*,
...., *District Clerk*.

NOTE.—In building a school-house, it is all-important to secure a plan of the building, with full specifications as to its dimensions, style of architecture, number and size of the windows and doors, quality of materials to be used; what kind of roof; number of coats of paint; of what material the foundation shall be constructed; its depth below, and its height above the surface of the ground; the number and style of chimneys and flues; the provisions for ventilation; the number of coats of plastering, and style of finish, and all other items in detail that may be deemed necessary. The plan and specifications should be attached to the contract, and the whole filed with the District Clerk. Before the building is commenced, the contract should be filed in the office of the County Clerk to prevent liens.

Form No. 46.—Form of Note for Money Borrowed.

.... N. J., ... 18.....

.... days after date, "The Board of Education, in the County of ....," in the State of New Jersey, promise to pay to................, or order,.........Dollars, with interest from the date thereof, at the rate of six per cent. per annum.

This note is given for money borrowed by the said Board for the purpose of............, pursuant to the statute entitled "An Act to Establish a System of Public Instruction," approved March 27th, 1874, and by the consent of the inhabitants of the said District lawfully given, at a meeting lawfully held on......... 18 .....

..................., *President.*

Attest ...., *District Clerk.*

Form No. 47.—Duties of District Clerk.

1. To prepare and post
   Notices for annual district meeting,
   Notices for special district meeting,
   and Notices for Trustee election.
2. To prepare and deliver notices for meetings of the Board of Education.
3. To act as Secretary of the Board of Education.
4. To record, in a book provided for that purpose, all the proceedings of trustee meetings and district meetings.
5. To keep an account of the finances of the District.
6. To pay out all moneys by issuing orders on the Township Collector.

7. To make a financial report.
>To County Superintendent,
>To Township Committee.

8. To make a report of the doings of the Board for the year to the annual district meeting for the election of Trustees.

9. To prepare and forward the annual report to the County Superintendent.

10. To notify County Superintendent and Township Assessor of the amount of district school tax ordered.

11. To notify County Superintendent of the election of members of the Board.

12. To superintend repairs of buildings; to buy fuel, crayons, and such other articles as the Board may direct.

13. To deliver to his successor all records and papers belonging to the District.

Teachers.

Form No. 48.—Directions Given to Candidates for Certificates Before Being Examined.

1. Write your name and the subject of the examination, distinctly, at the top of each page.

2. You need not copy the questions upon the paper, but be careful to number each answer to correspond with the question.

3. If unable to answer any question, write its proper number, and opposite the same write, "I cannot answer."

4. In answering questions in Arithmetic, Algebra, etc., give the work as well as the answer.

5. After beginning a set of questions, do not leave the room without the permission of the examiner in charge, until that exercise is completed.

6. During the examination avoid all communications with other candidates, with visitors, or with any one else, except the examiners,

whether by talking, signs, notes or otherwise. Any violation of this rule will cause your exercise to be rejected.

7. Referring to text-books, or to written or printed abstracts, or memoranda of any kind connected with the subject of examination, or having such book, abstract or memoranda in your desk or about your person, will cause your exercise to be rejected.

8. As soon as one exercise is finished, hand it to the examiner in attendance before beginning another.

9. Do not fold the paper containing your answers, and do not tear off any portion of the sheet that may remain after you have finished a set of questions, but leave the sheet whole, as the paper will be preserved.

10. A special average will be given for correctness in Orthography and Composition, and for legibility, order, neatness and general appearance of the examination papers.

11. Be careful to preserve this card of directions and questions. They will both be called for at the close of the examination.

Form No. 49.—Certificate that Child has Attended School.

I hereby certify that I am principal of School No. ......, in the Township of ...., County of ...., and that [*Name of child*] is the [*Son, daughter or ward*] of [*Name of parent or guardian*] residing at [*Street and city*]; that to the best of my knowledge and belief, said [*Name of child*] is .... years of age; and said [*Name of child*] has attended school under my charge, five days a week, for .... weeks, during the year preceding the date of this certificate.

Dated ...., 18......

...., *Principal.*

Form No. 50.—Teacher's Report to the County Superintendent when Leaving a School before the end of the School Year.

Report of the Teacher of Public School No. ...... in the Township of ...., in the County of ...., for the portion of the School Year commencing July 1st, 18......, and ending ...., 18......

[*The body of the Report same as Annual Report in the Register.*]
To ...., County Superintendent for ...... County :

Being about to leave my present School, I respectfully present the above record and statements as my report for the expired portion of the present School Year, as required by the laws of this State; which report I hereby certify has been carefully made out from the records contained in the School Register.

...., *Teacher*.

NOTE.—The law requires that a duplicate of the above report shall be made to the District Clerk.

Form No. 51.—Teacher's Report of the Suspension of a Pupil to the Board of Education.

To ...., District Clerk of the Board of Education of the Township of .... of the County of .... :

SIR:—You are hereby notified that I have this day suspended from my school .... for [*here state the cause for suspension.*]

Dated this .... day of ...., 18......

...., *Teacher*.

NOTE.—The School Law requires every suspension to be reported to the Board of Education.

Form No. 52.—Duties of Township Collectors.

1. To collect all school taxes.
2. To receive and hold in trust all school moneys, and to pay out the same only upon orders drawn in accordance with Forms 23 and 24.
3. To keep, in a book prepared for the purpose, an account with the Board or Education.
4. To make settlement with the Township Committee.
5. To transmit copies of the settlement made with the Township Committee to the County Superintendent and to the Clerk of the Township.

Miscellaneous.

Form No. 53.—Report of County Clerk to County Superintendent of the Names and Post Office Addresses of the Township Collectors and City Treasurers.

To the County Superintendent of........ County:

Sir:—I hereby report to you the names and addresses of the newly elected Township Collectors [*and City Treasurers, if there be any*], of this County, as follows:

Names of Township or City.	Names of Collectors and City Treasurers.	Address.

...., *County Clerk.*

Form No. 54.—Appeal to the State Superintendent.

........., N. J., ..., 18......

To ...., State Superintendent of Public Instruction:

Sir:—We herewith transmit a full and correct statement of the facts in the case of .... *vs.* ...., together with the decision of the County Superintendent thereon, from which decision we respectfully appeal for the following reasons: [*Here state the reasons for making the appeal.*]

We certify that the accompanying statements, together with the decision of the County Superintendent, are true to the best of our knowledge and belief.

Calendar for School Elections and Duties.

1. *State Board of Education.*—Meets on the first Tuesday of February, April and December, the last Tuesday in September, and on the last Thursday of June, annually.

2. *Trustees of the School Fund.*—Meet on the first Monday in April, annually, and at other times when called together by the Governor.

3. *State Board of Examiners.*—Meets on the first Thursday of June and December, annually, at the State Normal School.

4. *County Boards of Examiners.*—Meet on the first Friday and Saturday of February, May and October, annually.

5. *State Association of School Superintendents.*—Meets at the call of the State Superintendent.

6. *School Trustees.*—Elected on the third Tuesday in March, annually, and should meet on the first Tuesday after the first Monday in March, June, September and December, and oftener if necessary.

7. *District Clerks.*—Elected within ten days after the annual meeting for the election for members of the Board of Education; annually.

8. *District Meetings for Voting District Tax.*—Held on the third Tuesday in March, annually, or at the call of the Board of Education.

9. *Report of the State Board of Education to the Governor.*—On the first Tuesday in December, annually.

10. *Report of the State Superintendent to the State Board of Education.*—On the first Tuesday in December, annually.

11. *Report of County Superintendent to the State Superintendent.*—On or before the first of September, annually.

12. *Report of District Clerks to County Superintendent.*—On or before the first of August, annually.

13. *Report of Teachers to Board of Education.*—At the close of each quarter's teaching.

14. *Financial Statement of Township Collector to Township Committee and County Superintendent.*—On or before the first of August, annually.

15. *Financial Statement of District Clerks to Township Committee.*—On or before the first of August, annually.

16. *Financial Statement of District Clerks to the County Superintendent.*—On or before the first of August, annually.

17. *Assessor makes returns to Collector.*—Within fifteen days after the first Monday in September, annually.

18. *School Tax.*—Collected and due the Trustees by the first of December, annually.

19. *District Census.*—Taken during the month of May, annually.

20. *Apportionment of the State Appropriation to the Counties.*—Made by the State Superintendent, on or before the first Monday in May, annually.

21. *Apportionment of the State Appropriation and Township School Taxes to the District.*—Made by the County Superintendent on or before the first of June, annually.

22. *Copy of Apportionment.*—Made by the County Superintendent, and furnished to each Township Collector and District Clerk within twenty days after the apportionment is made.

23. *State Appropriation.*—One hundred thousand dollars paid in November, and the State School tax in the month of January following.

24. *Agricultural College.*—Candidates examined by the County and City Superintendents on the first Saturday in June.

25. *School Holidays.*—First day of January, twenty-second day of February, thirtieth day of May, fourth day of July, first Monday in September (Labor day), Thanksgiving day, Christmas day, any day upon which a general election shall be held for members of assembly, and also any day set apart by proclamation of the Governor of this State or the President of the United States for the purpose of public observance.

26. *School Year.*—Commences on the first day of July and ends on the thirtieth day of June.

27. *Fiscal Year.*—The school fiscal year of the State coincides with the school year.

Index.

INDEX.

A

	Page.
Abstract of apportionment to be given to certain persons, sections 14 and 29	7, 12
tax to be given to certain persons, sections 14 and 142	7, 48
Affidavit, County Superintendent may take, section 28	11
District Clerk may take, section 58	22
required to bills, section 58	22
Ages of children in census, section 38	14
factories, sections 205, 206, 254, 255 and 256	69, 90, 91
pupils in Deaf-Mute School, section 92	33
public schools, section 75	28
Agent for school books, school officers shall not act as, sections 117 and 118	40
Agricultural College, appropriation, sections 264 and 265	94, 95
examinations for, sections 261 and 263	93, 94
scholarships in, section 261	93
Annual district meeting, sections 115 and 164	39, 57
Appeal to Circuit Court, in case of condemnation of land, sections 219 and 223	75, 78
to County Superintendent, sections 67 and 70	26
to State Board of Education, sections 6, division VI, and 17	7, 8
to State Superintendent, sections 17 and 34	8, 13
Appointment of Census Supervisor, section 40	15
Child Labor Inspector, section 258	92
City Superintendent in second class cities, section 308	107
County Superintendents, sections 6, division III, and 25, and rule 44	6, 10, 133
District Clerk, sections 32 and 51 and decision No. 13,	12, 19, 143
State Board of Education, section 9	5
State Superintendent, section 9	7
School Trustees, section 31	12
Apportionment of school moneys, abstract to be given to certain persons, sections 14 and 29	7, 12
of balances of State moneys, section 159	54
of reserve fund, section 152	51
of State appropriations to counties, section 14	7
districts, sections 29 and 153 and rule 34	12, 51, 131
of State tax among counties, section 142	48
townships, sections 142 and 153	48, 51

(187)

	Page.
Apportionment of surplus revenue, sections 153 and 184	51, 65
Appraisement of school property, section 346	117
Appropriations, available for school year, decision No. 1	137
by city Boards of Education, sections 267 and 290	95, 102
city Boards may modify, section 272	97
districts paid by orders of County Superintendents, sections 29 and 155	12, 52
Deaf-Mute School, section 95	34
industrial schools, section 235	83
institutes, sections 137 and 138, division V	45, 46
libraries, sections 185 and 189	65, 66
manual training, section 235	83
Normal School, sections 86 and 138, division I	31, 46
penalty for exceeding, section 352	120
State school fund paid to counties by Comptroller, sections 13, 135, 136, 137 and 139	7, 45, 47
State school fund, sections 14, 135, 136, 137, 138, 140 and 235	7, 45, 46, 47, 83, 84, 85
withheld in certain cases, sections 15, 23 and 33	8, 9, 12
Arbor Day, sections 192 and 193	67
Assessment city school tax, sections 142 and 269	48, 96
district tax, sections 164, 170, 173 and 181, and decision No. 7	57, 60, 61, 62, 140
executions, to satisfy, section 62	23
State school tax, sections 141, 142, 143, 144 and 145	47, 48, 49
Assessor, apportion State tax among townships, section 142	48
appraise value of school property, section 346	117
bonds not taxable, section 182	64
compensation of, section 166 and decision No. 8	59, 140
district tax, to assess, sections 164, 170, 173 and 181 and decision No. 7	57, 60, 61, 62, 140
district tax to be separate item in levy, section 165	58
execution, to assess for, section 62	23
State school tax, sections 141, 142, 143, 144 and 145	47, 48, 49
Association of School Superintendents, sections 12 and 35	7, 13
Attorney-General to approve proceedings authorizing bonds, sections 172 and 179	61, 62
School Fund, member of trustees of, section 119	40
Award in condemnation of land, sections 217, 220 and 231	74, 76, 81

B

Ballot, appropriations at district meetings to be voted by, sections 45 and 168	17, 59
trustees elected by, section 45	17
Balances to be returned to county collector, section 161	13
repairs, may be used for, in certain cases, section 16	13

INDEX. 189

	Page.
Bills, affidavit required to, section 58	22
itemized, must be, section 57	22
Blanks for school officers to be furnished by State Superintendent, sections 16 and 180	8, 64
Boards of Education, affidavit to bills, to require, section 58	22
agent for school books, members shall not act as, sections 117 and 118	40
appeal from decision of County Superintendent, section 34	13
appeal from decision of State Superintendent, section 17	8
appointment of, by county superintendents, section 31	12
appointment of, in second class cities, section 302	105
appropriations from State moneys to be used for school year, decision No. 1	137
appropriations from State moneys to cities may be used for calendar year, section 276	97
appropriations for current expenses in cities, may be made by, in certain cases, sections 267 and 290	95, 102
appropriations in cities may be modified, section 272	97
appropriations, penalty for exceeding, section 352	120
appropriations withheld in certain cases, sections 15, 23 and 33	8, 9, 12
ballot, elected by, section 45	17
bills, affidavit required to, section 58	22
bills to be itemized, section 57	22
bills to be passed in open session, section 56	22
bonds, authority to issue in districts acting under general law, section 169 and decision No. 5	59, 138
bonds, authority to issue in cities, section 176	62
bonds, cancellation of, section 172	61
bonds, custodian of school funds to give, section 158	54
bonds, not taxable, section 182	64
bonds, officers to give, in certain cases, section 348	118
bonds, proceeds of sale of to be deposited with collector, section 158 and rule 35	54, 131
bonds, renewal of, section 171	60
books, power to provide, sections 53, division VIII, and 115	20, 39
books, to prescribe, sections 53, division VI, and 71	20, 27
boroughs, members of in, sections 47 and 48	18
borrow money, may, sections 53, division III, 109, 164, 290 and 319	20, 38, 57, 102, 109
bribery, penalty for, sections 351 and 354	118, 120

INDEX.

Page.

Boards of Education, building, may request township committee to erect, section 334...... 114
    buildings in districts, acting under general law, sections 53, division III, and 4...... 20
    buildings in first class cities, section 294...... 103
    census, to have taken, section 38...... 14
    certificate of transfer of children to be filed with, section 99...... 36
    cities of second class, sections 202, 203, 204, 205, 206 and 207......105, 106, 107
    children, school residence of, decision No. 6...... 139
    clerk of, in districts acting under general law, sections 33 and 51......12, 19
    clerk may take affidavit, section 58...... 22
    colored children, penalty for voting to exclude, section 73...... 27
    compensation of clerk in districts acting under general law, section 51...... 19
    condemn land for school purposes, in districts acting under general law, sections 215 to 225, and 231 to 234......73, 81
    condemn land for school purposes in cities, sections 226 to 234...... 78
    contagious diseases, may close school in cases of, section 60...... 23
    contagious diseases, prohibit persons exposed to from attending school, section 61...... 23
    contracts to be passed on in open session, section 56, 22
    contracts with teachers, section 66...... 25
    corporate name in districts acting under general law, section 50...... 19
    corporate name in second class cities, section 307...... 107
    course of study, shall prescribe, sections 53, division VI, and 71......20, 27
    current expenses in districts acting under general law, section 344...... 117
    current expenses in cities, sections 267, 273, 310 and 344......95, 97, 107, 117
    damages to buildings, to determine amount of, section 71...... 27
    dismissal of teachers, section 70...... 26
    district clerk appointed by County Superintendent, section 32...... 12
    district clerk, election of, section 51 and decision No. 13......19, 143
    district clerk may take affidavit, section 58...... 22
    district clerk may purchase supplies, section 57...... 22

INDEX.

191

	Page.
Boards of Education, election of, in districts acting under general law, sections 43, 44, 45, 46, 47 and 48	16, 17, 18
election of, in third class cities, section 318	109
examinations, to make rules for city, section 78	29
executions against, section 62	23
expel or suspend pupils, sections 53, division VII, and 67, and decision 3	20, 26, 138
expenditures, limit may be fixed in certain places, section 266	95
fire escapes, to provide, sections 102, 103, 105, 106 and 107	37
fire extinguishers, to provide, section 104	37
fiscal year in districts acting under general law, decision No. 1	137
fiscal year in cities, section 276	97
flags for school houses, to provide, section 347	118
hygiene, to be taught, section 197	67
holidays, section 66 and decision No. 11	25, 141
industrial schools, to certify that money has been raised for, sections 237 and 243	84, 85
industrial schools, to appoint trustees of, section 240	85
industrial schools, to make report of, section 244	86
institutes, teachers must attend, section 6, division IV, and rule 41	6, 132
insure school buildings, section 53, division IV	20
interest to be paid on school orders in certain cases, section 157	54
janitors, may employ, section 53, division I	20
legal voters, who are, sections 43 and 44	16, 17
libraries, may make rules for, sections 186 and 188	65, 66
manual training, to certify that money has been raised for, section 235	83
manual training, to make course of study in, section 235	83
manual training, to make report of, section 236	83
meetings of legal voters, may call, section 53, divisions IX and X	20
meetings of, regular, sections 51 and 55 and decision No. 2	19, 22, 137
meetings of, special, section 55 and decision No. 2	22, 137
minutes, to keep, section 52	19
mortgage school property in districts acting under general law, section 53, division III	20
mortgage school property in cities, sections 287 and 288	100, 101
notices for meetings of legal voters, to order, sections 43, 53, divisions IX and X, and 164	16, 20, 57

	Page.
Boards of Education, orders for school moneys, to draw, sections 52, 156 and 157	19, 52, 54
orders for school moneys to draw interest in certain cases, section 157	54
organization of, in districts acting under general law, section 51	19
penalty for excluding children from school, section 73	27
penalty for exceeding appropriations, section 352	120
penalty for failure to comply with school law, sections 15, 23, 33, 59 and 108, and rule 35	8, 9, 12, 23, 38, 131
penalty for failure to post notices for annual meeting, section 43	16
penalty for misuse of school moneys, sections 110 and 344	38, 117
petition for meeting of legal voters, section 53, division X	21
physiology, to have taught, section 197	67
plans for school-houses, section 24	10
polls, to designate time kept open, sections 45 and 46	17
powers of, under general laws, section 53	20
powers of, in second class cities, section 303	105
president of, under general law, section 51	19
president of, in certain cities, section 279	98
pupils, age of, section 75	28
pupils, may suspend or expel, section 53, division VII, and 67	20, 26
pupils, may pay for transportation of, section 100	36
religious services, section 119	40
rent school-houses, section 53, division IV	20
repairs to school property, section 53, division IV	20
report, annual report of, sections 37, 53, division XII, and 54	13, 21
salary of district clerk, to fix, section 51	19
salary of teacher, to fix, section 53, division I	20
school-house, plans for, section 24	10
school-houses, power to build, rent and repair, section 53, divisions III and IV	20
school-house, may permit use of for other purposes, section 53, division XI	21
school-houses in cities, may request loans for, sections 286 and 208	99, 104
school term, length of, section 15	8
school year, section 114	39
sinking fund, may establish, section 159	54

	Page.
Boards of Education, special laws, may be relieved from, sections 111, 112 and 113	38, 39
suitable school-house, penalty for failure to provide, sections 33 and 101	12, 36
superintendent in second-class cities, to appoint, section 308	107
supplies, not to be interested in furnishing, sections 118, 353 and 355	40, 120, 121
supplies, to provide, sections 53, division VIII, 57, 115 and 277	21, 22, 39, 98
suspend or expel pupils, sections 53, division VII, and 67, and decision No. 3	20, 26, 138
transportation of children, may provide for, section 100	36
taxes, sections 53, division IX, 100, 141, 156 and 164, and decisions 1, 7 and 8	20, 36, 47, 54, 57, 137, 140
teachers, employ and dismiss, sections 53, division I, 65 and 70, and rule 1	20, 25, 26, 125
technical schools, 237, 243 and 244	84, 85, 86
temporary loans in cities, sections 274 and 275	97
term of office under general law, sections 31, 47, 48 and 49	12, 18
term of office in second-class cities, section 302	105
term of office in third-class cities, sections 317 and 318	109
term, school, section 15	8
text-books, to prescribe, sections 53, division VI, and 71	20, 27
text-books, must provide, sections 53, division VIII, and 115	20, 39
township boards of, sections 47 and 48	18
township committee, may request erection of school-houses by, section 334	114
tuition fees, unlawful to charge, section 74	27
vacancy, how filled, section 31	12
vaccination of children, section 42	16
vote, penalty for accepting money for, sections 352 and 355	119, 120
women eligible as members, section 43	16
women may vote for, section 44	17
Bonds, proceedings authorizing to be approved by Attorney-General, sections 172 and 179	61, 64
assessment for payment of, sections 170, 173 and 181	60, 62
attested by District Clerk, section 169	59
authority to issue, sections 169 and 176	59, 62
blanks for, to be furnished by State Superintendent, section 180	64
cancelled bonds to be filed with State Superintendent, section 174	62
coupons, must have, section 169	59

	Page.
Bonds, custodian of proceeds of, section 169 and rule 35	54, 131
duplicate copy of proceedings to be filed with State Superintendent, section 169	59
interest, rate of, section 169	59
lien upon entire district, sections 169 and 172	59, 64
proceedings authorizing to be filed with State Superintendent, section 169	62
renewal of, sections 171, 172, 173, 174 and 175	63, 64, 65
report of amount of, to State Superintendent, section 183	64
tax not to be assessed on, section 182	64
township committee may issue, sections 335 and 336	114
Boroughs, separate school districts, section 97	35
may consolidate with township, section 97	35
Buildings, amount of bonds authorized in cities, sections 288 and 290	101, 102
bonds for, authorized in districts acting under general law, sections 169 and 315	59, 108
bonds for, authorized in cities, sections 176, 177, 274, 280, 290, 300, 301 and 315	62, 63, 97, 98, 102, 104, 108
bonds for, may be issued by township committee, sections 335 and 336	114
bonds for, not taxable, section 182	65
cities of first class, section 294	103
condemn land for, in districts acting under general law, sections 215 and 220	73, 76
condemn land for, in cities, section 226	78
damages to, who are liable for, sections 71 and 350	27, 119
doors to open outwardly, sections 33 and 102	12, 37
fire escapes, to have, sections 102 and 105	37
fire escapes, copy of act to be posted in, section 103	37
fire extinguishers, to have, section 104	37
flags for, sections 347 and 348	118
insurance on, section 53, division IV	20
mortgages in districts acting under general law, section 53, division III	20
mortgages on, in cities, sections 178, 287 and 288	63, 101, 100
penalty for failure to provide a suitable school-house, sections 33 and 101	12, 36
plans for, sections 18 and 24	9, 10
site, selection of, foot-note to section 164	57
suitable buildings, penalty for failure to provide, sections 33 and 101	12, 36
tax to build or repair, section 164	57
temporary loans in cities for, sections 299, 300 and 301	104
township committee to build, in certain cases, section 334	114
use of, for other purposes, section 53, division XI	21
Bribery, penalty for, sections 351 and 354	119, 120

INDEX. 195

C

	Page.
Census, ages of children in, section 38	14
blanks for, section 38	14
correction of, section 39	15
enumerators, appointment of, sections 38 and 39	14, 15
compensation of, sections 38 and 39	14, 15
revision of, section 39	15
supervisor of, section 40	15
salary of, section 40	15
term of office of, section 40	15
time when taken, section 38	14
vaccination of children to be reported, section 42	16
Certificates, average required, rule 3	125
branches required for county, section 199 and rules 15, 16 and 17	68, 127, 128
branches required for State, section 199, and rules 22, 23 and 24	68, 129
college diploma accepted, rule 7	126
contract not valid unless teacher holds a certificate. rule 1	125
County Superintendent, to be exhibited to, rule 1	125
County Superintendent to keep record of, rule 1	125
county certificates valid only in county where issued, rules 15, 16, 17 and 18	127, 128
diploma of Normal Schools in other States endorsed, rule 8	126
examinations, city, sections 12 and 78	7, 29
examinations, county, sections 12 and 77, and rules 3, 4, 7, 8, 9, 10, 11, 12, 15, 16, 17	7, 28, 125, 126, 127, 128
examinations, State, sections 12 and 76, and rules 3, 4, 7, 8, 9, 10, 11, 12 and 21	7, 28, 125, 126, 129
grammar schools, definition of, rule 18	128
high school, definition of, rule 18	128
Normal diplomas from other States endorsed, rule 8	126
Normal graduates, certificates issued to, rule 25	129
primary schools, definition of, rule 18	128
provisional certificates, rule 2	125
questions, State Superintendent to prepare, rule 19	128
record of, County Superintendents to keep, rule 1	125
revocation of county, sections 5, 23, 77 and 196, and rule 5,	9, 23, 67, 126
revocation of State, sections 23, 76 and 196, and rule 5	9, 28, 67, 126
special credits, rule 10	126
special examinations, section 77 and rule 19	28, 128
special certificates, rule 12	126
Cities, ages of pupils in, section 75	28
appeal to County Superintendent, foot note	13
appointment of superintendent in cities of second class, section 308	107

INDEX.

	Page.
Cities, appropriations, when available, section 276	97
appropriations withheld in certain cases, sections 15, 23 and 33	8, 9, 12
appropriations, modification of, section 272	97
appropriations, penalty for exceeding, section 352	120
Arbor Day, sections 192 and 193	66, 67
assessment for payment of bonds, section 181	64
assessment of school tax, sections 142 and 269	48, 96
balance of school moneys to be returned to county, section 161	55
boards of education in (see Boards of Education).	
boards of examiners in, sections 17, 76, 77 and 78	7, 28, 29
bonds, assessment for, section 181	64
bonds, proceedings authorizing to be approved by Attorney-General, sections 169 and 179	59, 62
bonds, custodians of school moneys to give, section 158	54
bonds for school houses, sections 169, 176, 177, 274, 280, 290, 300, 301, 315	59, 62, 63, 97, 98, 102, 104, 108
bonds not taxable, section 182	64
borrow money, sections 290 and 319	102, 109
bribery, penalty for, sections 351 and 354	119, 120
buildings in first class cities, control of, section 294	103
calendar year, State money may be used for, section 276	97
census in, section 38	14
colored children may attend any school, section 72	27
condemnation of land, sections 224, 225, 226, 227, 228, 229, 230, 231, 232 and 233	79, 80, 81, 82
contagious diseases, persons exposed to, may be excluded from schools, section 61	23
contagious diseases, schools may be closed in cases of, section 60	23
contracts with teachers, section 66	25
corporal punishment prohibited, sections 68 and 69	26
corporate name in second class cities, section 307	107
damages to school property, sections 71 and 350	27, 119
doors to school buildings to open outwardly, sections 33 and 102	12, 37
examinations in, sections 12 and 78	7, 29
expenditures, limit of, sections 266, 268 and 271	95, 96, 97
fire escapes and extinguishers, sections 102, 104 and 105	87
first class, control of buildings in, section 294	103
first class, custody of funds in, section 292	103
first class, loans in, sections 298, 299, 300, 301	104
first class, payment of teachers in, section 291	102
flags, to provide, section 347	118
graded schools, reports of, section 64	25
holidays, section 66 and decision 11	25, 141
hygiene must be taught, section 197	67
indigent children, section 278	98
industrial schools, sections 239, 240, 243 and 245	84, 85, 87
libraries in, sections 186 and 188	65, 66
limit of expenditures in, sections 266, 268 and 271	95, 96, 97

INDEX. 197

	Page.
Cities, loans for school houses, sections 169, 176, 280, 281, 283, 284, 299, 310 and 314	59, 62, 98, 99, 104, 107, 108
manual training, sections 235, 236 and 246	83, 87
mortgage school property, sections 287 and 288	100, 101
penalty for exceeding appropriation, section 352	120
penalty for failure to report, section 54	21
penalty for failure to maintain school nine months, section 15	8
penalty for failure to provide suitable school house, section 33	12
penalty for misuse of school moneys, sections 110 and 344	38, 117
penalty for violation of school law, sections 15, 23, 33, 59 and 207,	8, 9, 12, 23, 68
plans for school houses, section 24	10
physiology to be taught, section 197	67
pupils, age of, section 75	28
pupils, transportation of, section 100	36
religious services, section 119	40
residence of children, decision 6	139
reports of, sections 26 and 37	13
school term, section 15	8
school year, section 114	39
second class, superintendents in, section 308	107
second class, teachers in, payment of, section 316	109
special tax in, section 164	57
superintendents in second class, section 308	107
superintendents, powers of, sections 26, 36, 37 and 193, and decisions 4, 11, 13,	67, 138
supplies, officers not to be interested in furnishing, sections 352 and 355	120, 121
tax in, section 164	57
tax in, to be separate item in levy, section 165	58
teachers, payment of in first class, section 291	102
teachers, payment of in second class, section 316	109
technical schools, sections 237, 239, 240 and 243	84, 85
temporary loans for current expenses, sections 274 and 275	97
temporary loans for school houses, sections 280, 283 and 299	98, 99, 104
temporary loans, security for, sections 285 and 286	100
term, length of, section 15	8
tex-books, to supply, section 115	39
third class, election of boards in, section 318	109
transfer of children, section 99	36
transportation of children, section 100	36
tuition fees unlawful, section 74	27
truant officers in, section 210	71
vaccination of pupils, section 42	16
City Superintendents, appointment of, second class cities, section 308	107
penalty for failure to report, section 59	23
powers of, sections 26, 193 and 263	11, 67, 94
reports of, sections 36, 37 and 202	13, 68

INDEX.

	Page.
City Superintendents, salary, payment of, decision 4	138
association of school superintendents, section 35	13
College diplomas accepted, rule 7	126
Compulsory education, sections 204, 205, 206, 254, 255 and 256	69, 90, 91
penalty for violation of law, sections 209, 210 and 257	70, 71, 91
truant officers, appointment of, section 209	70
compensation of, section 209	70
powers of, sections 210 and 211	71
Condemn land, appeal to Circuit Court, sections 219, 223, 227, 232 and 233	75, 78, 79, 81, 82
award of commissioners, sections 217, 218, 220, 221, 224, 227 and 231	74, 76, 79, 80, 81
commissioners, appointment of, sections 217, 220 and 226	74, 76, 78
expenses, sections 230	81
jury trial, sections 224 and 233	78, 82
notice to owners, 217, 220 and 227	74, 79
taxable residents to vote, section 215	73
school-house, section 101	36
Contagious diseases, persons exposed to, may be excluded from schools, section 61	23
schools may be closed in cases of, section 60	23
Contracts between teachers and boards of education, section 66	25
County Collectors, balances to be paid to, section 161	55
duties of, sections 23, 141, 142, 148, 150, 151, 155 and 161	9, 47, 48, 50, 52
County Superintendents, affidavits, may take, section 28	11
agent for books shall not act as, section 117 and rule 32	40, 131
agricultural college examinations, to conduct, sections 261 and 263	93, 94
appeals to, sections 67 and 70	26
appeal from decision of, sections 17 and 34	8, 13
appoint district clerks, section 33	12
appointment of, sections 6, division III, and 25, and rule 44	6, 10, 133
apportion school moneys, 153 and 161 and rule 34	51, 55, 131
appropriations, to draw orders for, sections 29 and 155	12, 52
appropriations withheld in certain cases, sections 15, 23 and 33	8, 9, 12
Arbor Day, to prepare programmes for, section 193	67
association of, section 35	13
certificates, may grant, sections 30 and 97 and rules 2, 12, 15, 16 and 17	12, 28, 125, 126, 127

INDEX. 199

	Page.
County Superintendents, certificates, revoke, may, sections 23 and 196 and rule 5	9, 67, 126
condemn school-house, power to, section 101	36
course of study, may prescribe, sections 53, division VI, and 71	20, 27
District Clerk, may appoint, section 32	12
may remove, section 32	12
examinations for Agricultural College, to conduct, sections 261 and 263	93, 94
examinations for teachers' certificates, to conduct, sections 30 and 77, and rules 7, 9, 10, 11, 13, 14, 15, 16, 17 and 19	12, 28, 126, 127, 128
examiners, may appoint, section 77	28
expenses, amount of, section 27 and rule 43	11, 132
institutes, to hold, sections 6, division IV, 129, division V and 136, and rule 36	6, 45, 132
library for teachers, sections 189 and 190	66
office rent, no allowance for, rule 43	132
orders for examiner's salary, to draw, section 77	28
orders for school money, to draw, sections 29 and 155	12, 52
penalty for failure to report, rules 40 and 42	132
provisional certificates, may issue, rule 2	125
removal of, section 25	10
report of, sections 23, 26, 37, 39 and 202, and rule 40	9, 13, 68, 132
reports to, sections 52, 53, division XII, and 64,	19, 21, 325
salary of, section 26	11
supervise schools, section 26 and rule 28	11, 130
teacher's library, sections 189 and 190	66
term of office, section 25	10
text-books, may prescribe, sections 53, division VI, and 71	20, 27
trustees, to appoint, section 31	12
vacancy in office, how filled, rule 44	133
visit schools, section 26 and rule 26	11, 130
withhold school moneys, in certain cases, sections 15, 23, 33 and 101, and rule 35	8, 9, 12, 36, 131
Course of Study in Normal School, section 80	30
public schools, sections 53, division VI, and 71	20, 27
Custodian of school moneys in boroughs, section 156	52
cities of the first class, sections 155 and 292	52, 103
townships, section 156	52

D

	Page.
Damages to school property, sections 71 and 350	27, 119
Deaf-Mute School, appropriation for, section 95	34
contract, supplies to be furnished by, section 94	34
corporate name, section 89	31
expenses, how paid, section 95	34
fire-escapes, sections 102, 103 and 105	37
indigent pupils, sections 92 and 93	33
pupils, admission of, sections 90, 92 and 93	31, 33
pupils, age of, section 92	33
pupils, number of, section 90	31
pupils, qualifications of, section 90	31
pupils, term of instruction of, section 92	33
trustees of, section 4	6
superintendent of, section 90	31
teachers in, section 90	31
treasurer of, sections 90 and 91	31, 33
District Clerk, accounts to keep, section 156	52
advertise elections, section 43	16
affidavit, may take, section 58	22
agent for books, shall not act as, section 117	40
appointed by County Superintendent, section 37	12
appointed by trustees, section 51 and decision 13	19, 143
bonds to be attested by, sections 169 and 171	59, 60
bonds to draw orders for payment of, sections 173 and 181,	62, 64
census, to take, section 38	14
certify that register has been properly kept, section 63	24
compensation of, section 51	19
district meeting to post notices for, section 43	16
election of trustees, to advertise, section 43	16
election of trustees, post notices for, section 43	16
minutes, to keep, section 52	19
notices of district meetings to post, sections 43 and 164	16, 57
orders, to issue, sections 52 and 156, and rule 35	19, 52, 131
penalty for failure to perform duties, sections 15, 32, 43 and 57, and rule 35	8, 12, 16, 21, 131
register to certify, section 63	24
removal of, section 32	12
report of, sections 37, 52, 53, division XII, 156 and 183,	13, 19, 21, 52, 64
salary of, section 51	19
vacancy, how filled, section 32	12
District Schools, age of pupils in, section 75	28
appraisement of property, section 346	117
appropriations, when available, decision No. 1	137

INDEX. 201

	Page.
District Schools, appropriations withheld in certain cases, sections 15 and 22	8, 9
balances to be returned to county, section 161	55
balances may be used for repairs in certain cases, section 161	55
ballot, meetings to vote by, sections 45 and 168	17, 59
bonds in, sections 169, 170, 171, 172 and 182, rule 35, and decision No. 5	59, 60, 61, 64, 131, 138
boroughs, form separate districts, sections 47, 48 and 97,	18, 35
boroughs may consolidate with township, section 97	35
buildings, how provided, section 53, division III, 101 and 164	20, 36, 57
cities form separate districts, section 97	35
clerk appointed by County Superintendent, section 32	12
clerk appointed by trustees, section 51, decision 13	19, 143
colored children may attend any school, sections 72 and 73	27
condemn land for, section 215	73
contagious diseases, persons exposed to excluded, sections 60 and 61	23
corporate name, section 50	19
corporal punishment, sections 68 and 69	26
course of study in, section 53, division VI	20
damages to, sections 71 and 350	27, 119
debts of, section 96	35
disorderly conduct in, section 350	119
doors to open outwardly, sections 33 and 102	12, 37
election of trustees for, sections 43 and 44	16, 17
executions against, section 62	23
fire escapes, sections 102, 103 and 105	37
fire extinguishers, section 104	37
flags for, section 347	118
historical days, observance of, sections 194, 195 and 196	67
holidays, section 66 and decision No. 11	25, 141
hygiene to be taught, section 197	67
indebtedness to be reported to State Superintendent, section 183	64
insurance on, section 53, division IV	20
manual training in, sections 235, 236 and 246	83, 87
meetings, regular, sections 43 and 164	16, 57
meetings, special, section 53, divisions IX and X	20
meetings of trustees, section 55	22
meetings, notices for, section 43	16
mortgage on, section 53, division III	20
patriotism to be taught, sections 194, 195 and 196	67
penalty for damages to, section 350	119
penalty for excluding children from, sections 72 and 73	27

	Page.
District Schools, penalty for failure to maintain school nine months, sections 15 and 108	8, 38
penalty for violation of school law, sections 15, 23, 33, 101 and 202, and rule 35	8, 9, 12, 36, 67, 131
plans for, section 24	10
poll list at meetings, section 45	17
poll tax, sections 164 and 349	57, 119
polls, time kept open, sections 45 and 46	17
pupils, age of, section 75	28
pupils, suspension of, section 67	26
religious services in, section 119	40
residence of school children, decision No. 6	139
school month, section 66	25
school term, sections 15 and 108	8, 38
school year, section 114	39
sinking fund, section 158	54
site, selection of, foot note to section 164	57
special laws, may be relieved from, sections 111, 112 and 113	38, 39
suspension of pupils, section 67	26
tax for, sections 53, division III, and 164	20, 57
teachers, dismissal of, section 70	26
teacher's orders may draw interest, section 157	54
tellers at meetings, section 45	17
term, length of, section 15	8
text-books, must be provided, sections 53, division VII, and 115	20, 39
towns form separate districts, section 97	35
townships constitute school districts, section 96	35
trustees, appointment of, section 31	12
trustees, election of, sections 43, 45 and 331	16, 17, 113
trustees, organization of, section 51	19
trustees, term of office of, sections 47 and 48	18
trustees, vacancy, how filled, section 31	12
trustees, women eligible as, section 43	16
District school tax, amount of, section 164	57
annual and special meeting, may be ordered at, sections 53, division I, 115 and 164	20, 39, 57
assessment of, section 164	57
ballot, vote for, to be by, section 168	59
bonds, payment of, section 171	60
collection of, sections 154 and 164 and decisions Nos. 7 and 8	52, 57, 146
compensation for assessing and collecting, section 166 and decision No. 8	59, 140
condemnation of land, expense of, section 225	78
custodians of, sections 154 and 167 and decision No. 9	52, 59, 140

INDEX. 203

	Page.
District School tax, delinquent tax, collection of, decision No. 12	142
execution, to satisfy, section 62	23
flags, section 322	118
levy, separate item in, section 165	58
notice for, 164	57
payment of, sections 154 and 164	52, 57
poll tax, sections 164 and 349	57, 119
pupils, transportation of, section 100	36
special meeting, may be ordered at, sections 53, division IX, 115 and 164	20, 39, 57
taxable residents to vote on condemnation of land, section 215	75
text-books, section 53, division VI, and 115	20, 39
transportation of pupils, may raise for, section 100	36
Doors to open outwardly, sections 33 and 102	12, 37

E

Election of boards of education in third-class cities, section 318	109
towns, section 324	111
townships, time for, sections 43 and 46,	16, 17
townships, ballot to be by, section 45	17
townships, legal voters at, section 44	17
Evening schools, section 213	73
Examinations, Agricultural College, sections 261 and 263	93, 94
average required in county, rule 3	125
city, sections 12 and 78	7, 29
county, sections 77 and 199, and rules 2, 10, 11, 12, 13, 14, 15, 16, 17, 18 and 19	28, 68, 125, 127
record of, rule 6	126
report of, rule 6	126
special, section 77 and rule 19	28, 128
state, sections 76 and 199, and rules 2, 10, 11, 12, 21, 22, 23, 24 and 25	28, 68, 125, 126, 129
Examiners, city boards of, section 78	29
county boards of, section 77	28
county boards of, meetings of, section 77 and rule 13	28, 127
State Board of, sections 12 and 76	7, 28
State Superintendent a member of all boards of, section 12	7
Executions against school districts, section 62	23
Expenditures in cities, limit of, sections 266, 268 and 271	95, 96, 97
Expenses of County Examiners, section 77	28
County Superintendents, section 27 and rule 43	11, 132
industrial schools, section 138, division IX	46
institutes, section 137	45
School Fund, section 138	46

	Page.
Expenses of State Board of Education, section 7 and 138, division III........	7, 46
State Superintendent, section 6, division V, and 138, divisions II and VII	6, 46
Expulsion of pupils, sections 53, division VII, and 71............................	20, 27

F

Factories, ages of children in, sections 205, 206, 254, 255 and 256.......	69, 90, 91
certificate that child in, has attended school, sections 206 and 255...	69, 90
corporations, proceedings against for violation of act, section 214...	73
evening schools, children may attend, section 213.....................	73
hours children may labor, section 256..	91
inspector, sections 258 and 259..91,	92
penalty for violation of act, section 257.....................................	91
temporary schools, section 212..	72
Farnum School, appropriation for, section 138, division VIII....................	46
Fees of county examiners, section 77..	28
township assessor and collector, sections 147, 156 and 166, and decision No. 7..49, 52, 59,	140
Fire escapes, sections 102, 103 and 105..	37
extinguishers, section 104...	37
Flags for school houses, section 347...	118

G

Governor to appoint State Board of Education, section 1............................	5
to appoint State Superintendent, section 9...................................	7
appropriations for Deaf-Mute school, to approve, section 95.......	34
appropriations for industrial schools, to approve, section 235......	83
appropriations for manual training, to approve, section 235........	83
appropriations for school fund, number of trustees of, section 119,	40
number of trustees of industrial schools, to approve, section 240,	85
Graded Schools, reports of, section 64..	25
Grammar schools, definition of, rule 18..	128

H

High schools, definition of, rule 18..	128
Historic days, observance of, sections 194, 195 and 196............................	67
Holidays, legal school, section 66 and decision No. 11............................25,	141

I

Incidentals, orders for, to draw interest in certain cases, section 157..........	54
Incompatible offices, decision No. 10...	141
Incorporated town a separate district, section 97.......................................	35
board of education in, sections 324, 325 and 326............	111

INDEX. 205

	Page.
Industrial schools at Bordentown, sections 248, 249, 250, 251, 252 and 253,	87, 88, 89
appropriations for, sections 138, division IX, 236, 237 and 243	46, 83, 84, 85
custodian of funds of, section 242	85
reports of, sections 240 and 244	85, 86
trustees of, sections 240, 241 and 245	85, 87
Institutes, appropriations for, sections 137 and 138, division V	45, 46
expenses of, to be reported to Comptroller, section 143	48
organization of, rule 36	132
rules for, section 6, division V	6
teachers required to attend, rule 41	132
Union, section 137	45
Insurance on school buildings, section 53, division IV	20
Normal School, sections 81 and 138, division II	30, 46
Interest on bonds, rate of, section 169	59
district orders, section 157	54

J

Janitors, employment of, section 53, division I	20

L

Legal voters at school meetings, sections 43 and 44	16, 17
Libraries, school, amount of first payment, section 185	65
amount of subsequent payments, section 185	65
apparatus, may purchase, section 185	65
appropriations for, sections 138, division VI, and 185	46, 65
books, selection of, section 187	66
consolidation of, section 186	65
teachers', payment to, section 189	66
books, selection of, section 191	67

M

Manual training, appropriations for, section 235	83
course of study in, section 235	83
report of, section 236	83
Model School, section 85	31
Mortgage, by districts, section 53, division III	20
school fund not to be invested in, sections 126 and 147	43

N

Normal School, appropriations for, sections 86 and 138, division I	31, 46
certificates to graduates of, rule 25	129
course of study in, section 80	30
diplomas to graduates, section 80	30

	Page.
Normal School, examination for admission to, sections 82 and 83	30
pledge of pupils, section 83	30
principal of, member of State Board of Examiners, section 76	28
pupils, number of, section 83	30
repairs to, section 80	30
report of, section 80	30
supervision of, section 80	30
teachers in, sections 80 and 84	30, 31
treasurer of, section 80	30
trustees of, sections 3 and 80	6, 30
Notices for district meetings, sections 43, 53, divisions IX and X, and 164	16, 20, 57

P

Patriotism to be taught, sections 194, 195 and 196	67
Penalty for exceeding appropriations, section 352	120
excluding children from school, section 73	27
failure to post notices, section 43	16
misuse of school moneys, sections 110 and 344	38, 117
violation of school law, sections 15, 23, 33, 54, 59 and 108, and rule 35	8, 9, 12, 21, 23, 38, 131
Petition for district meeting, section 53, division X	21
Plans for school-houses, sections 18 and 24	9, 10
Poll-tax, section 349	119
Polls, time kept open, section 46	17
Primary schools, definition of, rule 18	128
Provisional certificates, rule 2	125
Pupils, ages of, section 75	28
books for, sections 53, division VIII, and 115	20, 39
contagious diseases, pupils exposed to prohibited from attending school, sections 60 and 61	23
corporal punishment prohibited, sections 68 and 69	26
course of study, sections 53, division VI, and 71	20, 26
damage to school property, liable for, sections 71 and 350	27, 119
expulsion of, section 53, division VII, and 71	20, 27
residence of, decision No. 6	139
suspension of, sections 53, division VII, 67 and 71, and decision No. 8	20, 26, 27, 138
teachers must submit to authority of, sections 67 and 71	26, 27
transfer of, section 99	36
transportation of, section 100	36
tuition fees not lawful, section 74	27
vaccination of, section 42	16

R

	Page.
Register, teacher to keep, section 63	24
Religious services in schools, section 119	40
Removal of District Clerk, section 25 and 32	10, 12
Report of City Superintendent, sections 36, 37 and 202	13, 68
County Superintendent, sections 23, 36 and 37 and rules 6, 39 and 40	9, 13, 126, 132
Deaf-Mute School, section 95	34
district clerk, sections 37, 53, division XII, and 54	13, 20, 21
indebtedness of districts, section 183	64
industrial schools, sections 240 and 244	85, 86
manual training, section 236	83
Normal School, section 80	30
school fund, sections 124 and 133	42, 44
State Board of Education, section 8	7
State Superintendent, section 21 and rule 7	9, 126
teachers, section 64	25
Reserve fund, apportionment of, section 152	51
Residence of school children, decision No. 6	139
Revocation of certificates, sections 23, 76 and 196 and rule 5	9, 28, 67, 126
Riparian lands, proceeds of sale of, to go to school fund, section 121	41

S

Salary of County Superintendents, section 26	11
district clerks, section 51	19
State Superintendent, sections 9 and 138, division IV	7, 46
teachers, sections 15, 23, 53, division I, and 157	8, 9, 20, 54
Scholarships in agricultural college, section 264	94
School Fund, apportionment of appropriation from, sections 14 and 29	7, 12
appropriations from, 6, 7, 9, 14, 24, 81, 86, 95, 126, 127, 135, 136, 137, 138, 235, 237, 240, 242, 243 and 264	6, 7, 10, 30, 31, 34, 43, 45, 46, 83, 84, 85, 95
appropriations from, paid by State Fund in certain cases, sections 135 and 140	45, 47
expenses of, section 138	46
investment of, sections 121, 122, 123, 124, 125, 126, 131, 132 and 175	41, 42, 43, 44, 62
report of, sections 124 and 133	42, 44
secretary of, section 134	45
treasurer of, section 124	42
trustees of, section 119	40
School-houses (see Buildings).	
meetings (see District Schools).	
month, section 66	25
term, section 15	8
trustees (see Boards of Education).	

	Page.
School year, section 114	39
Secretary of School Fund, section 134	45
State Board of Education, section 12	7
Sectarian schools, public moneys not to be given to, section 152	54
Sinking funds for schools, section 159	54
Special charters, sections 97, 340, 341 and 342	35, 116, 117
examinations, section 77 and rule 19	28, 128
teachers, rule 12	126
laws, districts acting under, may abandon, sections 111, 112, 113	38, 39
State Association of School Superintendents, sections 12 and 35	7, 13
State Board of Education, appeals to, sections 6, division VI, and 17	7, 8
appoint County Superintendents, sections 6, division III, and 25	6, 10
appoint census supervisor, section 40	15
appoint trustees of technical schools, sections 240 and 248	85, 88
appointment of, section 1	5
apportion reserve fund, section 152	51
compensation of, section 7	7
Deaf-Mute School, trustees of, section 4	6
duties of, sections 3, 4 and 5	6
examinations, to make rules for, sections 76 and 77	28
expenses of, sections 7 and 138, division III	7, 46
manual training, to approve course of study in, section 235	83
members of, section 1	5
Normal School, trustees of, section 3	6
quorum of, section 5	6
report of, section 8	7
secretary of, section 12	7
State School Tax, abstract of to be given to assessors and collectors, section 142	48
amount of, section 141	47
apportionment for collection, section 142	48
apportionment of reserve fund, section 152	51
apportionment by assessors, section 142	48
assessment of, sections 141, 142, 143, 144 and 145	47, 48, 49
balances, paid to successor by township collector, sections 156, 161 and 165, and decision No. 8	52, 55, 58, 140
balances may be used for repairs in certain cases, section 161	55
borrow money to pay, section 149	50
collection of, sections 141, 146, 147 and 151	47, 49, 50
custodian of, sections 156 and decision No. 9	52, 140
fourth class counties, payment by, section 151	50
orders for, section 156	52
payment to State Treasurer, sections 149, 150 and 151	50

	Page
State School Tax, payment to counties, sections 152 and 154	51, 52
to townships, section 155	52
report of, section 156	52
reserve fund, section 152	51
third class counties, payment by, section 151	50
transfer of, section 99	36
withheld in certain cases, sections 15, 23, 33 and 108,	8, 9, 1", 38
State Superintendent, appeals from decisions of, sections 6, division VI, and 17	7, 8
appeals to, sections 17 and 34	8, 13
appointment of, section 9	7
appoint County Superintendents, rule 44	133
apportion State appropriation, section 14	7
appropriations, to withhold in certain cases, sections 15 and 23	8, 9
blanks, to prepare, sections 16 and 180	8, 64
census, control of, sections 38 and 39	14, 15
certificates, may revoke, section 23 and rule 5	9, 126
examinations, to prepare questions for, rule 19	128
examiners, member of boards of, sections 12 and 76	7, 28
expenses of, sections 6, division V, and 138, divisions II and VII	6, 46
manual training, draw orders for, section 235	83
office, location of, section 10	7
penalty for violation of law, may remit, sections 54 and 109	21, 38
plans for school houses, to prepare, sections 18 and 24	9, 10
report of, section 21 and rule 7	9, 126
revoke certificates, section 23 and rule 5	9, 126
salary of, sections 9 and 138, division IV	7, 46
school laws, to print, section 16	8
seal of office, section 20	9
secretary of State Board of Education, section 12	7
term of office, section 9	7
Supplies, school officers not to be interested in furnishing, sections 118, 353 and 355	40, 120, 121
to be furnished to pupils, sections 53, division VIII, and 57	21, 33
Surplus revenue, sections 153 and 184	51, 65

T

Tax, local, sections 62, 115, 164 to 173, 181, 235, 237, 239, 243, 246	23, 39, 57, 62, 64, 83, 84, 85, 87
State, sections 141 to 163	47
Taxable residents to vote for condemnation of land, sections 215 and 220	73, 76

	Page.
Teachers, appeal to County Superintendent, sections 67 and 70	26
certificate to be exhibited to County Superintendent, rules 1 and 2	125
endorsement of, rule 8	126
required, section 65 and rules 1 and 2	25, 125
revocation of, sections 23 and 76 and rule 5	9, 28, 126
contract, sections 66 and 70 and rule 1	25, 26, 125
corporal punishment prohibited, sections 68 and 69	26
dismissal of, section 70	26
employment of, section 53, division I	20
examinations, city, sections 1, 78 and 199	7, 29, 68
examinations, county, sections 12, 77 and 199, and rules 3, 4, 6, 7, 8, 9, 10, 11 and 12	7, 28, 68, 125, 126
examinations, State, sections 12, 76 and 199 and rules 3, 4, 6, 7, 8, 9, 11, 12, 21, 22, 23 and 24	7, 28, 68, 125, 126, 129
historic days, to observe, sections 194, 195 and 196	67
holidays, section 66 and decision No. 11	25, 141
institutes, required to attend, rule 41	132
penalty for violation of school law, sections 15, 23, 64 and 196	8, 9, 25, 67
provisional certificates, rule 2	125
pupils, authority over, sections 67 and 71	26, 27
register, to keep, section 63	24
reports of, sections 64, 65 and 67	25, 26
revocation of certificates of, section 23 and rule 5	9, 126
salaries of, sections 15, 23, 157 and 316	8, 9, 54, 109
suspend pupils, section 67 and decision No. 3	26, 138
temporary certificates, rule 2	125
Technical schools, sections 237, 238, 239, 240, 243, 244 and 245	84, 85, 86, 87
Tellers at school meetings, section 45	17
Temporary certificates, rule 2	125
schools, section 212	72
Term, length of school, section 15	8
Text-books, to be supplied pupils, sections 53, division VIII, and 115	20, 39
Towns, separate school districts, section 97	35
boards of education in, sections 324, 325 and 326	111
custodian of school moneys in, section 327	111
incorporation of, section 322	110
tax in, section 328	112
Township, board of education in, sections 47 and 48	18
constitutes school district, section 96	35
elections in, sections 43, 44, 45 and 46	16, 17
Collector, balance paid to successor, section 154	52
balance paid to county, section 161	55
bonds of, liable for school money, section 159	54
compensation of, sections 147, 154 and 166, and decision No. 7	49, 52, 59, 140

Page.

Township Collector, custodian of school moneys, sections 154, 158, 159, 161, 213, rule 35 and decision No. 9..52, 54, 58, 85, 131, 140
    district tax, to collect, sections 62, 151, 169, 170 and 171...............23, 50, 57
    report of, sections 37 and 154..................13, 52
    State tax, collection of, sections 141, 146, 147 and 151,................47, 49, 50
    term of office of, section 156........ 52
Treasurer, Deaf-Mute School, sections 90 and 91................31, 33
    districts having special charters, section 338............ 115
    Normal School, section 80............ 30
    school fund, section 124............ 42
    town, section 328............ 112
Truant officers, sections 209, 210 and 211............71, 72
Tuition fees not legal, section 74 27

U

Ungraded school, definition of, rule 18................ 128

V

Vacancy, County Superintendent, how filled, rule 44............ 133
    district clerk, how filled, section 32 12
    incorporated town, board in, section 3 6............ 111
    township board, how filled, section 31............ 12
Vaccination of pupils, section 42............ 16
Visitation of schools, section 24 and rule 26............11, 130

W

Women, eligible as trustees, section 43............ 16
    vote at school meetings, may, section 44............ 17

BLANKS AND FORMS.

Page.

Forms for City Superintendents.
Bond for school-house loan, Form No. 20... 156
Manual training, application for, Form No. 28................................... 163

Forms for County Superintendents.
Appointment of District Clerk, Form No. 10....................................... 153
Appointment to fill vacancy in Board of Education, Form No. 9 152
Apportionment of balances, notice to Township Collector, Form No. 16... 155
Apportionment of balances, notice to District Clerk, Form No. 17....... 155
Certificate in cases of appeal, Form No. 18.. 155
Certificates, directions given to candidates for, Form No. 48.............. 178
Certificate, teachers', notice revoking, Forms Nos. 14 and 15.............. 154
Condemning a school-house, Form No. 19.. 156
County Collector, order for $100,000 appropriation, Form No. 4.......... 151
County Collector, order for balances, Form No. 7............................... 152
County Collector, order for State school tax, Form No. 5.................... 151
County Collector, order for interest of surplus revenue, Form No. 6.... 151
Examiners' salary, order for, Form No. 8.. 152
Examination of teachers, notice of, Form No. 13................................ 154
Expenses, statement of, Form No. 3.. 149
Institute, certificate of attendance, Form No. 2.................................. 149
Institute, notice of, Form No. 1... 149
Teachers' certificate, notice to District Clerk of revocation of, Form No. 15.. 154
Township Collector, order to withhold school money from a district, Form No. 12... 153
Township Collector, order to withhold school money from a teacher, Form No. 11... 153

Forms for District Clerks.
Affidavit to bill, Form No 39.. 172
Annual meeting for election of Trustees, notice of, Form No. 33......... 170
Annual meeting for ordering District tax, notice of, Form No. 35........ 171
Board of Trustees, notice of meeting of, Form No. 34......................... 170
Bonds, directions for proceedings, Form No. 31.................................. 167
Bonds, report of proceedings, Form No. 29... 163
County Superintendent, notice of vacancy in Board of Trustees, Form No. 40... 173
County Superintendent, notice of election of Trustees, Form No. 25.... 161
County Superintendent, report of amount of District school tax ordered to be raised, Form No. 21.. 158
Duties of, Form No. 47.. 177
Library, report of purchases, Form No. 27.. 163
Manual training, application for, Form No. 28................................... 163

Forms for District Clerks—Continued.
    Minutes of Trustee meeting... 165
    School tax, notice to Assessor of, Form No. 22............................... 159
    Various specifications of business to be transacted that may be inserted
        in any notice for District meeting, Form No. 47............................ 177

        Appeal to State Superintendent, Form No. 54................................ 181
        Application for State aid for library, Form No. 26.......................... 162
        Application for loan from school fund, Form No. 30 166
        Bonds to be issued for loan, Form No. 32....................................... 169
        Contract with teacher, Form No. 42.. 174
        Contract for building a school house, Form No. 45........................ 176
        Deed for school house site, Form No. 44.. 175
        Lease, form of, Form No. 43... 174
        Minutes of Trustee meeting... 165
        Note for money borrowed, Form No. 46 177
        Order for teachers' salary, Form No. 23.. 160
        Order for miscellaneous purposes, Form No. 24 161
        Special District meeting, notice for, Form No. 36........................... 171
        Vacancy in Board of Trustees, notice of, Form No. 40.................... 173
        Various specifications of business to be transacted that may be inserted
            in any notice for District meeting, Form No. 47........................ 177

Forms for Teachers.
    Appeal to State Superintendent, Form No. 54................................ 181
    Certificate that child has attended school, Form No. 49. 179
    Contract with district, Form No. 42.. 174
    Examinations, directions for, Form No. 48..................................... 178
    Report to County Superintendent when leaving a school before the
        end of the school year, Form No. 50... 179
    Report to trustees of suspension of pupils, Form No. 51..................... 180

Forms for Township Collectors.
    Duties of, Form No. 52.. 180

Forms for District School Meetings.
    Minutes of meeting authorizing the issue of bonds.......................... 165
    Notice to officers elected by district, Form No. 41........................... 173
    Order of business, Form No. 38.. 172

Miscellaneous Forms and Directions.
    Appeal to State Superintendent, Form No. 54................................ 181
    Calendar for school elections and duties... 182
    Certificates, directions for candidates, Form No. 48........................ 178
    Decisions by State Superintendent... 137
    Report of County Clerk to County Superintendent of names and
        post-office address of Township Collectors and City Treasurers,
        Form No. 53.. 181
    Rules and regulations prescribed by State Board of Education............ 125

Brown

New Jersey.

Amendments to School Law
AND
Rules of State Board of Education.

1896.

Amendments to School Law.

The following amends section 47 of the school law, edition of 1895:

<blockquote>

The board of education of any school district acting under the provisions of this act, and which district is not divided into wards, may divide said school district into eight precincts, which precincts shall be, as nearly as may be, equal in population, and in the formation of said precincts they shall be so constituted that each of said precincts shall contain at least one school-house unless said district contains less than eight school buildings, and hereafter upon the expiration of the term of office of a member of a board of education now in office, his successor shall be nominated from one of said precincts which now has no representation on the board of education, and thereafter, upon the expiration of the term of a member of the board of education, his successor shall be nominated from the same precinct in order that each of said precincts may at all times be represented on the board of education; and there shall also be one member at large nominated from the school district; *provided,* that whenever any district has heretofore or may hereafter vote to reduce the number of members of the board of education to either three or five, the board of education shall immediately re-arrange said precincts so that the number of precincts shall be one less than the number of members of the board of education of said district, so that there shall at all times be a member of said board of education from each of said precincts and one at large, and said members shall be elected at the same time and in the same manner as is now provided by law.

</blockquote>

Boards of education may divide districts into precincts. P. L. 1896, chap. 150, § 2.

Proviso.

[*Insert on page 17.*]

The following amends section 90 of the school law, edition of 1895:

The comptroller of this state shall be the treasurer of the New Jersey schools for deaf-mutes.

<small>Comptroller to be treasurer. P. L. 1896, chap 35, § 1.</small>

[*Insert on page 33.*]

Every district organized and acting pursuant to the provisions of the act to which this is an amendment, be and the same is hereby validated and confirmed as a legal school district, in accordance with and pursuant to the terms of the act to which this is an amendment, and all the official acts of boards of education or trustees of such school districts be and the same are hereby confirmed and legally established, as fully and to the same effect as if this amendment had not been passed, and that all obligations, debts and bonds incurred or issued by or on behalf of school districts organized under the act mentioned in the title of this act, entitled "An act to establish a system of public instruction" (Revision), approved March twenty-seventh, one thousand eight hundred and seventy-four, and all acts amendatory thereof or supplementary thereto, are hereby declared to be the legal obligations, debts and bonds of such school district.

<small>Districts validated. P. L. 1896, Chap. 150, § 4.</small>

<small>Acts of boards of education confirmed and established.</small>

[*Insert on page 43.*]

The following amends section 157 of the school law, edition of 1895:

It shall be the duty of the county superintendent of each county, on or before the fifteenth day of May, annually, to apportion to the districts of this county the state school moneys, together with the interest of the surplus revenue belonging to said county, in the following manner:

<small>County superintendents to apportion scho moneys. P. L. 1896, Chap. 150 § 1.</small>

I. He shall apportion to each district a sum equal to two hundred dollars for each teacher employed in the public schools in such district for the full time for which the schools in such district were maintained during the year next preceding such apportionment; *provided*, that when in the judgment of a majority of the board of education of any school district, any school within the district has needed and does need an additional teacher a portion only of the school year, the time to be determined by said board, and be not less than four school months, and said board shall certify the same to the county superintendent on or before the first day of April in each year, and the county superintendent shall thereupon further apportion to such district the sum of eighty dollars for every additional teacher thus certified to be needed, but said additional apportionment shall not be made to any district in which an additional teacher as aforesaid has not been employed for the term of four months in the year preceding that for which the apportionment is made.

<small>Amount.</small>

<small>Proviso.</small>

II. He shall apportion to each district the remainder of the school moneys belonging to his county on the basis of the last published school census.

<small>Remainder of moneys; how apportioned.</small>

[*Insert on page 55.*]

The following amends section 172 of the school law, edition of 1895:

It shall and may be lawful for the legal voters, either at the annual meeting or at a special meeting called for that purpose, by the consent of a majority of those present, to authorize the board of education, for the purpose of purchasing land for school purposes or for the purpose of building a school-house or school houses, or making additions, alterations, repairs or improvements in or upon such school-house or school-houses already erected, and the lands upon which the same are located, and for the purchase of school-furniture, to issue bonds of the district in corporate name of the district in such sums and in such amounts and payable at such times as the legal voters so met may direct, with interest at a rate not exceeding six per centum per annum, payable half-yearly; which bonds shall be signed by the president of the board of education and attested by the district clerk, and shall bear the seal of the district, and said bonds shall have coupons attached for current payment of interest, which coupons shall be signed by the district clerk and shall be numbered to correspond to the bond to which they are attached; and any bonds so issued shall be numbered and a proper registry thereof kept by the district clerk; and such bonds may be sold at public or private sale for the best obtainable price, but not less than par; said bonds shall be a lien upon the real and personal estates of the inhabitants of the district, as well as the property of the district, and the property of the inhabitants, as well as the property of the district, shall be liable for the payment of the same; and in all cases copies of all papers and proceedings authorizing the issue of such bonds shall be submitted to the attorney-general for his approval of the legality of the same, and duplicate copies of such papers and proceedings shall be sent to the state superintendent of public instruction.

Legal voters may authorize boards of education to issue bonds to purchase lands, etc.
P. L. 1896, Chap. 150, § 3

[*Insert on page 63*]

In all cases where bonds have been heretofore issued by the board of education or the trustees of any school district pursuant to the consent of a majority of the legal voters present at either an annual meeting or a special meeting called for that purpose, or where bonds have been voted as aforesaid, but not yet actually issued or delivered, the proceeds of the sale of said bonds having been applied, or to be applied, in whole or in part, to the building and furnishing of a school-house, and the only ground of the invalidity of the said bonds or proposed bonds is that they were issued, or are intended to be issued, in part for the furnishing of such school-house, such bonds so issued or intended to be issued, and the proceedings relating to the issuance and sale thereof are hereby declared to be legal.

<small>Bonds heretofore issued declared legal and valid. P. L. 1898, Chap. 09, ¿ 1.</small>

[*Insert on page 69.*]

The following amends section 243 of the school law, edition of 1895:

The trustees of schools for industrial education, to be hereafter appointed by the governor of this state for full terms under and by virtue of the acts to which this is a supplement or the supplements thereto, shall serve for terms of four years and not for terms of five years, as now required by law.

<small>Term of office of trustees. P. L. 1896, chap. 48, ¿ 1.</small>

[*Insert on page 89.*]

The following amends section 251 of the school law, edition of 1895:

Board of trustees; how appointed.
P. L. 1896, chap. 106, § 1.

In lieu of the trustees of the manual training and industrial school at Bordentown, New Jersey, designated in the act to which this is an amendment, the trustees of said school shall consist of the state superintendent of public instruction and the county superintendent of schools of Burlington county, ex-officio, and six persons to be appointed by the governor, who shall respectively hold their office as trustees for a period of three years, and until their successors, respectively, are appointed; the board of trustees herein provided for shall have and possess all the power and responsibilities heretofore conferred upon and held by the trustees of said school by the act to which this is an amendment.

[*Insert on page 92.*]

Boards of Education authorized to purchase land, erect school buildings and issue bonds
P. L. 1896, Chap. 33.

That in townships of this state now or hereafter having a population exceeding fifteen thousand inhabitants, as shown by any census taken under the authority of any act of congress, or of any law of this state, the board of education of such township shall have authority to purchase all necessary land for school purposes and erect all necessary school buildings thereon, and to authorize the issuance of bonds pledging the property of the whole township for the payment thereof and to provide for the payment of the principal and interest of said bonds, and possess all power with relation to the purchase of lands and the erection of school buildings now vested in any properly called annual or special school meeting, as now provided by law;

Proviso

provided, however, that no lands shall be so purchased, or school house or houses contracted to be erected, or erected thereon, and no bond issue authorized until the consent of the township committee to such proposed purchase of land, or the erection of such school building or buildings thereon, and to the necessary bond issue therefor, shall have been first obtained by a resolution duly passed by such committee and certificate thereof made to the board of education by the township clerk under the seal of the township.

[*Insert on page 118.*]

1. Whenever in any incorporated town in this state more or better school accommodations shall be needed it shall be lawful for the common council or other governing body of such town to borrow money to an amount not exceeding the sum of fifty thousand dollars, for the purpose of purchasing lands and erecting school-houses thereon, or adding to, enlarging or rebuilding such school-houses as may now be too small or unsuitable for school purposes, or for the erection of new school buildings on lands already owned by such town or the board of education thereof. *Towns may borrow money to purchase land and erect school-houses. P. L. 1896, Chap. 100.*

2. The said common council or other governing body of such incorporated town, to secure the payment of the sum or sums so borrowed, may issue bonds in the corporate name of such town, to be denominated "school bonds of the town of ———," not to exceed in the aggregate the sum of fifty thousand dollars, payable in not more than thirty years, bearing interest not to exceed the rate of four per centum per annum, pledging the faith and credit of such town for payment thereof, which bonds shall be sold the highest bidder at not less than par value; *provided, however,* that the purchase of lands for such purposes and the erection of school-houses with the money so borrowed shall be under the direction and control of the board of education of such town. *May issue bonds. Amount. Proviso.*

3. The common council or other governing body of said town shall provide for the payment of the principal and interest of said public school bonds in the manner and under the regulations prescribed for the raising of public revenues in such incorporated town. *Payment of principal and interest of bonds; how provided.*

4. If the charter of any such incorporated town in this state shall limit the amount of indebtedness that may be incurred, or by its terms prevent the carrying-out of the provisions of this act, the same shall not hereafter be held to apply to the raising of money under the provisions of this act, any other law to the contrary notwithstanding. *When provisions of act shall not hereafter be held to apply.*

[*Insert on page 118.*]

[*Insert at page 134.*]

1. Whenever it shall appear by the annual school census that there are between eight hundred and fifteen hundred children of legal school age in any school district now entitled by law to have but three trustees, then it shall be lawful for the legal voters of the said district at their next annual meeting for the election of school trustees to determine by a majority vote of those present whether the number of school trustees shall or shall not be increased to five. Voters to determine increase of number of trustees.
P. L. 1896, chap. 19.

2. In case it be decided to increase the number of school trustees in any such school districts to five, then the said legal voters shall proceed to elect, in the manner in which school trustees are now elected, two additional trustees, one to hold office for two years and one for three years, and annually thereafter a trustee or trustees shall be elected for the term of three years, and to fill the places of those whose terms expire. Election of trustees and term of office.

3. It shall be the duty of the district clerk in districts coming within the provision of the first section of this act, in his notice for the annual meeting of school trustees to insert a notice that there are within the district between eight hundred and fifteen hundred children of legal school age, and that it will be determined at said annual meeting whether the said board of school trustees shall consist of three or five ; *provided, further,* that no vote shall be taken on this subject unless public notice shall have been given as herein provided for. Duties of district clerk.
Proviso

1. Whenever in any incorporated town in this state more or better school accommodations shall be needed it shall be lawful for the common council or other governing body of such town to borrow money to an amount not exceeding the sum of fifty thousand dollars, for the purpose of purchasing lands and erecting school-houses thereon, or adding to, enlarging or rebuilding such school-houses as may now be too small or unsuitable for school purposes, or for the erection of new school buildings on lands already owned by such town or the board of education thereof. *Towns may borrow money to purchase land and erect school-houses. P. L. 1896, Chap. 109.*

2. The said common council or other governing body of such incorporated town, to secure the payment of the sum or sums so borrowed, may issue bonds in the corporate name of such town, to be denominated "school bonds of the town of ———," not to exceed in the aggregate the sum of fifty thousand dollars, payable in not more than thirty years, bearing interest not to exceed the rate of four per centum per annum, pledging the faith and credit of such town for payment thereof, which bonds shall be sold the highest bidder at not less than par value; *provided, however*, that the purchase of lands for such purposes and the erection of school-houses with the money so borrowed shall be under the direction and control of the board of education of such town. *May issue bonds. Amount. Proviso.*

3. The common council or other governing body of said town shall provide for the payment of the principal and interest of said public school bonds in the manner and under the regulations prescribed for the raising of public revenues in such incorporated town. *Payment of principal and interest of bonds; how provided.*

4. If the charter of any such incorporated town in this state shall limit the amount of indebtedness that may be incurred, or by its terms prevent the carrying-out of the provisions of this act, the same shall not hereafter be held to apply to the raising of money under the provisions of this act, any other law to the contrary notwithstanding. *When provisions of act shall not hereafter be held to apply.*

[*Insert on page 118.*]

[*Insert at page 134.*]

1. Whenever it shall appear by the annual school census that there are between eight hundred and fifteen hundred children of legal school age in any school district now entitled by law to have but three trustees, then it shall be lawful for the legal voters of the said district at their next annual meeting for the election of school trustees to determine by a majority vote of those present whether the number of school trustees shall or shall not be increased to five. Voters to determine increase of number of trustees.
P. L. 1896, chap. 19.

2. In case it be decided to increase the number of school trustees in any such school districts to five, then the said legal voters shall proceed to elect, in the manner in which school trustees are now elected, two additional trustees, one to hold office for two years and one for three years, and annually thereafter a trustee or trustees shall be elected for the term of three years, and to fill the places of those whose terms expire. Election of trustees and term of office.

3. It shall be the duty of the district clerk in districts coming within the provision of the first section of this act, in his notice for the annual meeting of school trustees to insert a notice that there are within the district between eight hundred and fifteen hundred children of legal school age, and that it will be determined at said annual meeting whether the said board of school trustees shall consist of three or five; *provided, further,* that no vote shall be taken on this subject unless public notice shall have been given as herein provided for. Duties of district clerk.
Proviso

Who to constitute board of trustees of the teachers' retirement fund. P. L. 1896, chap. 32.	1. The state superintendent of public schools, the members of the state board of education, and two representatives, to be selected annually by the public school teachers at the regular meeting of the state teachers' association, shall constitute a board of trustees that shall be known as "the board of trustees of the teachers' retirement fund."
Organization of board.	2. They shall organize as such board by choosing one of their number as chairman and one as secretary; the state treasurer shall be ex-officio treasurer of such fund; such
Board of trustees to have charge of fund, etc.	board of trustees shall have charge of and administer said fund as they shall deem most beneficial to such fund and to the beneficiaries thereof, and order payments therefrom according to the provisions of this act; they shall report annually to the legislature the condition of such fund, and the receipts and disbursements on account of the same, with a full and complete list of the beneficiaries of said fund and the amounts paid to each of them.
When teachers may be retired and annuity granted.	3. Whenever any teacher entitled to the benefits of this act has taught in the public schools of this state for a period of twenty (20) years, and shall become incapacitated from performing the duties of a teacher, such teacher shall, at his or her request, or may, at the discretion of the board of trustees of the teachers' retirement fund, without such request, be retired as a teacher, and shall thereafter receive an annuity out of said fund of a sum equal to one-half of the average annual salary received for the five (5) years imme-
Proviso.	diately preceding the time of retirement; *provided*, that no annuity granted under this act shall be less than two hundred and fifty (250) dollars or more than six hundred (600) dollars, but in case any teacher should be retired within five (5) years after the passage of this act, he or she must, in order to receive the benefits thereof, pay into the fund provided for in this act a sum equal to twenty per centum of his
Proviso.	or her annual salary at time of retirement; *and provided further*, that if at any time there shall not be sufficient money in said fund to pay the warrants drawn thereon as presented for payment, the treasurer shall register said warrants, and mark on the back of each these words: "Presented for payment this (giving day, month and year), and not paid for want of funds. Treasurer of state of New Jer-

sey;" and such warrants shall be paid in the order of registration and bear interest at five per centum per annum from date of registration.

4. Any teacher that shall have been a contributing member for five (5) years or more, who shall resign, or be otherwise honorably retired, shall, upon application within three (3) months after date of such retirement, be entitled to and shall receive one-half of the total amount paid by him or her into said funds. *Who entitled to receive one half of amount paid into the fund*

5. The public school teachers' retirement fund herein provided shall consist of the following, with the income and interest thereof: *Retirement fund, what to consist.*

(1.) The board of education of each municipality and the board of trustees in every school district or township outside of such municipalities, on the expiration of one month after the time when this act shall take effect, shall reserve monthly and pay over to the state treasurer one per centum of the salaries or annuities paid each month to the teachers who shall, prior to such date, elect to come under the provisions of this act; *One per centum of salaries of teachers to be reserved and paid to the state treasurer.*

(2.) All moneys and property received by donation, legacy, gift, bequest or otherwise, for or on account of said fund; *Moneys received by donation, etc.*

(3.) All other methods of increment as may be duly and legally devised for the increase of said fund. *All others.*

6. In addition to the powers hereinbefore granted to said board, it shall have the further power, first to subpœna and compel witnesses to attend and testify before it in all matters relating to the operations of this act, and any member of said board may administer an oath or affirmation to such witness, in the form prescribed in courts of justice; second, to provide for the payment out of said fund of all needful expenses, but the members of said board, as such, shall serve without compensation. *Powers of board.*

7. This act shall be binding only upon public school teachers who, after the passage of this act, shall sign and deliver to the board of education of the municipality, district or township in which they are employed, a notice in substantially the following form: *Act binding upon teachers signing notice.*

———— ————, 1895.

Form of notice or agreement.

To the board of education (or trustees, as the case may be) of ———— ————: You are hereby notified that I agree to be bound by, and desire to avail myself of, the provisions of the act of the legislature of New Jersey, approved ———— ————, eighteen hundred and ninety ————, entitled "An act to amend an act entitled 'An act to establish a system of public instruction in state of New Jersey.'"

————————,
Public School Teacher.

Notice to be given three months after passage of act to entitle to benefits.

And no teacher employed in the public schools of this state at the time of the passage of this act, failing to give such notice within three months, shall be entitled to any benefits under this act or subject to any of its burdens; and no teacher employed after the passage of this act, who within one year after such employment, fails to give such notice, shall share the benefits of or

Notices; to whom delivered.

be subject to the burdens of this act; such notices shall be delivered to the local board of education, and, at the same time, a duplicate copy of the same shall be sent to the board of trustees of teachers' retirement fund, and preserved as a record for their information.

Sections 369, 370, 371 and 372 of the School Law, edition of 1895, are repealed.

1. That whenever the board of education or other body having charge of the public schools in any city of the second class in this state shall, by resolution, determine that the property or buildings devoted to high school purposes in such city are improperly located, or said buildings are unsanitary, inadequate or otherwise unsuitable for high school purposes in said city, by certificate signed by the president, secretary or clerk of said board body, it shall be lawful for the common council or other governing body of such city or board having charge of the finances of such city, by resolution, to appropriate such sum of money, not exceeding one hundred and eighty thousand dollars, as they, in their discretion, shall determine, for the purchase of lands and the erection of buildings or for the repair and improvement of buildings used or to be used for high school purposes.

<small>Cities may make appropriation for erection of buildings for high school purposes. P. L. 1896, chap. 21, § 1.</small>

<small>Amount.</small>

2. Such city, by or through its common council or other governing body, or board having charge of the finances of such city, may, from time to time, or at once, as may be deemed most advantageous for the credit of such city, borrow the money so appropriated by the common council or other governing body of such city, pursuant to the provisions of this act, and may issue bonds of such city to the amount so appropriated and may negotiate and sell the same at any sum not less than par; and the money so raised by the sale of such bonds shall, upon the books of the said city, be carried to the credit of the board of education or other governing body having charge of the public schools of such city, to be used by such board or body for the purposes provided for in this act and for no other purposes whatsoever; said bonds so to be issued shall be made payable in not less than twenty nor more than thirty years, shall bear interest at a rate not greater than four per centum per annum, payable semi-annually, and may be registered or coupon bonds or may be registered and coupon bonds combined, at the option of the city; and there shall be raised by tax in each year the interest on the whole amount of the bonds so issued, together with at least three per centum per annum for the purposes of a sinking fund, to be paid to the commissioners of the sinking fund of said cities for the purpose of meeting the said bonds as they may become due.

<small>May borrow money and issue bonds.</small>

<small>Interest, how raised.</small>

<small>Board of education to purchase lands, erect buildings, &c.</small>

3. When, pursuant to the provisions of this act, the common council or other governing body of any such city or board having charge of the finance of such city, shall have appropriated for the purpose of this act any sum or sums of money, it shall be the duty of the board of education or other body having control of the schools of such city to at once proceed to purchase lands and erect buildings suitable and adequate for high school purposes in said city, or to re-

<small>Proviso.</small>

construct, repair, improve such buildings; *provided, however*, that no land shall be purchased for the purpose of erecting thereon a high school, except with the concurrence and approval of the common council or other governing body of such city or board having charge of the finances of such city, which concurrence shall be expressed by resolution of the said common council or other governing body or board having charge of the finances of such city, and the title to all lands so purchased shall be in the corporate name of such city.

<small>Moneys raised by sale of bonds; how carried.</small>

4. All the moneys raised by the sale of bonds, or otherwise, pursuant to the terms of this act, and carried to the account of the board of education or other body having charge of the public schools in any city of the second class in this state, shall be carried in an account to be designated

<small>Warrants; how stamped or printed.</small>

"High School Construction Account," and all warrants drawn by the board of education or other body having control of the public schools in any such city upon this account shall have stamped or printed thereon conspicuously the words "High School Construction Account," and such warrants in other respects shall conform to the warrants now required by law for the drawing of moneys from the city treasury or the construction of other school buildings in such cities.

<small>Act inoperative until adopted by legal voters at charter elections.</small>

5. This act shall take effect immediately, but its provisions shall remain inoperative in any such city until assented to by a majority of the legal voters thereof voting at an annual charter election to be held in such city, of which the city clerk of such city shall cause public notice of the time and place of holding the same to be given, by advertisements signed by himself and set up in at least twenty public places in such city, and published in two or more daily

newspapers printed therein, for at least six days previous to the day of such election; and that such assent or assents shall be expressed upon the regular ballots to be used at such election by the words printed or written, or partly printed and partly written, "For the adoption for this city of the provisions of an act entitled 'An act concerning cities of the second class in this state, and providing for the purchase of lands and the construction and repair of buildings for high school purposes in such city,'" or "Against the adoption for this city of the provisions of an act entitled 'An act concerning cities of the second class in this state, and providing for the purchase of lands and the construction and repair of buildings for high school purposes in such city,'" and the election officers shall return to the common council, or other legislative body of such city, a true and correct statement in writing, under their hand, of the result of said submission, the same to be entered at large upon the minutes of said body; and upon such adoption, and not otherwise, this act shall in all respects be and become operative in such city.

[*Insert on page 112.*]

Rules and Regulations

Prescribed by

The State Board of Education.

1896.

Rules for the State and County Examinations.

Prescribed by the State Board of Education in Conformity with the Act Entitled "An Act to Establish a System of Public Instruction," Section 2, Clause 1.

I. GENERAL INSTRUCTIONS RELATING TO BOTH STATE AND COUNTY CERTIFICATES.

1. No person shall be employed as a teacher by any board of education unless he holds a regular teacher's certificate in full force and effect at the time that the engagement is made. Any person accepting a position as a teacher in any school in this state shall, before taking charge of such school, exhibit his or her certificate to the county superintendent of the county in which such school is situated; and the board of education shall, within five days after making a contract with a teacher, report to the county superintendent the name of such teacher, the length of time for which he or she is employed, the kind and grade of certificate held by said teacher, the amount of salary and the times of payment, and any contract entered into between any teacher and any board of education shall not be valid until the requirements of this rule are complied with. It shall be the duty of the county superintendents to keep a record of such certificates.

2. Any person desiring to obtain a position as a teacher in any school in this state between the dates of the regular examinations, and who is not in possession of a regular certificate in full force and effect, may obtain from the state or county board of examiners a provisional certificate, good in the subjects it covers until the next regular examination in those subjects; *provided*, that such provisional certificate shall not be renewed or extended; *and provided*, that the applicant have an appointment depending on the certificate.

3. No certificate shall be issued to a teacher whose average in any subject covered by the examination falls below 70.

4. All candidates are required to furnish testimonials as to their moral character, and as to the times and places in which they may have taught, and their success in teaching. Such testimonials shall be retained by the board of examiners and form part of their permanent records.

5. Any certificate may be revoked for cause, either by the board which issued it or by the state board of examiners. Every such case shall be reported to the state board of education in writing.

6. Every board of examiners shall keep a full and correct list of all certificates issued, together with the names and addresses of the holders. Such list shall be transmitted to the state superintendent within ten days after every examination, and shall be printed as part of the annual report of that officer.

7. In all examinations for teachers' certificates the diploma of a college in good standing shall be accepted in lieu of an examination in the academic subjects prescribed.

8. The state board of examiners may indorse the diploma of any normal school or training college or the permanent certificate issued by a state superintendent, or board of examiners, of another state, when the course of study of such normal school or training college, or the requirements for such certificates, are, in the judgment of the state board of examiners, equivalent to those required for similar diplomas or certificates in this state, and provided, that such other state shall grant reciprocal privileges to those holding certificates from this state; and when so indorsed, such diploma or certificate shall have full force and effect as if issued in this state.

9. With the exception of reading, elocution, music, school gymnastics, drawing and manual training, all examinations are to be conducted in writing.

10. A special average will be given for correctness in orthography and composition and for neatness and order in the general appearance of the examination papers. Special credit marks will be given for ability to teach elocution, music, school gymnastics, drawing and manual training.

11. Any board of examiners shall accept from any applicant for a second or first grade county certificate, or for any state certificate, any certificate of any grade, in full force and effect at the time the appli-

cation is made, in lieu of further examination in the academic subjects covered by said certificate; *provided*, that the applicant shall have attained a general average of 85 per cent., and shall present satisfactory evidence of having been a teacher in good standing during the time subsequent to the granting of said certificate.

12. Applicants for employment as special teachers to give instruction in any subject not prescribed in the certificates granted by the state or county boards of examiners, may be examined by the board of examiners in such subject, and when satisfied of the fitness of the applicant to teach any of the branches referred to, said board of examiners may issue a special certificate to said applicant. Such certificates shall remain in force three years, and shall be valid as licenses to teach the subjects for which they are issued, within the jurisdiction of the board of examiners granting the certificates.

II. COUNTY EXAMINATIONS.

13. The county superintendent, together with those persons whom he may appoint as county examiners, shall hold three stated meetings during each year for the examination of teachers, in such places in the county as are most convenient of access to the teachers. The first examination shall be held on the first Friday and Saturday in October; the second on the first Friday and Saturday in February, and the third on the first Friday and Saturday in May; *provided*, that when any of these days falls upon a legal holiday the examination shall be postponed one week. The October and February examinations shall be for second and third grade certificates, and the May examination for first, second and third grade certificates. At the May examination the subjects shall be given on the days, and in the order following:

Friday—(1) Penmanship, (2) orthography, (3) arithmetic, (4) geography, (5) grammar, (6) reading, (7) temperance physiology, (8) theory and practice.

Saturday—(*All grades.*) (1) Temperance physiology and physiology, (2) theory and practice, (3) school law of New Jersey; *second grade*—(4) history, (5) composition, (6) book-keeping; *first grade*—(4) history of education, (5) algebra, (6) civics, (7) physics.

At the October and February examinations the order for second and third grade subjects shall be as above given.

It is recommended that examinations be completed on the days named. Still it will be the privilege of the board of examiners to allow any applicant for a third grade certificate to postpone examination on temperance physiology and theory and practice of teaching until the morning of the following day (Saturday). Also, to permit any applicant for a first or a second grade certificate to take theory and practice of teaching, and school law of New Jersey on the afternoon of the previous day (Friday). To render the above plan practicable the state superintendent shall prepare two sets of questions on the following subjects, viz., temperance physiology, ~~physiology~~, theory and practice of teaching, and school law of New Jersey. In case an applicant has no license and desires a second grade certificate, it is recommended that he shall take all third grade subjects on Friday and all second grade subjects on Saturday. If a first grade *is applied for* then all the subjects that are *allowed* on Friday are to be taken on that day, and those remaining on Saturday. Otherwise he will be required to advance from grade to grade at different, though not necessarily successive examinations. Applicants who are required to be examined in one or more of the professional subjects only (theory and practice, school Law of New Jersey, history of education) are required to be present at the opening of the session on Saturday.

14. A teacher holding a certificate *of any grade*, having a general average not less than .85 per cent., and having engaged to teach in a county other than the one in which such certificate was issued, may secure such endorsement as will render it valid by passing an examination in the professional subjects of his grade in the county where employed.

15. The county superintendent will issue certificates of the three grades to be known respectively as the first, second and third grade county certificates. County certificates of the first grade, issued prior to March 15th, 1893, will be valid in any part of the State during the time for which they were issued, but no county certificate issued after said date shall be valid outside of the county in and for which it is issued.

16. It shall be the privilege of any teacher holding a certificate in full force and effect to present himself at not more than two subsequent examinations of corresponding grade for the purpose of improving his record in any subject or subjects; and such improvement shall be recorded on the certificate already received. This concession

shall serve to increase his general average, but will not prolong the term for which the certificate was originally issued.

17. Special certificates for each grade shall be issued to those teachers whose minimum standing in any one branch is not less than 80, and whose general average in all the studies is not less than 90, and who have completed the prescribed course of professional reading; *provided*, said teachers, in the judgment of the county superintendent and the local board of education, shall possess *exceptional skill in the organization, management and advancement of a school*. The aforesaid special certificates may be granted at any time, shall bear the same date, and be valid for the same term as the regular certificates which they replace. They are authorized as a measure of justice to teachers of the second and third grades who evince exceptional aptitude and skill as instructors; and to such teachers of the first grade as, through experience, progressiveness and devotion to duty shall achieve marked distinction as educators. They are also designed to subserve the further purpose of furnishing committees and boards of education with reliable evidence of professional ability. County superintendents are therefore required to exercise due caution and discretion in their issue. *They are to be granted in no case until after a careful personal supervision and inspection of school work.* The state superintendent shall be duly notified of the issue of all said special certificates, and will keep a record of the same in the department of public instruction. The regular certificates, known simply as first, second and third grade, shall be regarded as indicating the same degree of merit as heretofore.

18. Candidates for the third grade county certificate are to be not less than eighteen years old. No experience in teaching will be required. Applicants for third grade certificates will be examined in orthography, reading, penmanship, geography, arithmetic, English grammar, and the theory and practice of teaching. The certificate will continue in force for one year from date, and will be valid as a license to teach in an ungraded school or in a primary school or department. The third grade county certificate shall not be issued to the same person more than three times, unless said teacher shall secure the special certificate. In this case he will, after three years, be entitled to two years' renewal of the same by passing a satisfactory examination *each year* in theory and practice of teaching and school law of New Jersey.

19. Candidates for second grade county certificates are to be not less than nineteen years old, with an experience in teaching of not less than one year. The examination will be the same as that for the third grade certificate, with the addition of English composition, physiology, the history of the United States, school law of New Jersey, and book-keeping. The certificate will continue in force for three years from date, and will be valid as a license to teach in any school or department not above the grade of a grammar school. Any teacher who shall hold either a special or an ordinary second grade certificate shall, at the end of the term for which it was issued, be entitled to a renewal of the same by passing a satisfactory examination in theory and practice of teaching, school law of New Jersey, and history of education. No certificate shall be renewed, or shall be issued to a teacher whose average in any subject covered by the examination falls below 70.

20. Candidates for first grade county certificates are to be not less than twenty years old, with an experience in teaching of not less than two years. The examination will be the same as that for the second grade certificate, with the addition of algebra, physics, history of education, and civics. The certificate will remain in force for five years from date, and will be valid as a license to teach in any school or department in the county. A first grade county certificate may be renewed without a re-examination, but only in the county in which it was originally issued.

21. In view of the growing popularity and superior effectiveness of departmental instruction, it is further required that county superintendents shall by all the opportunities afforded them ascertain whether certain teachers are, through natural taste, aptitude and acquirement, especially qualified to give instruction in particular branches or departments; and when he shall so determine, shall record the same on the teacher's license.

22. An ungraded school is defined as one in which but a single teacher is employed. A graded school is one in which more than a single teacher is employed, and which is divided into at least two departments. A primary school or department is defined as one having the first four years of the usual school curriculum, consisting of studies similar to those prescribed in the primary department of the State Model School. A grammar school or department is defined as one having the second four years of the usual school curriculum, con-

sisting of studies similar to those prescribed in the grammar department of the State Model School. A high school is defined as a school, the curriculum of which includes more advanced instruction than that of a grammar school, as herein defined.

23. A new set of questions shall be prepared for each county examination under the direction of the state superintendent of public instruction, and ten questions will be given in each study. Since all examinations are held on two consecutive days, the questions assigned to each shall be printed on different sheets and forwarded to county superintendents in separate packages. Each package shall remain sealed until opened on the day of the examination in the presence of the candidates. No special examination shall be held unless the consent of the state superintendent of public instruction has been first obtained, and no questions shall be used at any regular or special examination except those issued or approved by the state superintendent. County superintendents, on granting certificates at special examinations, may grant them in the usual form; or, if they deem it advisable, they may grant them to be good only until the next regular examination.

24. Upon each county certificate shall be written the special average in each study gained by the holder, and his or her general average, each marked as a percentage upon the scale of 100.

III. STATE EXAMINATIONS.

25. The state board of examiners will grant certificates of three grades, to be called respectively first, second and third grade state certificates, the third or lowest grade ranking one degree above the highest grade issued by a county board of examiners. Two examinations for state certificates, and only two, shall be held each year, in the city of Trenton, beginning on the first Thursdays of June and December respectively. These examinations shall be public, and the questions used shall be approved formally by each member of the board of examiners.

26. Candidates for third grade state certificates are to be not less than twenty years old. No experience in teaching will be required. They will be examined in all the subjects required for a first grade county certificate, together with psychology, plane and solid geometry,

chemistry, geology, botany and free-hand drawing. The certificate will remain in force for seven years from date, and will be valid as a license to teach in any school in the state. It may be renewed without re-examination.

27. Candidates for second grade state certificates are to be not less than twenty-one years of age, with an experience in teaching of not less than two years. The examination will be the same as that required for a third grade state certificate, together with the philosophy of education and the principles of manual training and physical training. The license will remain in force for ten years from date, and will be valid as a license to teach in any school in the state. It may be renewed without re-examination.

28. Candidates for first grade state certificates are to be not less than twenty-five years old, with an experience in teaching of not less than five years. Candidates will be required to present satisfactory evidence that their teaching has been in every way successful. The examination will be the same as that required for the second grade certificate. The certificate will remain in force during the life of the holder, unless revoked for cause (see Rule 5), and will be valid as a license to teach in any school in the state.

29. Graduates of the State Normal School who have completed the three years' course shall be entitled to a second grade state certificate, good for life.

IV. COUNTY SUPERINTENDENTS.

30. It shall be the duty of each county superintendent to visit the schools in his county as often as may be necessary; *provided*, that he shall visit every school under his jurisdiction at least once in each year; *and provided further*, that the total number of visits made during the year shall equal at least twice the number of schools under his jurisdiction; the additional visits to be made to such schools as, in his judgment, most need his encouragement and advice.

31. He shall note at such visits, in a book provided for the purpose, to be designated "The Superintendent's Visiting Book," the condition of the school buildings and out-houses, the appearance and correctness of the records kept in the school registers, the efficiency of the teachers, the character, record and standing of the pupils, the methods of instruction, the branches taught, the text books used, and

the discipline, government and general condition of each school; and from the notes thus taken he shall ascertain and report the relative grade of merit of each school.

32. He shall labor in every practicable way to elevate the standard of teaching and to improve the condition of the schools in his county; shall give such directions in the science, art and methods of teaching as he may deem expedient, and shall be the official adviser and constant assistant of the school officers of his county.

33. He shall distribute promptly all reports, forms, laws, circulars and instructions which he may receive from the state superintendent or the state board of education, and in accordance with their directions.

34. He shall take care that the decisions of the state superintendent or the state board of education, upon controversies relating to the school laws of the state, or to the rules and regulations prescribed by the state board of education, be complied with by the parties concerned; and in case such decisions are not complied with, he shall inform the state superintendent thereof, and state the circumstances connected therewith.

35. He shall carefully preserve all reports of school officers and teachers, and all examination papers of teachers examined by the county board of examiners, and, generally, shall carry out the provisions of the law "Establishing a system of public instruction," and the rules and regulations prescribed by the state board of education, and at the close of his official term shall deliver to his successor all records, books, documents, papers, and property belonging to the office.

36. No county superintendent shall act as agent for any author, publisher or bookseller, nor directly or indirectly receive any gift, emolument or reward for his influence in recommending or procuring the use of any book, or school apparatus, or furniture of any kind whatever in any public school; and anyone who shall violate this provision shall be subject to removal from office.

37. He shall meet each township board of education at least twice each year, which meetings shall be held at such times and places as he may appoint.

38. He shall ascertain from the township collectors, within five days after the annual town meetings, the amount of school tax ordered to be assessed in each township, and on or before the fifteenth day of May of each year, he shall apportion, according to law, to the several townships and school districts of his county, all the school moneys to

which they are entitled for the following year, whether received by state appropriation or ordered to be assessed as township school tax.

39. It shall be the duty of the district clerk of any school district to deposit with the township collector, or other legal custodian, all moneys received by the board of education, from tuition, loans, proceeds from the sale of bonds, or other school property, or from any other source, and disburse the same only by orders upon the collector of the township in which said school-house is located; and in case of the refusal of a district clerk to comply with the above, it shall be the duty of the county superintendent to serve the collector with a written notice forbidding him to honor any drafts against the state moneys until the provisions of this rule be complied with.

40. Every county superintendent shall encourage and assist in the organization and management of county institutes, as the committee on education may direct, and be present at and preside over the same.

41. Every county superintendent shall, in the manner now provided by law, prepare and establish a uniform course of study in the schools under his supervision, and he shall adopt a uniform system of examinations, by which the promotion of pupils from grade to grade and the requirements for final graduation shall be determined. The aforesaid course of study and questions for final examination shall be submitted to the state superintendent for his approval.

42. Every county superintendent shall, by such means as he shall deem most practicable, establish a county pedagogical library, and he shall designate courses of pedagogical reading ~~and a system of examinations,~~ subject to the approval of the state superintendent, for the several grades of teachers under his supervision.

43. The state superintendent shall prepare, have printed and furnish blank diplomas to be awarded by county superintendents to all pupils who shall successfully complete the prescribed course of study, also diplomas suitable to be granted to such teachers as shall, from copious notes from the same, prove that they have intelligently completed the course of professional reading adapted to their respective grades.

44. At the close of their official terms, or on the vacation of their office, by resignation or otherwise, should the same occur during the scholastic year, all county superintendents shall report to the state superintendent for the portion of the year that may have expired, as provided for in the forty-seventh section of the school law, with refer-

ence to their annual reports; and no order shall be given for their last quarter's salary until such reports are received in a manner satisfactory to the state superintendent.

45. That in case of the failure of any county superintendent to make his report to the state superintendent on the first day of September, as required by law, the state superintendent shall not give to such county superintendent any order for the payment of salary for the quarter next succeeding such delinquency, except by special resolution of the state board of education for this purpose.

46. All teachers are required to attend the annual institute held for the county in which they are teaching; and no deduction shall be made by the board of education from the salary of any teacher for the time he or she is in attendance upon said institute.

47. When it is within the knowledge of the state superintendent that a county superintendent is not attending to the duties of his office, he shall withhold from such county superintendent orders for his quarterly salary until the board shall direct such orders to be drawn.

48. No allowance shall be made for office rent in the expenses of the county superintendents.

49. Whenever there is a vacancy in the office of county superintendent, the state superintendent is hereby authorized to appoint a suitable person as county superintendent *pro tempore;* said appointment to be approved by the president of the state board of education.

50. The committee on education shall examine into the qualifications of candidates for the position of county superintendent, by personal interviews with such candidates, and in such other ways as the committee may determine, and shall report upon the same at the meetings of the board at which elections of county superintendents are to take place.

www.ingramcontent.com/pod-product-compliance
Lightning Source LLC
Chambersburg PA
CBHW031729230426
43669CB00007B/297